Fictive Domains

The Bucknell Studies in Eighteenth-Century Literature and Culture

General Editor: Greg Clingham, *Bucknell University*

Advisory Board: Paul K. Alkon, *University of Southern California*
Chloe Chard, *Independent Scholar*
Clement Hawes, *The Pennsylvania State University*
Robert Markley, *University of Illinois at Urbana-Champaign*
Jessica Munns, *University of Denver*
Cedric D. Reverand II, *University of Wyoming*
Janet Todd, *University of Glasgow*

The Bucknell Studies in Eighteenth-Century Literature and Culture aims to publish challenging, new eighteenth-century scholarship. Of particular interest is critical, historical, and interdisciplinary work that is interestingly and intelligently theorized, and that broadens and refines the conception of the field. At the same time, the series remains open to all theoretical perspectives and different kinds of scholarship. While the focus of the series is the literature, history, arts, and culture (including art, architecture, music, travel, and history of science, medicine, and law) of the long eighteenth century in Britain and Europe, the series is also interested in scholarship that establishes relationships with other geographies, literatures, and cultures of the period 1660–1830.

Titles in This Series

http://www.departments. bucknell.edu/univ_epress

Fictive Domains

Body, Landscape, and Nostalgia, 1717–1770

Judith Broome

Lewisburg
Bucknell University Press

Associated University Presses
2010 Eastpark Boulevard
Cranbury, NJ 08512

The paper used in this publication meets the requirements of the American National Standard for Permanence of Paper for Printed Library Materials Z39.48-1984

Library of Congress Cataloging-in-Publication Data

Broome, Judith, 1952–
    Fictive domains : body, landscape, and nostalgia, 1717–1770 / Judith Broome.
        p.   cm.
    Includes bibliographical references and index.
    ISBN-13: 978-0-8387-5634-8 (alk. paper)
    ISBN-10: 0-8387-5634-4 (alk. paper)
    1. English literature—18th century—History and criticism.   2. Nostalgia in literature.   3. Nostalgia—Great Britain—History—18th century.   4. Home in literature.   5. Nature in literature.   6. Desire in literature.   I. Title.

    PR448.N67B76 2007
    823'.509353—dc22

                                                                2006012994

In memory of my father, George Broome

When the real is no longer what it was, nostalgia assumes its full meaning.

—Jean Baudrillard, *Simulacra and Simulation*

Contents

7

Acknowledgments

THIS BOOK CAME INTO BEING WITH THE SUPPORT OF MANY MENTORS, colleagues, and friends. I would especially like to thank Tassie Gwilliam, who nurtured this project from its very inception and whose guidance, support, and friendship have been constant. Thanks, also, to my other mentors and readers — Frank Stringfellow, Patrick A. McCarthy, John Paul Russo, and Barbara Woshinsky — for their thoughtful observations and recommendations. Special thanks go to the College of Humanities and Social Sciences, William Paterson University of New Jersey, for the released time that allowed me to complete this book. I would also like to thank Greg Clingham of Bucknell University Press for his support of this project and for his wise suggestions.

Many colleagues have shared ideas, read drafts, and made suggestions throughout the life of this book. Robert Healy read *Clarissa* along with me and discussed the novel over endless lunches; Kathryn Kruger was a source of invaluable suggestions for revisions of early drafts; Blas Falconer helped me see this project through to the end and has been a wonderful friend and colleague. For the gift of unconditional friendship, I wish to thank Susan Pomeranz and Kathy Morgan.

I am indebted to my mother, Patricia Broome, who taught me to love books, and to my father, George Broome, who was always so generous with his praise. Most of all, I thank my daughter, Sarah Victoria Mesa-Pelly, whose love, support, and sense of humor have made this book possible.

I am grateful to the University of Chicago Library, Special Collections Research Center, for permission to reprint the frontispiece from the 1764 edition of Sarah Scott's *A Description of Millenium Hall, and the Country Adjacent*.

Fictive Domains

1
Introduction: Toward a Theory of Nostalgia

IN HIS ESSAY "ON TRANSIENCE," FREUD RECALLS A SUMMER WALK IN the country with two friends, one characterized only as "taciturn," the other "a young but already famous poet." The poet was dejected at the impermanence of the natural beauty of the countryside, an attitude that was confusing to Freud, who observes that "the proneness to decay of all that is beautiful and perfect can, as we know, give rise to two different impulses in the mind. The one leads to the aching despondence felt by the young poet, while the other leads to rebellion against the fact asserted."[1] Freud, who refutes the claims of his two friends that the "worth" of natural beauty is diminished by its transience, observes that their reactions are occasioned by a "foretaste of mourning" over the imminent decay of the natural scene before them. Freud closes this short essay with his observations on the war and the violence with which it changed not only the face of the landscape, but also his country's cultural wealth and the morale of its people. Freud's memory of his walk in the country is, it seems, less a meditation on his friends' reaction to the transience of natural beauty than on his own bittersweet longing—a mood that we commonly call nostalgia—for a simpler time when the delicacy of nature might have been a primary concern; in 1915, Freud knows, such a conversation could never take place again in exactly the same way. His memory is of a more innocent time, a pastoral interlude that afforded emotional, sensual, and intellectual stimulation. Most significantly, Freud's longing has inspired a creative act: the writing of his essay.

The desire that we call nostalgia is a peculiar mix of sadness and pleasure, and while the longing is not new, the name is relatively modern: it was not until 1678, when Johannes Hofer coined the term in his University of Basel doctoral dissertation, that a single word existed to describe a homesickness so intense that it could cause physical illness or even death. The disease Hofer called *nostalgia*—from the Greek terms for "grief" or "pain" (*algia*) and "to return home" (*nostos*, literally, return)—was a disease of both the body and the mind, with specific physical symptoms. While *nostalgia* has sometimes been associated, or even conflated, with the concepts of *melancholy* or *melancholia*, a distinction among the words should be made: *melancholia* has traditionally been used to describe a medical condition, while *melancholy* has typically been ascribed to a mood or a personality type. Such uses of *melancholy* can be traced back as far as the fourteenth century, but the split between the terms became especially prominent in the sixteenth and seventeenth centuries in Britain, with the Elizabethan "melancholic" personality, who was frequently represented on stage and in literature. *Melancholy* has retained its association with aesthetic or cultural practice, while *melancholia* has remained a part of medical discourse. Recently, however, there has been some attention paid to nostalgia as a pathological condition, versus the pleasurable nostalgic "mood" with which we are all familiar.[2]

It took some time for *nostalgia* to enter the English language: the word is still too new to appear in Samuel Johnson's *Dictionary* of 1755, but an early mention is found in 1770, when Sir Joseph Banks, writing in his journal on board the H.M.S. *Endeavour*, notes that many of the sailors on board were suffering from "the longing for home, which the Physicians have gone so far as to esteem a disease under the name of Nostalgia."[3] Later in the century, medical writers such as R. T. Crosfield, John Clark, Francis Spilsbury, and Thomas Trotter considered homesickness and misery to be causes of the scurvy suffered by sailors on extended voyages; Trotter, calling this variety of homesickness "scorbutic Nostalgia," found it to be a symptom as well as a cause of scurvy.[4] While the term *nostalgia* may have remained within medical discourse, the desire for something elusive, something lost, nevertheless surfaced in the cultural productions of the eighteenth century. Embedded in the very origins of nostalgia, or homesickness, are the body and the land. The cultural nostalgia that pervaded the eighteenth century—a nameless longing—manifested itself in cultural constructions of body and landscape, specifically sentimental bodies and picturesque landscapes.

Nostalgia emerged as a cultural construction at a time of accelerated social change and increasing social instability, as a response to the anxiety produced by such social transformations. The appropriation of a new term created a distinguishing category that allowed social and aesthetic value to be attached both to the past and to a present that seemed in jeopardy. At stake in the creation of literature or systems of aesthetics that are interested in the ways bodies and landscapes "ought to be," or "used to be," was a conservative interest in preserving the status quo.

NOSTALGIC REPARATIONS

With its blushes, sighs, tears, palpitations, and swoonings, the sentimental body of eighteenth-century literature savors its grief and reserves its tenderness for innocence or weakness that has been exploited or corrupted by an evil world. A sentimental body prominently displays its feelings, marking such a body as that of a "good man," like Samuel Richardson's Sir Charles Grandison, or an innocent victim, like Richardson's Clarissa Harlowe. Such tenderness, however, represents a displacement of certain economic and social circumstances of the time. As Robert Markley has pointed out, sentimental ideology reinforced conservative and essentialist values by aligning "victims of social inequality—men, women, and children—with 'feminine' powerlessness."[5] Sentimentality served the interests of cultural nostalgia by creating an aesthetic escape valve for anxiety about social inequity and victimization, and the threat any social change might offer to a growing middle class interested in preserving its tenuous status.

Bodies themselves were problematic. As "investments," like land, bodies were gradually slipping out of the control of those who had the most to gain by their exchange. Marriage in the sixteenth through the eighteenth century was being reconceived as a companionate match, rather than a straightforward consolidation of family interests through the joining of estates.[6] It is likely that the changes in attitudes toward marriage and romantic love, or what Lawrence Stone has termed "affective individualism," were more gradual and less clearly defined than Stone's study allows; nevertheless, companionate marriages would have represented an erosion of patriarchal power, making it increasingly difficult to exchange the body of a daughter or son in a tidy financial arrangement that would benefit the interests of the estate. Such a struggle over control of bodies as a result of changes in attitudes is played out in detail on the body of Clarissa Harlowe, for example. Clarissa's body—caught in a struggle between her desire and will to control both her body and her future and her family's and Lovelace's plans to control her body by exchange or corruption—gradually wastes away in response to her overwhelming sensibility.

Similar and related ideological struggles are located in eighteenth-century representations of landscape; at issue was control of the land rather than the body. In eighteenth-century Britain, the rise of merchant capitalism tilted the balance of social and economic power between the landed aristocracy and the newly moneyed urban bourgeoisie. The money accrued by London merchants, however, did not confer social status, and many London merchants exchanged capital for land or country estates. Increasingly, land was becoming a commodity to be measured and mapped by surveyors, and ultimately exchanged; at the same time, commons were being increasingly enclosed and converted into private property subject to sale. Traditional meanings associated with land were quickly dissolving; in response to that symbolic instability, landscape—a scene that can be taken in with the eye, or visually consumed—became highly valued, both in its representation in literature and painting and in its construction and cultivation at the hands of its new owners.

Henri Lefebvre has described a "double illusion" at work in the cultural construction of space; these illusions, I would argue, are active in the cultural construction of the body as well. One illusion is that of "transparency," a perception of space as "innocent" and "free of traps or secret places." That which is hidden or false, and therefore threatening, according to Lefebvre, is "antagonistic to transparency, under whose reign everything can be taken in by a single glance from that mental eye which illuminates whatever it contemplates."[7] Such an illusion would seem to be built into visual consumption, which assumes the completeness or totality of that which can be seen.

The other illusion described by Lefebvre is the "realistic" illusion that calls on "naturalness," or on an opaque materiality or "substantiality." These two illusions, far from contradicting each other, actually embody and feed on one another. Moreover, Lefebvre notes, "the shifting back and forth between the two, and the flickering or oscillatory effect that it produces are thus just as important as either of the illusions considered in isolation. . . . The apparent translucency taken on by obscure historical and political forces in decline (the state, nationalism) can enlist images having their source in the earth or in nature, in paternity or in maternity. The rational is thus naturalized, while nature cloaks itself in nostalgia which supplants rationality."[8] The idea of nostalgia emerged at precisely the right time to negotiate the social contradictions that were becoming increasingly apparent during the course of the eighteenth century. By attaching itself to representations of body and landscape, cultural nostalgia served to preserve and control, in fantasy, material bodies and landscapes that were rapidly passing out of the control of the aristocracy.

Cultural nostalgia manifested itself in two important aesthetic concepts that flourished during the eighteenth century—the sentimental and the picturesque. Representations of the sentimental body and picturesque landscape were constructions that served cultural nostalgia in several ways. Certainly, this nostalgia was consumable in the form of novels, poetry, painting, and picturesque travel. More significantly, cultural nostalgia offered the possibility of emphasizing an aesthetic experience at the price of history; sentimental novels and picturesque paintings or poems tended to obviate social or historical analysis by their highly visual and aesthetically pleasing representations of body and landscape. Bodies and landscapes came to carry new meanings as the sites of nostalgic "investment," bearing what Ludmilla Jordanova describes as "important qualities [that] express dense psychic and social concerns."[9] Moreover, once bodies and landscapes are commodified as images or symbols, the gloss of aesthetic practice obscures history and underlying social relations.[10]

Nostalgia, imbued with supportive illusions, is a self-constituting performance that needs to be constantly repeated. Nostalgia has only an imagined referent; the lack of any historical referent is concealed by the repetition of a performance in and by nostalgic cultural products. Such repetition is a deferral that provides the ground against which contemporary nostalgia can be viewed; yet, as Judith Butler points out in a different context, the subordination of a nostalgic evocation of a golden age to its purported originary moment is nothing more than a "ruse" in which the golden age is actually derived from its own contemporary performance. The "irrecoverable past" provides the ground for nostalgic "memory" that conceals the lack of an originary moment, or any true golden age;[11] the performance of nostalgia in and by various forms of aesthetic practice is symbolic work that fends off loss, absence, and melancholia. The peculiar pleasures of nostalgia make it especially appropriate for creative work that becomes a symbolic and material substitute for the object of nostalgic desire.[12]

Because nostalgia was originally linked to the idea of home, these constructions are "fictive domains"—imaginary places to return to, naturalized spaces that carry the illusion of being originary. We reside in our bodies and in the surrounding landscape; moreover, we relate to the landscape through our bodies, in terms of both proportion and location.

For Susan Stewart, the idea of "fictive domains" describes a space out-side the body that aids us in thinking about the body in history: "Within the development of culture under an exchange economy," Stewart writes,

> the search for authentic experience and, correlatively, the search for the au-thentic object become critical. As experience is increasingly mediated and abstracted, the lived relation of the body to the phenomenological world is replaced by a nostalgic myth of contact and presence. "Authentic" experi-ence becomes both elusive and allusive as it is placed beyond the horizon of present lived experience, the beyond in which the antique, the pastoral, the exotic, and other fictive domains are articulated. In this process of distanc-ing, the memory of the body is replaced by the memory of the object, a mem-ory standing outside the self and thus presenting both a surplus and lack of significance.[13]

The cultural nostalgia present in sentimental bodies and picturesque landscapes suggests a desire in the eighteenth century to construct bod-ies and landscapes that, as the objects of a controlling gaze, would pres-ent an imaginary resolution to social contradictions, and at the same time function as objects for visual consumption. Such cultural spaces could not be free of competing discourses or uneven development.

In his discussion of "Golden Ages" in *The Country and the City*, Ray-mond Williams notes that "old forms" and "old ways of feeling" linger well into periods of new development and obvious social change; the concept of what appears to be an "old order" or a "'traditional' society" keeps resurfacing as a yardstick "against which contemporary change can be measured." The "old order" that Williams cites is an illusion, however: "The structure of feeling within which this backward refer-ence is to be understood is then not primarily a matter of historical ex-planation and analysis," Williams writes. Of interest is the "particular kind of reaction to the fact of change."[14]

Such anxiety about social change necessarily contains certain class and gender implications, which are present in Hofer's concept of nostal-gia as disease and which bear some examination. Hofer found the dis-ease to be one primarily of conscripted soldiers, although some young women, who had left their families to go into service, were also subject to nostalgia, an idea that would persist well into the nineteenth cen-tury.[15] Clearly, nostalgia was not primarily an aristocratic malady in Hofer's scheme. The traditional association of melancholy and the artist or the aristocrat did not obtain; while melancholy was restricted to the upper and middle classes, nostalgia was accessible to everyone, in one form or another.

The nostalgia that acted upon the bodies of the lower class in the form of disease was adopted as a cultural stance by what Williams has called the "shifting intermediate groups," for whom the idea of a golden age was "a myth functioning as a memory." These intermediate groups suffered, more than from anything else, from the instability of their condition: having achieved "a place in the altering social structure of the land, [they were] continually threatened with losing it." Williams observes that these groups abstract a certain "moral order" from the feudal economy and attempt to impose it on their own unstable economic conditions.[16] Williams locates these "shifting intermediate groups" throughout history; because of the acceleration of industrialization and capitalism in the eighteenth century, however, I would argue that social instability became a more widespread anxiety than, perhaps, ever before.

The idealization of the past—nostalgia—in contrast to a present seen as chaotic and uncertain requires "forgetting" the actual contradictions of the past. Such "forgetting" is nothing more than repression, as Fredric Jameson points out: while the concept of repression is originally political, in psychoanalytic theory, repression is not violent; it is, rather, "looking away [or] forgetting." Repression, Jameson notes, is "reflexive, that is, it aims not only at removing a particular object from consciousness, but also and above all, at doing away with the traces of that removal as well, at repressing the very memory of the intent to repress." Forgetting, then, "marks the spot where something painful is buried."[17] Such an imaginary response occasions representations of both body and landscape as fictive domains in which nostalgic fantasies are played out. As the land is increasingly engrossed and enclosed, or as it passes from the hands of the aristocracy into those of newly moneyed London merchants, the idea of a "natural," picturesque—that is, suitable for visual representation—landscape accrues value. The sentimental body, in which feelings and thoughts—and the goodness of the "heart," or moral virtue—are manifested by and on the body through blushes, tears, sighs, or even wasting and disease, is above all a visible body that is frequently displayed. In both cases, representations of body and landscape are overdetermined, attesting to the energy required by mystification, and by the continual process of selection and exclusion of those elements that would threaten the temporary stability achieved by these fragile constructions, a continuing process that fends off symbolic collapse.

In this book, I examine the history of nostalgia as a medical condition, a disease that affected the body as well as the mind, and its implications in the cult of "sensibility"; and nostalgia as a source of a cultivated "taste" for the picturesque, elements of which appear in travel narratives and poetry throughout the century, and which is finally theorized at the end of the century by Uvedale Price. But nostalgia cannot be satisfied and seems to resist interpretation; it is the "desire for desire" as Susan Stewart has observed.[18] For this reason, the manifestations of nostalgia as cults of sensibility or the picturesque tend to be short lived. Part of my project, then, is to examine the ways in which these constructs need to be constantly reworked in order to resist the wearing off of gloss or mystery. Beyond the sentimental body and the picturesque landscape, I consider the intersections of bodies and landscapes as they appear in novels of the later eighteenth century, and the ways in which the political unconscious surfaces in these novels.

Fredric Jameson's model of the political unconscious posits history as the Real, to which we have access only through a text (or, I would suggest, other types of material production, including the plastic arts or landscape gardening); history, Jameson stresses, "is *not* a text, for it is fundamentally non-narrative and nonrepresentational" and "can be approached only by way of prior (re)textualization."[19] History must be read *through* the text. The social contradictions of history are often not explicitly present in the text itself, although the text is charged with their energy; at the moment of material production, the Real of history interacts with the unconscious of the writer or artist to produce a text that both remembers and forgets. The social contradictions of the present, what might be called history-in-process, also surface in the material production, not as memories, but as anxieties that demand palliation through the distancing effect of nostalgic constructions of sentimental bodies and picturesque landscapes.

As must history, nostalgia must be (re)textualized, to borrow Jameson's terminology, in the material productions of sentimental literature or picturesque gardens. The wasting away of the fictional Clarissa Harlowe's body generates the body of text that is *Clarissa*. Later in the century, landscape improvers such as Uvedale Price, Humphrey Repton, or Lancelot "Capability" Brown rework bodies of land into picturesque gardens, material productions that enact the nostalgia of the period.

Bodies and texts intersect in other ways as well. Pope's "Eloisa to

Abelard" constrains bodily passion and desire within the rigid scheme of rhymed couplets; Pope's poem is all the more passionate for its tight control. Eloisa's convent cell and her moral restraint are embodied on the page by the rigor of poetic form; Pope nevertheless maximizes the silences and hesitations within the poem, ultimately adopting Eloisa's passion as his own as he writes himself into the end of the poem. Rousseau's *Julie, ou la nouvelle Héloïse* is the nostalgic recreation of a mother's body, a passionate body brought under control by Julie's own internalization of patriarchal ideology. In both instances, female passion is utilized by Pope and Rousseau as a creative source but reined in by the authors' own discourse.

Of all these texts, I ask the same question: what is at stake for these writers? To reduce the answer to a single common denominator would be an oversimplification, even if it could be done. By examining the perceived losses of these writers, and the ways in which they attempt to negotiate those losses and construct bodies of text that serve as symbolic reparations, I locate a unifying thread: that of a desire for wholeness or coherence, and an overarching concern with defining that wholeness against a sense of fragmentation, loss, or otherness that is dangerous, threatening, overwhelming, or bewildering—in other words, a desire for the familiar, or home, in the face of uncertainty and alienation. That desire is nostalgia.

TEXTUAL BODIES

As the site of uncertainty, mystery, and nostalgia, the body, and especially the female body, represents a territory to be explored, appealing to what Peter Brooks, in *Body Work*, calls "epistemophilia," or the desire to know.[20] Brooks contends that since the eighteenth century, narratives have been concerned with assigning meaning to the body itself; these bodies, imbued with meaning, in turn drive narratives, a process he calls the "somatization of story." The mind, according to Brooks, needs to recover the body in order to define itself through the body's otherness; the resulting curiosity leads to the desire to know the body fully as a source of pleasure, knowledge, and power.[21] The body in the eighteenth century was a site of psychic conflict and desire; the culturally constructed body of art or literature was a site where social conflict and desire are inscribed. The nostalgia of this period was a response to a society undergoing rapid change and is similar to other psychic conflicts of loss and separation, specifically the loss of the mother's body, as Freud and, more particularly, Melanie Klein have observed. Brooks suggests that we also share a "certain romanticized nostalgia" about the body; that is, we imagine that there exists in history another period "of more unified sensibility" when the body, sex, and death "were more fully integrated in human consciousness as 'natural' parts of life." Brooks points out that "we can think back to, or invent, such unity only through our present consciousness of division."[22] If the body precedes language, that we invest it with nostalgia for a prelapsarian time, or even a certain innocence, is not surprising.

The construction of the sentimental body in eighteenth-century literature shares this desire to recover the body within the narrative, as well as the desire to know: consider a novel such as Sterne's *Tristram Shandy*, in which the narrator attempts to write the story of his own conception. The detailed articulation—"to the moment"—of the tears, swoons, blushes, and palpitations of Clarissa Harlowe or Harriet Byron provides the reader with insight into the mental and emotional workings of Richardson's heroines as well as a palpable sense of their bodily experiences. The swoons and palpitations of the sentimental novel encode the sexuality that cannot be openly expressed; for Clarissa and Harriet at least, sexuality must necessarily be confined to satisfaction within marriage. When faintings and flushes overwhelm the body, as they do for many of Richardson's female characters, the body is given up to illness, suggesting that sexuality easily tips over into illness if not satisfied within marriage.

The highly variable categories of health and illness are brought forward as sensibility—and its more dangerous variation, sexuality—becomes excessive. The idea that female celibacy could lead to illness is present in the earliest accounts of Greek medicine and appears in the writings of Galen, Robert Burton, and Ambrose Paré. In "Nuns, Maids, and Widows," Burton elaborates a lengthy description of all the possible symptoms suffered by unmarried women and suggests that "the best and surest remedy of all is to see them well placed, & married to good husbands in due time; hence these tears, that's the primary cause, and this the ready cure, to give them content to their desires."[23] Contradictory social forces exerted their pressures on women: although medicine, from classical times forward, asserted that sexual activity was necessary for good health, the need for a stable system of property distribution, even prior to early capitalism, required that female sexuality be controlled. Unmarried women, without places as wives or mothers, were

themselves "excessive" in a patriarchal society. Without a socially sanc-
tioned outlet for their sexual drives, they were prone, according to Burton and other medical thinkers, to "melancholy"; their difference was
diagnosed as illness, containing and isolating them. The establishment
of categories of health and illness is both socially and historically determined, and subject to change over time; if illness is a category, the discovery of "new" illnesses is often the result of a change in perceptions.

The medical sociologist Bryan Turner notes that "the meaning of illness reflects anxieties about patterns of social behaviour which are
deemed acceptable or otherwise from the point of view of dominant social groups."[24] A diagnosis of illness, then, can be utilized as an instrument of control, a means by which to mark certain feelings, perceptions,
or behaviors as deviant in some way. The sentimental body, as presented by Richardson, Mackenzie, Goldsmith, Fielding, and others,
helped codify and explain, and thereby control, what Turner calls "the
deviance of body surfaces": blushes, flushes, tears, and other involun-
tary or uncontrollable bodily reactions that, occurring as visual signs on
the exterior of the body, are subject to "cultural surveillance."[25] The
sentimental body that appears in eighteenth-century fiction is above all
a performing body that constructs and defines the self.

External signs of fixed social status eroded with the growth of early
capitalism, and by the eighteenth century, merit and achievement began
to compete with titles and inheritance as markers of gentility, a trend
that, although contested, continued into the nineteenth century. Education, possession of land, and the accessibility of consumer goods, such
as clothing and household items such as china, also blurred the distinction between the aristocracy and the middle class. It was necessary,
therefore, to find a way to distinguish those individuals of fine sensibility and superior moral fiber; a "new aristocracy"—but one with profoundly middle-class roots—was being created. The attempt to refix
social lines of demarcation was a nostalgic, conservative gesture; the
sentimental body performed the cultural work of establishing and maintaining a newly created social hierarchy based on such subjective qualities as sympathy for the unfortunate and goodness of heart. Such
sympathy conferred a benefit: "Let me imprint the virtue of thy sufferings on my soul," Harley tells Old Edwards in Mackenzie's *The Man
of Feeling.*[26] Although, as John Mullan notes, in the sentimental novel
sensibility is "constituted . . . out of an opposition to a 'world' of masculine desire, commercial endeavour, and material ambition,"[27] the consumer of sentimental fiction could partake of the virtue of suffering,

assimilating this virtue through its aesthetic representation. Moreover, the circulation of sentimental fiction offered a model of bodily comportment that readers aspiring to upward social mobility could adopt and emulate.

HOMESICKNESS: THE MEDICAL SUBTEXT OF NOSTALGIA

The official medical history of the "disease" of nostalgia begins with Johannes Hofer's dissertation *De Nostalgia oder Heimwehe*, published in Basel in 1678.[28] Hofer's assertion that he was the first physician to describe the condition is not entirely accurate. Spanish doctors had earlier diagnosed an illness they called *el mal de corazón* among soldiers of the Spanish army of Flanders; another variation of this malady, marked by despair and hopelessness among forcibly conscripted soldiers with little or no possibility of leave, was termed *estar roto*. Spanish records from the period 1634–44 report at least six soldiers discharged as a result of *mal de corazón* and another soldier released for being "broken."[29] French-speaking physicians in Switzerland had called a similar illness *maladie du pays*, but Hofer's *nostalgia* would prove to be the most durable.[30]

Unlike the generalized (and essentially nonphysical) concept we now hold of nostalgia (a longing for the past, or for a time when matters were "better" or "simpler"), nostalgia, in the early medical literature, was a disease marked by a wide array of physical symptoms, including "continuing melancholy, incessant thinking of home, disturbed sleep or insomnia, weakness, loss of appetite, anxiety, cardiac palpitations, stupor, and fever."[31] Hofer, while asserting that nostalgia is precipitated by the imagination, theorizes a physiological response to a troubled mind: the vital spirits, continually agitated by thoughts of home and loved ones, fail to flow to the parts of the brain that serve bodily functions, resulting in poor appetite and digestion. The body, in turn, produces a decreasing quantity of vital spirits, which are soon exhausted, resulting in slower heartbeat, general weakening, and eventually, death. Recommended treatments included purgatives, to eliminate poorly digested food; emetics, to relieve nausea; and venesection, to relieve the excess of blood in the circulatory system known as "plethora." Narcotics were suggested to alleviate insomnia and restlessness. A major component of the course of treatment that Hofer recommended was to give the patient hope that he or she would be able to return home as soon as possible. In the event that none of the palliatives are successful, however, the patient was to be sent home anyway, as the trip home almost always resulted in a cure. As evidence, Hofer cites the case of a young student in Basel, homesick for Bern, whose symptoms included a low-grade fever, anxiety, and palpitations. Although his death appeared imminent, an apothecary advised that he be returned to his native city, a pronouncement that resulted in immediate improvement of the student's condition. By the time he was returned to Bern, he had already recovered. [32]

Hofer's clinical description of nostalgia resulted in a spate of dissertations and essays on the subject, and by the middle of the eighteenth century, nostalgia was accepted in medical nosology, appearing in contemporary medical dictionaries. The German *Onomatologia medica* of 1755 defines nostalgia as a disease that "not only leads the mind into foolish, odd and even bizarre eccentricities, but also impairs the individual's physical health. The individual's vitality, both as to color and activity, declines, and little by little his health deteriorates leading to complaints and serious diseases, some affecting the body alone, others the mind as well, and can even degenerate into a kind of melancholy. As long as this strong impulse and desire [to return to the native land] cannot be satisfied, all medicaments and arguments are useless. Indeed, there are even cases where death has resulted when this most ardent desire could not be gratified."[33] Physicians who expanded on Hofer's work added recommendations for treatment, including a diet of easily digested food, including fresh fruit and vegetables; fresh air and light exercise; and modest diversions and entertainment.[34] The advice of Mr. Goddard, the apothecary who first pronounces Clarissa Harlowe's "case to be grief," is consistent with contemporary medical protocol: "he ordered for the present only innocent juleps by way of cordial; and as soon as her stomach should be able to bear it, light kitchen-diet; telling Mrs Lovick that [the diet], with air, moderate exercise, and cheerful company, would do [Clarissa] more good than all the medicines in his shop."[35]

Clarissa's symptoms of wasting and breathlessness, which undoubtedly cause Margaret Doody to conclude that she suffers from consumption, are consistent with nostalgia as it was understood within the context of eighteenth-century medicine. Leopold Auenbrugger, the Viennese physician who claims to have developed the clinical practice of percussion, writes of changes in the lungs of patients suffering from nostalgia. In his *Inventum novum* of 1761, Auenbrugger notes that he has detected "a dull sound (*sonitus obscurus*) on one side of the chest" when percussing nostalgic patients. Moreover, Auenbrugger asserts, he has "opened many cadavers of those who died of [nostalgia] and have always found the lungs firmly adherent to the pleura; the lobes on the side where the sound was dull were callous, indurated, and more or less purulent."[36] Stanley Jackson observes that the changes Auenbrugger attributes to nostalgia were most likely the result of tuberculosis;[37] yet, in the eighteenth century, the connection between disordered emotions and pathological changes in the body was well-accepted.

In the eighteenth century, nostalgia was considered a form of melancholia, but later physicians dissent from such a strict classification. Nostalgia incorporates much more than just dejection or sadness. In the nineteenth century, Dominique Jean Larrey, while classifying nostalgia as a form of melancholia, nevertheless describes a primary stage of the disease as one that includes "an exaggeration of the imaginative faculty." Nostalgic patients do not recall their homes as those homes really are, but rather as "delightful and enchanting, no matter how rude and poverty-stricken they may be," and family members are recalled as affectionate, genial, and "richly clothed." [38] The patient effectively rewrites his or her actual history in order to construct an idealized object of desire.

More recently, Harvey Kaplan has proposed a psychoanalytic model of nostalgia that removes nostalgia from the broader category of melancholia. Observing that nostalgia contains "pleasurable components" that depression or melancholia lack, Kaplan suggests that nostalgia is "a compromise formation, the function of which would be the fulfillment of secret and repressed wishes that protect the ego from anxiety arising from undischarged instinctual tensions in the present. This effort would be aimed at fulfilling unsatisfied wishes through the creation of an imagined situation in which the wish was represented as being fulfilled."[39] Through such a formation, Kaplan notes, "the present is enhanced, sensations heightened, the world becomes full, not empty," in contrast to depression, which is marked by "sadness, loss, emptiness, and self-loathing."[40]

Kaplan's concept of enhancement and fullness is consistent with the tendency of nostalgia to generate text or other aesthetic production.[41] Enhancement, however, only lasts as long as the fantasy can be sustained. *Clarissa*, replete with letters "written to the moment," is nothing other than enhancement of the present moment; at the same time, the novel retains a certain "historicity," or, as Fredric Jameson puts it, "a relationship to the present which somehow defamiliarizes it and allows us that distance from immediacy which we call historical." The epistolary form allows us to "draw back from our immersion in the here-and-now (not yet identified as a 'present') and grasp it as a kind of thing— not merely a 'present,' but a present that can be dated."[42] The letters of *Clarissa* are an obsessive form of remembering, in which nothing can be left out; dialogue is painstakingly recorded, and even sighs, tears, laughter, and tone of voice are included. Such obsessive and all-inclusive "remembering" functions as a screen for the social contradictions at work in the novel.

NOSTALGIA AND THE BODY

In Samuel Richardson's *Clarissa* (1748) and *Sir Charles Grandison* (1753–54), the body becomes a text that can be read. What happens when repressed social contradictions surface on the body of the text? My reading of Richardson's novels turns on the categories of health and illness, and the ways in which gender plays a part in the construction of those categories.

The wasting and diseased female bodies that appear in *Clarissa* and *Sir Charles Grandison* can be seen as updated versions of those of Sir Robert Burton's melancholic or lovesick women. Many writers, including Timothy Bright and Thomas Browne, had written about "the English malady," but Burton's monumental *Anatomy of Melancholy* (1621) became the definitive text in the field. While Burton's tome helped establish the melancholic man (including him) as an exquisitely sensitive being, given to aesthetic pursuits, his female examples are merely sufferers of an illness that participates in no elite cultural category.

Some of Burton's theories regarding the management of melancholia and lovesickness dovetail neatly with theories advanced in the eighteenth century for the management of the body. Burton blames melancholy on idleness, particularly the idleness of the wealthy and aristocratic. Moreover, wealth made possible the consumption of rich and exotic diets that, combined with idleness, resulted in bodily and social disorder. Burton's theories surface in Dr. George Cheyne's *The English Malady* (1733), a text that had considerable influence in the years following its appearance.

Cheyne, Richardson's close friend and personal physician, believed that the expansion of trade and a growth in wealth had led to a dangerous overconsumption of imported and highly spiced food and drink, which, in turn, made the population prone to melancholy and other nervous diseases. Cheyne's cure, which he practiced at Bath, was the "low diet," consisting of vegetables, milk, and seeds; alcohol and animal flesh were to be strictly avoided. Also included in the regimen were exercise, regular evacuation, vomits, and useful industry.[43] Cheyne's ideas were disseminated to the general public through writers such as Richardson and were also adopted by John Wesley as the basis of his *Primitive Physick* (1752). Cheyne's diet and regimen were consistent with Methodist asceticism, in which the individual exercised a stewardship over the body, considered the "temple of Christ," and therefore not to be abused. The management of diet was no longer just a bodily practice; it had become a matter of morality and served to control unruly desires that held the potential for social disorder.

Concurrent with Cheyne's and Wesley's writings on the healthy and well-managed body was the development of the sentimental body. My examination of Richardson's sentimental bodies takes up the issue of whether those bodies are considered "healthy" or "ill," how gender plays a part in determining health or illness, and how these categories are distributed throughout *Clarissa* and *Sir Charles Grandison*. Why, for example, do the sentimental heroines, Clarissa Harlowe, Clementina della Porretta, and Harriet Byron, fall ill of their grief, while Sir Charles Grandison's good "heart" and tender emotions result in bounding good health and good cheer? Or why is physical illness or weakness in a male character displaced onto Jeronymo—an Italian, whose gender is rendered ambiguous by intimations of castration? The representation of illness in Richardson's novels is double edged in that the body becomes the site of anxiety about conflicts between virtue and desire, and about the control of bodies; hence, contemporary concerns, such as those surrounding the control of daughters' bodies and the transfer of property, or the development of domestic ideology, are played out on the weak, diseased, or dying female body that displays its illness for a male gaze.

Richardson's own nostalgia for wholeness and coherence, I argue, is held in place by the displacement of disorderly or dangerous elements onto "other" bodies and landscapes. Such displacement reveals itself, however, in the form of textual disruption, specifically, Clarissa's "mad" papers and the unusual Italian travel section of letter 39 in Volume 4 of *Sir Charles Grandison* that seems so obviously not to have been written by Richardson at all, but interpolated into the text, perhaps from personal correspondence.[44] In the case of *Clarissa*, madness—the most extreme, and most spectacular episode of Clarissa's illness—takes on material form as the letters are printed askew on the page; her violated body "speaks" through the disorder of her letters, which Richardson the printer cleverly produces for visual consumption. In the case of the letter from Mr. Lowther, the physician who accompanies Sir Charles to Italy, to his brother-in-law, the textual disruption is subtler; nevertheless, the narrative that describes the crossing of the mountains into Italy is peopled with not-wholly human characters with strange customs, and set in a cold and sinister landscape. In this depiction of Italy, Sir Charles's kindness and goodness stand out in relief.

Chapter 3 of this volume concerns the textual bodies that recall the story of Heloise and Abelard. In Pope's "Eloisa to Abelard" (1717) and Rousseau's *Julie, ou la nouvelle Héloïse* (1761), desire struggles against bodily or social control. In Pope's formally rigid poem, desire peeks through the rhymed couplets as the sensuous Eloisa peeks through the window of her convent cell. But the longing and pain reflected in Eloisa's desire are a displacement of the pain and loss that cannot be spoken, except by the body's "tears, and burning blushes"[45]: that of Abelard's castration. Abelard, imprisoned in a cruelly mutilated body, is present only through his writings and Eloisa's desire for him. Pope's nostalgia for a whole and healthy body reveals itself in this poem of loss and longing; moreover, Pope inserts himself as the object of feminine desire by assuming Abelard's position of mastery over Eloisa's discourse and desire. The writing of the poem constructs a body through which Pope's own desire reveals itself, a body that speaks in a feminine voice.

Rousseau's novel also creates the body of a woman; specifically, that of a mother—a passionate mother, for the Julie whose letters bear the imprint of her erotic desire for her lover, Saint-Preux, ultimately dies for love of her child. In my examination of Pope's and Rousseau's texts, I move outward from the body itself and into the landscape against which the body is displayed. Julie's garden is so private, so very much her own, that it becomes a natural extension of her body, while Eloisa's convent—dark, moldering, confining, ruined—is at odds with her desire and vitality. In Rousseau's *Julie*, the imprisonment of Pope's Eloisa in a convent evolves into Julie's prison of domesticity and superior moral virtue. Both texts construct bodies that offer the writers symbolic substitutes that conceal the anxiety of gender difference and reveal their longing for whole and coherent bodies that effectively cover over the threat of castration or disorderly female desire.

The cloisters and ruins of Pope's "Eloisa," written early in the century, and the gardens and enclosures of Rousseau's *Julie*, written over forty years later, reflect the growing interest in landscape and gardens that would become a significant aesthetic category in the eighteenth century. In chapter 4 of this book, I examine representations of the landscape and body in Pope's "Windsor Forest" (1714) and Oliver Goldsmith's "The Revolution in Low Life" (1762) and *The Deserted Village* (1770), with a particular focus on the pleasures of the picturesque. My interest in the ways gender and class affect our notions of space influences my reading of Goldsmith's novel *The Vicar of Wakefield* (1766), in which I examine the spaces of the home and the domestic ideology at work within the Vicar's family.

The seeds of the picturesque took root early in the century, as early as Addison's *Remarks on Several Parts of Italy* (1705), which served as a guidebook to young men on the "Grand Tour" in the first half of the eighteenth century. Anxieties about changes in the English landscape were palliated by a nostalgic response that manifested itself in an increasing interest in antiquities, ruins, and sublime landscapes—elements that eventually found their way into the "taste" for the picturesque, which was codified in William Gilpin's *Three Essays: On Picturesque Beauty; On Picturesque Travel; and On Sketching Landscape* (1792). Unlike the Grand Tour, domestic tourism to picturesque locations, such as the Lake District, was available to the British middle classes; one did not have to own land in order to enjoy it. But by the end of the century, Uvedale Price moved to theorize the picturesque in his *Essay on the Picturesque* (1794), and thereby to recuperate nostalgia for the upper classes. Price's *Essay*, as Ann Bermingham has observed in *Landscape and Ideology: The English Rustic Tradition, 1740–1860*, is an ideological project. Responding to the "improvements" of Lancelot "Capability" Brown and Humphrey Repton, Price attempts to codify an aesthetic of the picturesque—one available only to those with the education to enjoy it and the resources to allow their land to "become" picturesque the old-fashioned way: by leaving it alone. As Bermingham points out, "The value of the picturesque landscape was that no amount of money could bring it about."[46]

Price's *Essay* also represents an interesting attempt to find a middle ground or third term between Burke's concepts of the sublime and beautiful. The fact that the picturesque was, by definition, that which was appropriate for a painting or sketch implies a certain sense of control or mastery that is missing from Burke's sublime. The picturesque may amuse, or even produce wistfulness, but it never terrifies—if only because picturesque elements such as crumbling cottages or Gypsy camps are always kept at a distance, always aestheticized. The social conditions that result in ruined cottages are elided in the picturesque scene.

Concerns about the effect of social change on the English landscape (and way of life) surface in much of the literature, but perhaps nowhere so tenderly as in Oliver Goldsmith's *The Deserted Village*. Goldsmith's investment in his own nostalgia for a better, simpler time, or perhaps his own longing for home—he had long ago left his native Ireland—is captured in his most famous poem, which eulogizes not a dying body, but a dying village. The village Goldsmith's narrator mourns is that of his childhood; he can never return in the same way, yet his nostalgia for his own memories is put into the service of art. The deserted village of the poem is an eloquent "dying body" in the picturesque twilight of its life. The nostalgia of *The Deserted Village* reappears in *The Vicar of Wakefield* (1766), in which the placid Dr. Primrose's desire to enjoy the simple life is constantly thwarted—not just by circumstance, but also by his wife and daughters, who are charged with the burden of his nostalgia at the expense of their own modern and occasionally unruly desires.

The final chapter of this volume explores the possibility of feminine nostalgia in Sarah Scott's 1762 novel, *A Description of Millenium Hall*. In this novel about a utopian community of women, Scott attempts a radical rearticulation of space and narrative production; in *Millenium Hall*, the women create their own society and households and tell their own stories. By creating a community based on close relationships, Scott attempts to dismantle traditional power structures in the space of the estate, but this utopia is not without its contradictions and internal tensions, and a close look at the novel reveals the unevenness of Scott's narrative and ideology.

The nostalgia of Richardson, Rousseau, Pope, Goldsmith, and Scott is a conservative response to social change. Nostalgia is a pleasurable repetition; it is not mourning, which defers a complete separation from the past, but a way of indulging the pleasures of melancholy without the dangers of tipping back into the semiotic. Cultural nostalgia reinforces subjectivity by offering a sense of continuity with the past, a reassurance that the self is still intact. Unlike mourning, which defers acknowledgment of loss and refuses to move forward, nostalgia can be enjoyed from within the fantasy of full subjectivity. The nostalgic subject looks back at loss from a safe vantage point, but the burden of tradition and nostalgia is borne by those who are other; in the texts examined here, those others are most often women and the poor. Clarissa, Julie, Eloisa, Deborah Primrose, and the nameless female characters of Goldsmith's sweet Auburn weep, suffer, waste away, or even die in the service of nostalgia.

The modern self is one who narrates, who tells the tales of those who bear the burden of the past. The cultural nostalgia of the eighteenth century sought reparation in aesthetic production and would go on to drive the literary production of the poets and novelists of the nineteenth and twentieth centuries, as those writers attempted to negotiate social change and construct illusions of wholeness and permanence in a world that was scarcely free of social contradictions.

2

"Pronouncing her case to be grief": Nostalgia and the Body in *Clarissa* and *Sir Charles Grandison*

WHAT AILS CLARISSA HARLOWE? CRITICS HAVE ATTRIBUTED THE death of Clarissa to various causes: Margaret Doody declares that Clarissa dies of "galloping consumption"; Terry Eagleton observes that "clinically speaking, Clarissa dies of depression"; G. J. Barker-Benfield believes her illness "should be thought of as a nervous disorder in extremis"; and Donnalee Frega, while refusing to declare Clarissa anorexic, nevertheless interprets her "starvation" as "a powerful, erotic, and dangerous form of discourse."[1] While Clarissa's symptoms may suggest a specific illness such as consumption, depression, or a nervous disorder, Samuel Richardson is careful not to allow any such diagnosis to appear in his 1748 novel *Clarissa, or the History of a Young Lady*. While the causes of other deaths in the novel, such as Mrs. Sinclair's death of gangrene, or Mr. Belton's death of consumption, are clearly defined, Clarissa's doctors can only "pronounc[e] her case to be grief."[2]

But to say that Clarissa dies of "grief" or "depression" is to ignore the rich subtext of her death, for Clarissa's is a death that generates narrative. Clarissa herself dates her death from the tenth of April, the day that she leaves her parents' home; her protracted dying, then, accounts for approximately two-thirds of Richardson's mammoth novel. Any attempt to diagnose Clarissa's illness from a twenty-first-century perspective would be reductive; on the other hand, Clarissa's death takes on meaning when we read her illness and death within the context of nostalgia, an affect that leads not away from language into the asymbolia of depression, but toward language, and toward a pleasurable profusion of words that constructs a "new" body, that of Richardson's text.

The sentimental body—of which Clarissa Harlowe's body and Sir Charles Grandison's body are prime examples—served the cultural nostalgia of the eighteenth century. Both sentiment and sensibility intersected with categories of health, illness, gender, and class. The sentimental male body, as we shall see in the case of Sir Charles Grandison, can be simultaneously healthy, vigorous, and emotional, in contrast to the female sentimental body, which is delicate, ill, or "suffering" from the very same emotions that mark the male body in a positive light. How are the traditional signs of the sentimental body—blushes, tears, swoons, palpitations, sighs—read differently in male and female bodies? And what is at stake in such interpretations?

One of the differences between male and female sentimentality was apparent in the contemporary theoretical link between sensibility and sexuality: the male body showed signs of high moral character through its sensibility, while the female body showed dangerous signs of sexuality. G. J. Barker-Benfield suggests that unhindered expression of "heterosocial pleasure" and "individual pursuit of self-expression" result from the cult of sensibility and remarks that such practices were "epitomized by the figure of the rake."[3] Pope's often-quoted dictum that "e'vry Woman is at heart a rake"[4] expresses an anxiety that was common to the age, one to which Robert Lovelace, the quintessential rake, certainly subscribes. The pleasure and self-expression available to men in the form of unrestricted behavior, rakish and otherwise, were assumed to be equally desirable to women, despite the social restrictions on their public demeanor. The belief that women were rakes "at heart" hints at a rampant sexuality and a love of pleasure that are only barely kept under control by social mores and domestic surveillance.

This ancient version of female sexuality was in the process of being displaced by what Thomas Laqueur calls the "newly discovered 'contingency' of delight," the fact that female orgasm was not necessary for conception, but was instead a biological "bonus." Such a shift in thinking, corresponding to the altered concept of the one-sex to the two-sex model of the body, "created a space in which women's sexual nature could be redefined, debated, denied, or qualified,"[5] and we see this conflict and transformation being worked through in Clarissa. This contradictory attitude toward women's sexuality, comprising both fear and titillation, allowed an ideological construction of the female body as weak, subject to unpredictable sexual urges, and susceptible to illness and disease: in short, a body unsuitable for work, and in need of control.

THE IDEOLOGY OF THE SENTIMENTAL BODY

If the body is the threshold where nature and culture meet—the body is always at once natural and social—then the sentimental body represents a shared social body image. More than just a code of behavior, the sentimental body offers a way to imagine the body in society, responding—with physical sensations, genuinely experienced—to a wide array of social phenomena. The sentimental body is nostalgic in its *performance* of empathy for the suffering or unfortunate; just as the picturesque will later attempt to "recapture" a landscape undergoing change, sentimentality attempted to "recapture" a social benevolence perceived as disappearing, or to preserve, in fantasy, a "moral order" that, according to Raymond Williams, the middle classes abstracted from a feudal economy.[6] Whether any genuine social benevolence really existed is, of course, debatable: as Judith Butler points out, the object of nostalgic desire is always an imaginary referent, constituted by the performance of nostalgia.[7] The social benevolence "remembered" in the performance of sentimental empathy may well have been paternalistic control, which was cruel as often as it was helpful.

Empathetic sentimentality, however, belongs to Harley, in *The Man of Feeling*; Tristram Shandy; or Sir Charles Grandison. Another type of sentimentality is reserved for Clarissa Harlowe and Harriet Byron. In what way is feminine sentimentality nostalgic? The sufferings of Clarissa or Harriet (or Jeronymo della Porretta) are decidedly *not* the mark of social empathy; instead, their swoons, tears, and blushes spring from their own physical delicacy. Their sentimentality is located not in their elevated sense of social morality, but in the weakness of their bodies. While the observation of—and empathy with—suffering "imprints" virtue on masculine souls, feminine sentimentality is more often marked as illness, a spectacle to be observed and co-opted for the vicarious virtue it offers through its suffering. The construction of feminine sensibility as weakness or delicacy served cultural nostalgia by contributing to a developing domestic ideology that increasingly confined women to the private sphere of the home; sentimentality, ultimately, helped to construct and reinforce sexual difference. The sentimental bodies appearing in eighteenth-century novels allowed contemporary readers to partake of vicarious virtue and to participate in a larger social body image, in which all the members of that social body would be able to recognize each other. Because of the growing separation of public and private spheres, this social body image was masculine; feminine sensibility, on the other hand, was private.

Anthony Ashley Cooper, third earl of Shaftesbury's, *Characteristics of Men, Manners, Opinions, Times* (1711) is considered a seminal text in the history of sensibility. Interestingly, Shaftesbury's attitude toward sensibility is ambivalent: although he posits an innate moral sense, a theory possibly derived from the influence of Locke (who was employed by the first earl of Shaftesbury to supervise his grandson's education), Shaftesbury resists any democratization of sensibility, proposing instead a nostalgic agenda that recuperates sensibility for himself and his fellow aristocrats.[8] The sensitive self that Shaftesbury extols is above all inherited, and therefore not universally available; the ideal modern man, as described in his *Characteristics*, evokes Sir Charles Grandison: manly, reasonable, polished, well bred. The new man would maintain a certain inner control, enabling him to direct his own destiny. Shaftesbury's modern hero would be a man of learning and ideas, but not a Hercules of physical strength. His ambivalent stance toward the sensible man, his resistance to "effeminacy," may be the mark of his own sickly body on his writing; Shaftesbury suffered from chronic poor health, and particularly from asthma.[9] Unable to emulate his ancient heroes, Shaftesbury constructed, out of his nostalgia, a modern hero to validate his own existence as a writer and man of ideas and to retain the authority of the scholar or the artist for those born to the calling.

Male and female versions of the sentimental body were read in different ways. Contemporary readers saw Clarissa Harlowe's suffering and death as the mark of her virtue and her impeccable moral character, but her sensibility did not change or enhance her class status. Clarissa simply wastes away and dies. Clarissa's virtue does not assure her an active role in the social order; she assumes her role as virtuous heroine only through her death. Harriet Byron falls ill, as does Clementina della Porretta, not from grief, but from love of Sir Charles Grandison. While sentimental female bodies are languishing, sentimental male bodies are accruing superior moral virtue through the suffering of others, a contrast to Shaftesbury's modern man, whose virtue derives from his own superior inner qualities.

Peter Brooks points out the differences in the treatment of male and female bodies, noting that in patriarchal societies, the male body is "ostensibly deproblematized . . . and concomitantly more thoroughly hidden."[10] Despite, or perhaps because of, its function as the norm, as an unmarked category, the male body is not available for view; it is not the object of the gaze. Hence we see Tristram Shandy's trying—unsuccessfully—to write his own bodily experience from within; the elusiveness of his body, Tristram's inability fully to grasp his bodily existence, keeps the novel going in a frustrating attempt to "catch up" to the real history of his body. On the other hand, the textual body of

Clarissa increases as Clarissa Harlowe's body wastes away, a process that is always on display for the reader.[11] The male bodies in *Sir Charles Grandison* with the most textual presence are those that are mutilated or injured, such as those of Jeronymo, who suffers a groin wound; Sir Hargrave Pollexfen, who loses his teeth; and Mr. Merceda, who is nearly castrated by an irate husband. Sir Charles's body may be there in the text, but its presence is defined by female desire: the desire that Clementina tries to suppress at the expense of her mental health, the desire that leads Olivia to declare that she is willing to live as Sir Charles's mistress, and the desire that Harriet Byron is finally able to domesticate through marriage.

The sentimental body helped to explain and legitimate the unpredictability of body surfaces, those blushes, tears, sighs, and even palpitations that could be seen behind delicate handkerchiefs. But deviances of the internal body—disease and illness—were subject to what Bryan Turner calls "moral evaluation,"[12] and the signs of sentiment, so unequivocally positive in men, were often read as signs of illness in women. Those nonspecific diseases—hysteria, lovesickness, grief, "vapours"—whose symptoms are so similar to the emotions of sentiment were nearly always diseases of women or of men turned somehow womanly. The melancholy suffered by the sensitive man was a badge of distinction that conferred a superior sensibility upon the sufferer and held the added bonus of endowing the melancholic with artistic tendencies. Unlike melancholy, nostalgia had never been a malady of aristocrats, allowing it to be easily adopted by the middle classes as a cultural posture.

These different ways of reading symptoms underline the importance of studying the cultural and ideological work done by illness. These "maladies" are, on the one hand, social constructions that reinforce an image of women as weak creatures, in need of male protection, and best suited to roles within the private, domestic sphere. Burton and others, including Freud, recommend marriage as a form of social restraint that will provide mental stability and personal happiness for women. But, from the point of view of the "sick" woman, some value might accrue to the sick role.

The modern concept of the "sick role," according to Talcott Parsons, describes a person who willingly seeks out assistance from a health care professional, thereby adopting the social position of one who does not enjoy a commonly accepted sense of "health." Such a role usually includes social factors, including withdrawal from activities such as work, school, or chores. The "sick role" can be temporary, as in the case of acute illness, or permanent, in the case of chronic disease.[13] The sick role itself, however, is nothing new: variations on such a role have always existed, although their manifestations have conformed to specific periods in history.

Parsons suggests that adopting a "sick role" indicates a willingness to withdraw from a certain level of activity and social contact; similarly, perhaps, the *assignment* of a "sick role" to another would serve to restrict activities and social contacts of the person designated as "sick," effectively removing the sick person from circulation. The control of social movement and circulation of women through the assignment of the sick role is implicated in the notion of the sentimental body, which, in *Clarissa* and *Sir Charles Grandison*, is inextricably linked to categories of health versus illness, organized along gendered lines.

The fear that voluntary adoption of a sick role meant the feigning of "nervous illnesses" was a subject of concern in the eighteenth century. Despite the materialistic basis of the primary theories of the nervous system, many writers, including Dr. George Cheyne, Richardson's friend and personal physician, worried that women could feign illness to their personal advantage. G. J. Barker-Benfield suggests that women discovered that headaches, fainting, and fits could help them resist men's sexual approaches. Moreover, women were thought to be excessively fond of increasingly available consumer goods and luxuries, specifically tea, coffee, or chocolate, all generously fortified with sugar, the ingestion of which was suspected to have a deleterious effect on the delicate female nervous system.[14] But another factor was the supposed female pursuit of pleasure: spas such as Bath or Tunbridge Wells, which offered lively social scenes in addition to their therapeutic springs, were revived as husbands and fathers escorted wives and daughters to "take the waters" and brace up their nervous constitutions.[15] The same anxiety that Pope exhibits in his contention that "evr'y woman is at heart a rake" is evident in the view that some women feigned illness in order to procure a trip to a spa town, where, in the imagination of some writers, they could engage in sexual dalliances when they were not indulging their tastes for consumer luxuries at the shopping parades, or enjoying the evening dances and places of public entertainment. It is true that there may be some benefit in the adoption of the sick role: being ill can be a creative act in its own right, used to manipulate family members, to achieve a certain status within the household, or to excuse oneself from activities of various kinds. When other means of resistance or rebellion are ineffective or unavailable, the body itself may be used to subvert or resist authority.

As the threshold where nature and culture meet, the body is socialized in various ways, but particularly through consumption. Eating, the most literal form of consumption, is thoroughly imbued with social components; it is often more "social" than "natural," entailing elaborate rituals, preparations, celebrations, and various family or community events.[16] Clarissa Harlowe's resistance to her father's authority is acted out in her refusal to consume either food or the goods that would make up her trousseau in preparation for a marriage to Mr. Solmes. Clarissa effectively withdraws from society—that is, from the circumscribed domestic sphere that constitutes her social realm—when she stops consuming. But Richardson's sentimental heroine apparently cannot live outside society; her refusal—or inability—to consume ultimately results in the death of her body.

Turner observes that attempts to control the body are likely to fail.[17] But the contingent nature of the body only makes it a more tempting subject of artistic control through the creation of a symbolic body that can perform ideological work. As does the land, which is also considered "natural," the body offers both a threat and a promise: the threat of disorder, but the promise of an essence—Freud's "bedrock" of biology—that is a comfort to the nostalgic writer, such as Richardson, at the middle of the eighteenth century.

DYING BODIES AND THE BODY OF TEXT

The textual body that is Samuel Richardson's *Clarissa* comes into being at the expense of the physical, if fictional, body of Clarissa Harlowe. Clarissa's body is a site at which many eighteenth-century social contradictions intersect, and where the very real social changes of Richardson's time—a move, for example, from marriages arranged by families to "companionate" marriages—are played out, for the forces that ultimately converge to lead Clarissa to take that fatal step outside her father's garden wall have their origin in the conflict between Clarissa's own desire and the "will" of her family, especially that of her father, and her brother, James. Richardson, in the midst of social change, "writes to the moment" of history: he responds to those changes with a massive novel that incorporates the past and the present. *Clarissa* is at once a "history" and an epistolary novel, a collection of letters that gives the illusion that the events recounted in its letters are happening as we read them. Ultimately, however, *Clarissa* is a "whole" textual body that accommodates and unifies the textual fragmentation of the letters and the historical fragmentation produced by social tensions. Clarissa's lingering death allows the text of *Clarissa* to come into being, the body of text taking on materiality as the fictional Clarissa's body wastes away to nothing.[18]

The gaps in the chronology of *Clarissa* generate text. The abrupt ruptures in the novel—Clarissa's departure from her father's house and her rape by Lovelace—cannot be represented at the moment of their occurrence; they are recounted only subsequently, and only obliquely in the case of the rape. Clarissa's nostalgia for her home and for her innocent body generates text in the form of letters that describe her extended suffering and her death, which is a slow decline rather than a single violent occurrence. Clarissa's body gradually loses materiality at the same time her soul gains strength, a process that is minutely recorded in the profusion of letters exchanged between the tenth of April and the seventh of September, the last day of Clarissa's life.[19]

Clarissa's letter to Anna Howe of Tuesday morning, one o'clock, April 11, is jarring to the reader. The sense of being in the present of the novel is abruptly shattered when we realize that Clarissa's tensely awaited departure from her father's house—or more properly, Lovelace's abduction of Clarissa—has already taken place. The event is missing from the chronological sequence of events. Moreover, we must wait to hear the story, and by the time it is recounted, it is clearly "history." This type of textual disruption makes sense, if we consider that Clarissa's flight from her father's house is the event that creates a "history" for Clarissa; as long as Clarissa is living in her father's house, time—and her own actions—are not irrevocable. Her threatened marriage to Mr. Solmes is continually deferred to the future; her status within her family, although diminished by the Harlowes' displeasure at her refusal to marry Solmes, is able to be resolved or even restored to its previous position—on the condition, of course, that she comply with her father's and brother's wishes.

Once she leaves the garden in the company of Lovelace, however, nothing can ever be the same. "Oh that I were again in my father's house, stealing down with a letter to you," Clarissa laments to Anna (L94/382). With this statement, Clarissa's own nostalgia asserts itself; her feelings about her father's house—lately a place of confinement and misery—have been converted into a pleasant affect, a warm memory that relieves the terrible anxiety and uncertainty of the present. From this point until her death, when her wish will be realized in a theological and metaphorical sense, Clarissa's overwhelming desire is to return to "her father's house."

This nostalgic desire overcomes the erotic desire for Lovelace that seems to peek through the text while Clarissa is still at home. Her sexual desire clearly underpins the conflict between Clarissa and her family. Clarissa repeatedly affirms her revulsion at Solmes's "person": she describes him as "odious," a "bent and broad-shouldered creature" who "squats" and "stalks." Clarissa is disgusted and offended when Solmes sits too close to her: "He took [a] chair," Clarissa writes to Anna, "and drew it so near mine, squatting in it with his ugly weight, that he pressed upon my hoop" (L16/87), a clear, if metaphorical, expression of sexual disgust. Her feelings toward Lovelace, despite his reputation as a libertine, reflect no such disgust; on the contrary, Clarissa seems tempted to see him, and, despite her family's vehement opposition, she finds excuses to continue corresponding with him. Clarissa's desire for Lovelace is never explicitly expressed in her own letters (although it is articulated in Anna Howe's remarks). Once Clarissa suspects that he has tricked her into fleeing her father's house, her desire seems to disappear, to resurface only in her "mad" letters; in several comments in which Clarissa tells Lovelace that she once could have loved him; and in her ambiguous references to her "fault," a term that she later defines as her "pride," a definition that overrides any hint of sexual desire. Such desire, it seems, can only exist for Clarissa within the patriarchal framework of marriage, or the relatively "safe" structure of her father's house, that timeless place where nothing is irrevocable.

Clarissa's sexual desire is rechanneled into the service of nostalgic desire, which is increasingly eroticized. Desire generates narrative in this novel, while the completed sex act, the end of desire, does not in any direct way. Witness the novel's shortest, yet most famous, letter: Lovelace's letter 257 to Belford, in which he reports, "And now, Belford, I can go no farther. The affair is over. Clarissa lives" (883). As does Clarissa's letter to Anna reporting her flight, Lovelace's letter points to a major gap in the text, that of the rape itself. The tension of Lovelace's attempts to seduce Clarissa has been unbearably prolonged, and the absence of the rape itself from the chronology of the letters is like a black hole "toward which this huge mass of writing is sucked only to sheer off again," as Terry Eagleton characterizes it. "Lovelace's sexual climax," Eagleton goes on to say, "is also the novel's great anticlimax, a purely impersonal act of violence which refuses entry into discourse."[20] But while Clarissa's departure from her family home is reported after only a brief delay, the rape is never really fully reported, for Clarissa is drugged at the time of the rape, and her vague description of what she can remember does not appear until much later.

Lovelace's rape of Clarissa is his encounter with Clarissa's unmediated body and can only be rewritten, presented in retrospect, constructed in fantasy. If the rape effectively mutes Lovelace (albeit temporarily), the violation of Clarissa's body effects a disruption of her textual production: the "mad" letters, so full of words, yet empty of memory. "And thought, and grief, and confusion came crowding so thick upon me," Clarissa writes to Anna, ". . . so I can write nothing at all—only that, whatever they have done to me, I cannot tell; but I am no longer what I was in any one thing" (Paper I, 890). As Leah Price notes, in the mad papers, Clarissa's own narration ceases and is replaced by quotations: Paper X comprises quotations from Dryden, Otway, and Shakespeare, among others, followed by meditations that are "pieced together from biblical quotations." Moreover, "the rape prompts Clarissa's project of compiling other characters' letters to form the corpus that will eventually become the novel. Instead of narrating, Clarissa "'collects.'"[21] Clarissa's act of collection is reparative but lacks the authenticity of her own narrative; she attempts to "piece together" her damaged body, but the resulting text is no longer a representation of her unviolated self.

The materiality of Clarissa's mad papers acts out what Clarissa cannot remember: Paper I is "torn in two pieces"; Paper II is "scratched through, and thrown under the table"; the lines of Paper X are strewn all over the page (890–93). The torn and scattered pages represent the violation of her body and the fragmentation of her sense of self. But Clarissa's madness, like the rape, is never really present in the text; her mad writings are contained within Lovelace's letter to Belford, transcribed by Dorcas when Lovelace finds that he "can write no more of this eloquent nonsense myself; which rather shows a raised, than a quenched, imagination" (L261/890). Lovelace edits Clarissa's writing, in effect reassembling Clarissa, choosing to include only "some of the scraps and fragments" (L261/889) that Clarissa writes. Presumably, there are others that he leaves out or does not see.[22] Despite ample evidence to the contrary, Lovelace assures Belford that Clarissa's "memory, which serves her so well for these poetical flights, is far from being impaired" (L261/894). As Frances Ferguson has observed, Lovelace is not prepared for Clarissa's transformation "into a version of the disorderly letter";[23] his reconstruction of the "mad" Clarissa is, for him, "whole" and unified.

In his desire to reconstruct Clarissa, Lovelace fantasizes a second rape in which Clarissa is a more willing partner. For Lovelace, a second sexual encounter would help rewrite the first one, which has left him so unsatisfied. In Lovelace's fantasy, "Mother H," a somewhat benign version of Mrs. Sinclair, is in bed with Clarissa as Clarissa tells her "sad story." When Mother H leaves the bed to search for a cordial to calm her colic, she drops her candle, allowing Lovelace to take her place in bed. Although Clarissa, in Lovelace's imaginary scenario, is shocked to find Mother H replaced by "a young person of the other Sex," she is nevertheless relieved to find that the young man is Lovelace himself: "it was a matter of some consolation to her . . . that she had been still the bedfellow of but *one* and the *same* man" (L271/922). Clarissa's relief at seeing Lovelace rather than a stranger constitutes, for Lovelace at least, a facsimile of desire. Most importantly, Clarissa's relief acknowledges the first rape and reassures Lovelace that he has indeed succeeded in finally "knowing" Clarissa's body and penetrating it with his own—a satisfaction that seems to be lacking in the curious absence of the rape from the text, and in Lovelace's terse commentary in his letter 257 to Belford.

The fantasy goes well beyond the moment of the rape (which is imagined in scarcely any detail) to include the sequelae: "Then," he writes to Belford, "as quick as thought (for Dreams thou knowest confine not themselves to the Rules of the Drama), ensued Recoveries, Lyings-in, Christenings, the smiling Boy, amply, even in *her own* opinion, rewarding the suffering Mother" (L271/922). The "smiling Boy" who is finally able to convince Clarissa that her suffering has been worthwhile, converting her pain to joy, is nothing other than Lovelace's own nostalgic reincarnation of himself, a triumph of sameness over Clarissa's sexual difference that carries with it, moreover, Clarissa's own concurrence. Lovelace's fantasy reproduction of himself—the deed made flesh— negates his guilt, allows him to rewrite the first rape, reassures him of the stability of sexual boundaries by making Clarissa a mother, and results, ultimately, in the transcendence of those boundaries in the form of a son.

But Clarissa steadfastly rejects Lovelace's attempts to reconstruct her. By refusing to marry him, a move that would retroactively negate the rape, she takes herself "out of circulation" within the patriarchal economy, effectively denying any possibility of recuperating her former status within her family even as she claims to long for reconciliation with them. Clarissa refuses to allow Lovelace to act on his theory of "Marry and repair, at any time" (L470/1344) and insists on living henceforth as the raped and "miserably abused" Clarissa (L261.1/896), who has no place within the surrounding social structure. Tassie Gwilliam observes that Clarissa's death thwarts Lovelace's possession of her by rejecting the possibility of desire, pregnancy, or death in childbirth: "by not defining herself as a body disintegrated by the rape or as one whose essence is possessed by another, by not acquiescing in her commodification, Clarissa engages in a self-transformation that arrests change."[24]

By her refusal to be "rewritten," Clarissa assumes a new identity as a tragic heroine, whose suffering and dying body is a lingering reproach to her family and to Lovelace, all of whom have refused to recognize Clarissa as an independent subject. Observing that Clarissa refers to her violated body as "nothing," and her self as "nobody's," Terry Eagleton notes that such a denial is "a radical refusal of any place within the 'symbolic order,' a rebuffing of all patriarchal claims over her person. The dying Clarissa is nothing, errant, schizoid, a mere empty place and non-person; her body occasions writing—her will, the whole text of the novel—but is itself absent from it, and will be literally nothing when we come to read the book."[25] Indeed, the book comes into being as a result of the dissolution of Clarissa's body.[26]

But Clarissa's assertion that she is "nothing" should not be understood only within the context of a shattered self-image or a Puritan ethic that attributes no importance to the deceased body. Clarissa's declaration represents her attempt to define her own subjectivity outside the patriarchal system of marriage and family. Through her beautiful wasting away, Clarissa evades the restrictive categories of her patriarchal family and of Lovelace, distancing herself from traditional conceptions and uses of women's bodies. Clarissa's laments that she is "nothing" and "nobody's" express both anxiety and pleasure.[27] Outside the protection of her paternal home or of marriage, she has no legal or social status; by writing of her misery, however, she effectively defines a "new" Clarissa who can live outside the patriarchal system, if only in writing. In fact, the world of Clarissa's family *does* need her—as a token of exchange, by which they might increase their wealth or position—but they do not want an independent Clarissa, and they certainly have no use for a nonvirginal Clarissa, whose status effectively takes her off the marriage market.

The difference between Clarissa's virginal body and her violated body is a crucial concept in the novel, since that difference represents the difference in Clarissa's value as a wife, a daughter, or, to Mrs. Howe, a friend of one's daughter. Because the actual rape is repressed, its various representations distributed throughout the text, and because Clarissa's memory of the rape is erased (except for a few hazy images of "female figures flitting . . . before [her] sight" [L314/1011], memories that do not necessarily spring from the moment of the rape itself), the difference in Clarissa's body becomes very much a matter of construction. Clarissa is different to the world only when everyone becomes aware of what has happened. Although Clarissa is never explicit in her letters, she clearly *feels* different. By focusing on the rape as a pivotal event, Clarissa creates a history for her body. Just as the history of her life in her father's house begins when she steps outside the garden door, the moment her body is violated—although she may not recall it, she believes it has happened—also creates history.[28]

Clarissa focuses obsessively on this bodily history in her letters, as if she needs to make her body—that is, her own body image—public (even though she also imagines a private madhouse as her destination). Her letters display her grief at the loss of her innocent body, a loss with which her correspondents can commiserate; Clarissa's nostalgia, her longing for "home" and her desire to become her father's daughter once more, is deeply embedded in and represented through her grief at the loss of her virginal body. Clarissa's virginity is very much a question of knowledge; it exists because everyone knows it exists. By publicizing the rape and revealing the loss of her virginity, Clarissa appropriates her loss for herself. The significance of Clarissa's frankness about the rape is not lost on Lovelace. "There never, surely, was such an odd little soul as this," he writes to Belford, "Not to keep her own secret. . . . What would become of the peace of the world, if all women should take it into their heads to follow her example? What a fine time of it would the heads of families have? Their wives always filling their ears with their confessions; their daughters with theirs; . . . the whole world would either be a scene of confusion, or cuckoldom" (L371/1149).

The sexual desire that is destroyed by the rape is sublimated within Clarissa's prolonged death. In a very real sense, the social tensions created and expressed by a conflict between the will of the father and the will of the daughter become material in the death of Clarissa's body.

But by ceaselessly "writing" her own death, Clarissa also enjoys a certain pleasure: the sexual desire forbidden to her is displaced onto an eroticized desire for death: "I have much more pleasure," Clarissa writes to Anna, "in thinking of death, than of such a husband" (L359/1115). Later, she will tell Anna, "As for me, never bride was so ready as I am. My wedding garments are bought . . . [and they will] be the easiest, the happiest suit, that ever bridal maiden wore" (L446/1339).[29]

All of Clarissa's desire becomes invested in her own death. The coded letter that she sends to Lovelace is laced with bittersweet pleasure: "I have good news to tell you. I am setting out with all diligence for my father's house [and] . . . I am overjoyed with the assurance of a thorough reconciliation" (L421.1/1233). There is nothing of grief in this letter. Her "father's house," of course, is heaven, and her "reconciliation" will be with Christ. Although the letter is really a ruse to keep Lovelace away from her, the pleasure is real enough. Clarissa has erected a nostalgic compromise that satisfies her "wishful fantasies" and creates an idealization in which death has been accorded "glamour and fascination."[30]

Deprived of her family home and the home that she rightfully owns, her grandfather's Dairy House, Clarissa designs and purchases her ultimate "house," her coffin. She pays for her coffin by selling her clothes, thus "dressing [her] soul for death" and "renouncing the world and the flesh."[31] Clarissa takes pleasure in designing the "devices" that grace the lid of her coffin: "a crowned serpent, with its tail in its mouth, forming a ring, the emblem of eternity"; a winged hourglass; an urn; and "the head of a white lily snapped short off, and just falling from the stalk," combined with quotations from the book of Job, and Psalms 116 and 103 (L451/1305–6). But, despite her protests that the undertaker has taken the coffin up to her room earlier than expected, shocking Belford, Mrs. Lovick, and Mrs. Smith, Clarissa's coffin is very much an item of display: she keeps it in her room, "under her window not far from her bedside" (L451/1305), and often uses it as a desk upon which to read and write. Margaret Doody finds Clarissa's coffin "one of the most bizarre and surprising things in the novel," a baroque memento mori, but it is just such dramatic display that allows Clarissa to place herself within the tradition of the melancholic literary figure, or suffering saint. For Clarissa, notes Doody, death "is the great adventure, which fascinates her imagination."[32]

The death of Clarissa also fascinated the imagination of Richardson, who uses Belford to describe the image of Clarissa's dying body in repose: "We beheld the lady in a charming attitude. Dressed, as I told you before, in her virgin white . . . one faded cheek rested upon [Mrs. Lovick's] bosom, the kindly warmth of which had overspread it with a faint, but charming flush; the other paler, and hollow, as if already iced over by death. Her hands, white as the lily, with her meandering veins more transparently blue than ever . . . hanging lifelessly. . . . Her aspect was sweetly calm and serene" (L474/1351). Clarissa's body is both dead and alive. The strange juxtaposition of pale and "hollow" cheeks "already iced over by death," and lily-white hands that hang "lifelessly," with Clarissa's "charming attitude" and "sweetly calm and serene" aspect testifies to the very real social contradictions that are played out on the body of Clarissa. Although Clarissa's death allows her to refuse appropriation of her body through marriage, the aestheticization of her dying body in this description by Richardson/Belford nevertheless makes Clarissa's body into an object for visual consumption and pleasure: the description of Clarissa's static body, with its blue veins "meandering" through lily-white hands, could easily be that of a marble sculpture.

Richardson's own ambivalence toward Clarissa is evident here. Although he allows Clarissa to withdraw from circulation within the patriarchal economy through her death, her dying body, as an aesthetic object, is quickly reabsorbed into that economy. That Belford, as Richardson's narrator, can at once lament Clarissa's death and view her dying body as "charming" and "sweetly calm and serene" is a disturbing mark of the unevenness of social development: Belford knows Clarissa's death is wrong, but he cannot escape his role as master subject. Clarissa's agency, no matter how radical, can go only so far.

Richardson's investment in Clarissa's body as a nostalgic site is tenuous and must be held in place by setting off the immaculate death of Clarissa's body against the death of Mrs. Sinclair's polluted body. While Clarissa has rejected sex, pregnancy, and corporeality, Mrs. Sinclair's body bears the burden of all the materiality that Clarissa's body abjects.

"Oh Lovelace!" writes Belford, "I have a scene to paint in relation to the wretched Sinclair, that if I do it justice will make thee seriously ponder and reflect, or nothing can" (L499/1386). When Jack Belford "paints" the scene of Mrs. Sinclair's death, his intention is explicit: to shock an already "disordered" Lovelace into an "immediate change of life and manners" (L498/1386). Where repeated verbal exhortations and descriptions of Clarissa's dying body have failed, Belford hopes that another kind of spectacle will succeed. Visual imagery is already well established as part of Belford's writing strategy,[33] but his portraits of the saintly Clarissa—her immaculate body and clothing against the sordid background of her garret prison (letter 334), or her dying body in repose (letter 481)—have not succeeded in conclusively reforming Lovelace. Belford's hope is that the horror of Sinclair's death scene, and the contamination that seems to exude from her dying body and the corrupted bodies of the prostitutes who surround her deathbed, will shock Lovelace's sensibilities so thoroughly that he will follow Belford's advice to reform.[34]

The spectacle that Belford presents—for the benefit not only of Lovelace, but of fellow rakes Mowbray and Tourville as well—is a variety of purge or emetic, intended to act on the body as well as on the mind. By presenting the scene of Sinclair's death as physically repulsive, replete with disgusting details, Belford hopes to "cure" Lovelace by purging his rakish desires. The loathsome sight of dying and putrefying bodies, Belford hopes, will force Lovelace to redefine his "self" against and by the abjection of those bodies. For, just as Belford eliminates any hint of body or sex in his portraits of Clarissa, he explicitly calls on a tradition of misogyny that abhors female flesh, presenting the bodies of Sinclair and her "girls" as overflowing in an excess of feminine odors, sights, and sounds. The displacement of all the unpleasant bodily elements of death onto Mrs. Sinclair renders the misogyny of this scene especially intense. The real horror of Sinclair's death scene is constituted by nothing so much as sexual difference.

The dead body is the height of abjection. Unable to be named, defined, imagined, or desired, the abject is that which must be continually excluded or jettisoned in order to establish and maintain identity. The corpse is what we, as living beings, are not: "the most sickening of wastes . . . a border that has encroached upon everything," the sight of which goes beyond signification, notes Julia Kristeva. Moreover, the corpse is spectacle: "as in true theater," Kristeva writes, "corpses *show me* what I permanently thrust aside in order to live. [In the presence of a corpse], I am at the border of my condition as a living being. My body extricates itself, as being alive, from that border."[35]

For Belford, the border at stake is not only that between life and death (to be sure, one of his aims may be to jolt Lovelace out of his temporary madness and to prevent his friend from harming himself); it is also the border between male and female. If a corpse is "death infecting life,"[36] the sight of Sinclair's gangrenous female body and the corrupted bodies of the prostitutes threatens to infect a masculinity held in place by difference, and constantly under the threat of contamination through sexual contact. By scapegoating Mrs. Sinclair, Richardson is able to stave off the abjection inherent in Clarissa's dying body.

As are those of Clarissa and Belton, Sinclair's is a public death; she suffers in full view of the prostitutes in her employ and calls for Belford's unwilling presence. The scene that Belford witnesses (and reports) is terrifying: Sinclair is represented as animalistic, a body without a soul. Since the previous night she has been raving and "howling," her screaming "more like that of a wolf than a human creature," or "more like that of a bull than of a woman" (L499/1387); her eyes are described as "flaming-red as we may suppose those of a salamander" (L499/1388), the creature assumed to be able to survive the flames of hell. Sinclair's life of depravity has hardened her heart; she is unable to repent or even to cry and refuses any spiritual consolation from clergy. Her body, invaded by gangrene, is rotting from the rapid spread of infection; unlike Clarissa's body, which seems to dissipate slowly as she dies of "grief," Sinclair's "misfortune" actually seems to have "increased her flesh," Belford notes (L499/1388).

Read carefully, the description of Sinclair's agony hints at another type of suffering, one that is coded exclusively as feminine: that of childbirth. The victim of a "fall," Sinclair's body is grotesquely swelled; her suffering, as does that of labor, has lasted many hours. "Behold her then," writes Belford deictically, "spreading the whole tumbled bed with her huge quaggy carcase: her mill-post arms held up, her broad hands clenched with violence." Her body threatens to overflow the bed (the site, at some distant point, of sexual pleasure) as she clenches her fists and screams in agony. Her hair is "grizzly" and "matted" by sweat and "wickedness," and her lips are "parched." Her wide-open mouth, like a vagina forced open by an emerging infant's head, "split[s] her face, as it were, into two parts; her huge tongue hideously rolling in it," as "heaving, puffing as if for breath;" her deformed, "bellows-shaped and various-colored breasts" rise and fall "with the violence of her gaspings" (L499/1388). Screaming, panting, her "flesh increased," and her face contorted by pain, she exhibits little difference, in Belford's description, between death and birth.[37]

But if Sinclair's body is abject in the throes of death, the bodies of the prostitutes who surround her bed (as do a laboring woman's gossips) are abject even in life. Only partially dressed, without stays or hoops, they wear makeup that is "lying in streaky seams not half blowzed off, discovering coarse wrinkled skins"; the hair of some

women reveals "divers colours" amid evidence of a blacklead comb that
has lost the battle with their "natural brindle," while the hair of others
has been "plaistered with oil and powder, the oil predominating." Their
"shocking dishabille" consists of "trollopy" gowns "tangling about their
heels," and some of the women are stockingless, all of them "underpetti-
coated"—an interesting observation when compared with Clarissa's
concern about Solmes's "pressing" on her hoop. Their bodies, so mea-
gerly covered by their shabby clothes, are prematurely old, Belford
observes: "half of them (unpadded, shoulder-bent, pallid-lipped, feeble-
jointed wretches) appearing from a blooming nineteen or twenty perhaps overnight, haggard well-worn strumpets of thirty-eight or forty"
(L499/1387–88). Compared to Clarissa's nineteen-year-old body,
which is beautiful even after death, the bodies of these women are more
dead than alive.

But the corruption that has decayed the bodies of Sinclair and the
prostitutes threatens to infect anyone in contact with them. Belford
twice mentions his anxiety about the "effluvia arising from so many
contaminated carcasses," at one point throwing open a window for relief, and later stating that he "never was so sensible of the benefit of
fresh air as I was the moment I entered the street" (L499/1390, 1393).
Mrs. Sinclair's sickroom, Belford notes, is particularly offensive: in addition to medicinal items, the room reeks with "the stenches of spiritu-
ous liquors" imbibed by the prostitutes. "And yet," he observes, "this is
thought to be a genteel house of the sort: and all the prostitutes in it are
prostitutes of price, and their visitors people of note." Such visitors, of
course, would include Lovelace and Belford himself. Not coinciden-
tally, Belford's next comment makes his observations personal: "Oh
Lovelace! what lives do most of us rakes and libertines lead! What company do we keep!" The "generality of men of our class," he says, are
"miry wallowers" and "filthy sensualists, whose favourite taste carries
them to mingle with the dregs of stews, brothels, and common-sewers"
(L499/1393).

Belford's comments here echo those of Dr. George Cheyne, who
writes of the pollution and waste produced in crowded cities such as
London, and the consequent dangers to health:

> London (where nervous Distempers are most frequent, outrageous, and un-
> natural) is, for ought I know, the greatest, most capacious, close, and popu-
> lous City of the Globe, the infinite Number of Fires, Sulphureous and
> Bituminous, the vast Expence of Tallow and foetid Oil in Candles in Lamps,

under and above Ground, the Clouds of stinking Breaths, and Perspiration, not to mention the Ordure of so many diseas'd, both intelligent and unintelligent Animals, the crouded Churches, Church-yards and Burying Places, with putrifying Bodies, the *Sinks, Butcher-Houses, Stables, Dunghils,* &c. and the necessary Stagnation, Fermentation, and Mixture of such Variety of all Kinds of Atoms, are more than sufficient to putrify, poison and infect the Air for twenty Miles round it, and which, in Time, must alter, weaken, and destroy the healthiest Constitutions of Animals of all Kinds; and accordingly it is in such like cities, that these Distempers are to be found in their highest and most astonishing Symptoms.[38]

The "Distempers" Cheyne refers to are nervous diseases: vapors, "lowness of spirits," and the like. Such nervous disorders, nevertheless, are occasioned by physical contact with waste and contamination, the "Mixture of such Variety of all Kinds of Atoms." If nervous disease is a consequence of modern living, then the cure must be found in a simpler way of life. Cheyne suggests a pastoral cure: "Seldom any lasting or solid Cure is perform'd till the Diseased be *rusticated* and purified from the infectious Air and Damps, transubstantiated into their Habits, by a great City, and till they have suck'd in and incorporated the sweet, balmy, clear Air of the country, and driven the other out of their Habit. . . . [T]he Nitre or Acid of fresh, new Air, is as necessary towards Life and Health as fresh balmy Food."[39] The only "solid" cure is a move — both physical and ideological — away from the city, the site of modern life. Cheyne's nostalgia locates the healthy body and mind in a pastoral life free of the pollution of the city, and the excessive consumption of rich and exotic food and drink. Belford, recognizing that "it is not in a man's own power to reform when he will" (L499/1393), paints the shocking scene of Sinclair's dying body and the corruption of the prostitutes' living bodies in an attempt to engender disgust in Lovelace for "mingl[ing]," or for Cheyne's "Mixture." By presenting a visual spectacle of horror, Belford writes to Lovelace's body (and, perhaps, to the bodies of profligate readers); where intellectual persuasion has failed, Belford hopes that physical revulsion will prevail.

While the fellow rake Belton's slow death of consumption may be sad, it is not horrifying; rather, it is a death in which any rake might envision his own. We might even say that Belton's death is a logical end to a body that has consumed itself through the indulgence of excessive appetites. The bodies of Sinclair and the prostitutes, on the other hand, represent that which the rake's body consumes or incorporates; these female bodies, "so unprepared for being seen," as Belford observes (L499/1388), are truly something "horrible to see at the impossible doors of the invisible."[40] The shock of Belford's "painting" is the dissolution of borders: Sinclair's death throes evoke images of birth; the prostitutes are both dead and alive; the very air in the room, reeking of feminine bodies, threatens the contamination of sexual difference. Belford intends his "spectacle" to make Lovelace share his revulsion and ends his letter with a celebration of sameness and union, the hope that "we, who have been companions in (and promoters of one another's) wickedness, might join in a general atonement to the utmost of our power" (L499/1394).

Belford's desire for unity, for the safety of clearly defined borders and separate spheres—indeed, his desire to "reform" Lovelace, Mowbray, and Tourville—is a nostalgic desire that backs away from difference. Belford seeks consolation in a pure and healthy body, which can only flourish away from the contamination of sexual difference. While Cheyne locates health in a pastoral setting, Belford finds health and well-being in nondifferentiation. By abjecting the bodies of Sinclair and the prostitutes, Belford—and Richardson—scapegoat them in order to apotheosize Clarissa, who is essentially different.

The horror of sexual difference at the heart of Sinclair's death scene suggests that the scene may be juxtaposed not only to the death scenes of Clarissa and Belton, but also to Lovelace's rape of Clarissa. The experience that leaves the usually loquacious Lovelace speechless—his encounter with Clarissa's body, on which the burden of gender definition rests, as Tassie Gwilliam has suggested[41]—is not narrated, but merely tersely announced. Lovelace fails to describe that moment in which he confronts the difference of Clarissa's sexed body. The task of describing difference then falls to Belford, who is able to do so only from a position within frantically constructed borders.

Samuel Richardson's *Clarissa* attempts to reconcile the contradictions produced by social change; as the point of mediation between the individual subject and the experience of history, the concept of nostalgia suggests a way of thinking about *Clarissa* as a response to those social changes. A reading of Clarissa's wasting away as an "illness" is, perhaps, an ideological investment. Some may suggest that she starves herself to death. But is self-starvation necessarily an illness? Would it perhaps not be fairer to say that, with her reality being continually invalidated, Clarissa attempts to write her reality in two ways: through her letters and on her body? Her property is denied her; her ability to act is severely curtailed; ultimately, her body is her only possible arena for resistance. Perhaps we should say that Clarissa falls victim to Richardson's own nostalgia for a world that seems simpler and easier to understand, with more clearly defined borders and categories. Underneath nostalgic desire, however, lie contradiction and ambivalence.

What emerges within *Clarissa* are categories: pollution and purity, danger and safety, illness and health. The establishment of categories such as these helps fend off the anxiety produced by ambivalence and contradiction, the same anxiety reflected in Cheyne's concern with the mixture of atoms, or Belford's revulsion at mingling with the contaminated bodies of prostitutes. These categories surface in *Clarissa* as displacements of gender and class; the suturing of gender and class into these other categories then reinforces concepts of difference. As gender and class are absorbed into the discourses of other categories of difference—health and illness, for example—differences in gender and class gradually become "invisible," while the other categories are overdetermined. That very invisibility, however, is a mark of their hegemonic status. At stake for Richardson in his writing is stability in the face of change. Not only does he attempt to establish categories and borders that emerge even more clearly in *Sir Charles Grandison*, but his loving creation of the book itself—the material body of *Clarissa*—is a means by which he can "fix" his own aesthetic creation, make his ideas permanent, and provide his work with an extended life that his human body lacks.[42]

Difference is written into the textual body that is *Clarissa*. The graphic and material display of Clarissa's madness in the form of her "mad papers" skewed across the page provides the reader with physical evidence of Clarissa's disordered mind and effectively establishes her sanity prior to the rape and after her "recovery," as she prepares for death. The extreme brevity of Lovelace's letter 257, followed immediately by Richardson's comment, set off by black lines, directing the reader to letters 312, 313, and 314, in which "the whole of this black transaction is given by the injured lady to Miss Howe," makes the violation of Clarissa's body visual and material and marks off a space that delays representation, a moment of resistance by both Lovelace and Richardson himself.

Despite any sense of agency that my own reading may assign to Clarissa Harlowe's death, her suffering nevertheless reinforces the categories set in place by a patriarchal gender system and reflects

Richardson's own interpretation of female psychology, as well as his own mediation between the radical alternatives imagined by Clarissa and the social conservatism voiced by Lovelace. We may well question Richardson's need to kill Clarissa, but I would suggest that Clarissa's death offers resolution to the contradictions a living Clarissa presents, for, as Lovelace expresses it, "What would become of the peace of the world, if all women should take it into their heads to follow her example?"

WRITING THE "GOOD MAN"

You are offered a man, whose perplexities have not proceeded from the entanglements of intrigue, inconstancy, perfidy; but from his own compassionate nature. . . . —Who?
—Sir CHARLES GRANDISON—For whom so many virgin hearts have sighed in vain! (Lady G. to Harriet Byron)[43]

Richardson's third novel, *The History of Sir Charles Grandison* (1753–54), may have lacked a narrative plan, as Jocelyn Harris suggests in her introduction to the novel (vii); nevertheless, Richardson, who began the project by exploring his ideas through his correspondence, was keen to write and define a "good man" to complement his portrait of the virtuous woman, Clarissa Harlowe. The result of this project is a clearer definition of the binary categories that we see emerging at the end of *Clarissa*.

Richardson's project—to write "the good man"—reveals his nostalgia for what he perceives as a simpler life, when difference was more clearly defined, when social categories were fixed, and when paternalistic economic and social ethics obtained. Richardson's contemporary world seems confused and chaotic because the traditional aristocracy has abandoned its social responsibilities; it is up to the "new" aristocrats of sensibility, such as Sir Charles, to assume their rightful place and responsibilities in society.[44] Without the leadership of "good men" such as Sir Charles, whose paternalistic project for civic improvement promises to restore traditional class and gender boundaries, modern society is threatened with confusion and dissolution.

The social project envisioned by Sir Charles counts on women and the poor to bear the burden of tradition; in the novel itself, it is the bodies of women that most often bear the burden of masculine nostal-

gia. A continuum of delicacy, weakness, illness, disease, and death
marks the physical condition of women in Richardson's novels. In turn,
these physical debilities reinforce gender differences, offering reassurance to a nostalgic Richardson that the world possesses some sort of
continuity. Richardson begins *Sir Charles Grandison* with two categories
firmly established. The more obvious, of course, is Richardson's division of the characters according to the "Names of the Principal Persons," which are listed as "Men," "Women," and "Italians." Such a
curious mode of classification exoticizes the Italians by consolidating
Italian men and women into a single category determined by geography, as if their "foreignness" overpowers all other characteristics, even
those of gender. Clearly, the Italians are "different" from the English
characters, whose nationality is invisible, an unmarked category against
which the world can be evaluated. Their nationality made hypernorma-
tive, in contrast to the otherness of the "Italians," the English characters
are defined in terms of gender, which advance Richardson's project of
drawing the portrait of a "good man" in Sir Charles Grandison.

The division of characters reflects the other category in place as the
novel begins, geography. The action takes place in both England and
Italy; throughout, the two locales define each other by difference, an
ancient contrast, with England as the site of propriety, civility, and
rationality, and Italy as the site of passion, violence, and mystery, a
transgressive space. By representing Italy as exotic and ambiguous,
Richardson purifies his English characters, particularly Sir Charles
Grandison—and perhaps the English "experience" in general—by filtering out troublesome elements that threaten to disrupt the neat char-
acterization of Sir Charles as both infallible and desirable.

Many readers have commented on Grandison's lack of presence in
the novel, the lack of any evidence of his interior life, and the contradictory or ambiguous nature of his personality.[45] Richardson's attempt at
presenting the model of a good man results in a curious emptying out
of Grandison's character. By the time Richardson finishes distilling the
character so that all deviance and disorder are drawn off, thereby leaving only the essence of a good man, there seems to be very little left;
ultimately, he is a cipher. Such a vacuum is certainly troubling as well
as intriguing: it points, as does the rape of Clarissa, or Lovelace's letter
257, to an absence in the text. In this case, however, the text is organized around, or perhaps in spite of, the resistance to representation of
any interior life that Sir Charles may possess.

Tassie Gwilliam observes that Richardson takes a "relentlessly social view of character" in *Grandison;* that is, Sir Charles is constructed, by default, as that which everyone else *is not.*[46] Other bodies suffer illness or maiming, while that of Sir Charles remains healthy; other characters are greedy, villainous, or violent, while Sir Charles is a model of benevolence and good temper. Neither the reader nor Sir Charles's many female admirers can really know what lurks behind his glossy surface. He is created a hero, as Gwilliam notes, by an "accretion of interpretation and praise" from other characters, and as a lover by the declarations of love from the female characters.[47] The lack at the heart of Richardson's novel results in a text that is driven by female desire for the generally unattainable hero, and by the reader's own desire to know whether Sir Charles possesses any interior life at all.

This lack and the desire it generates hint at a subtle subtext of castration and desire, a subtext that is more fully developed in other works of the century: the story of Eloise and Abelard. It is no accident that Sir Charles is Clementina's "tutor"; his relationship as "guardian" to Emily Jervois is equally troubling. He is the object of everyone's desire, yet his own desire cannot be known, and he is prevented from acting upon it. All of Sir Charles's desire is deeroticized and channeled into sentiment; his tears, tremblings, hesitations, disappointments, and grief are set down to his good nature and sympathetic heart. The manifestations of sensibility on his body are anything but sexual. He is metaphorically castrated by the total absence of his sexuality; this castration is overdetermined in its distribution among all the other characters, including Jeronymo with his groin wound, Sir Hargrave Pollexfen with his missing teeth and facial injuries, Clementina with her madness and spectacularly bleeding arm, Olivia with her bandaged wrist, and Harriet with her melancholic vapors.[48]

The sentimental male body that Richardson attempts to assign to the "good man" must be a healthy body; hence, the categories of health and illness are foregrounded, joining gender and class as a means of categorization.[49] Indeed, the idea of health has already been alluded to in the editor's "Preface," in which Richardson reveals that after the completion of *Clarissa* "the Editor apprehended he should be obliged to stop, by reason of his precarious State of Health" (4). The very existence of *Sir Charles Grandison*, then, depends on Richardson's own good health. By nostalgically foregrounding the now-lost health of his own body, Richardson calls the body to his readers' attention.

John Wiltshire notes that health is generally an "absence" in a realist text, a ground against which illness or disease can be presented. The body itself, observes Wiltshire, "is normally merely enabling, transparent, taken for granted: it is only when it becomes painful or dysfunctional that its workings become disclosed to consciousness." Furthermore, the "ground" of writing is "precisely the functional competence of the bodily existence."[50] Aside from calling the body to the readers' consciousness, Richardson attempts to increase his readership's appreciation of his newest novel by telling them that it very nearly never came to be. Without the healthy body of the novelist, the history of the good man cannot have material existence.

Richardson's own "precarious" health shares in the distribution of health and illness among the characters, with all the health awarded to Sir Charles Grandison, and with all the illness and weakness displaced onto other characters. When Harriet Byron writes a description of Sir Hargrave Pollexfen in a letter to Lucy Selby, she observes that "his complexion is a little of the fairest for a man, and a little of the palest" (1:44). Sir Charles, in contrast, is described as being possessed of "florid health": "His complexion seems to have been naturally too fine for a man: But as if he were above being regardful of it, his face is overspread with a manly sunniness [I want a word] that shews he has been in warmer climates than England" (1:181, brackets in original). The "sunniness," for which Harriet lacks an adequate word, sets him apart from the pale and sickly-looking Sir Hargrave. The "manly sunniness" derives not from England, as Harriet points out, but from Italy, and it also from Italy that the strongest hint of Sir Charles's sexuality will emerge, particularly in connection with the Lady Olivia. But while Italy has a positive effect on Sir Charles's body, the bodies of the Italian males do not fare as well. Bodily illness and weakness, in the form of a wound to the hipjoint, is displaced onto Jeronymo della Porretta, who is geographically and culturally distant from Sir Charles. Considered incurable, Jeronymo is "cured" nevertheless through his friendship with Sir Charles, who procures an English doctor to treat him. Jeronymo's illness further reinforces Sir Charles's image of strength and health.

The female characters absorb disorders of the mind or the spirit. Harriet Byron and Clementina della Porretta suffer from lovesickness; they are "sick," of course, with love for Sir Charles, whose divided heart prohibits him from making a definitive choice between his two faithful admirers. The Italian character, as we shall see, suffers more intensely and dramatically than her English counterpart. Harriet succumbs to her love for Sir Charles with a lingering malaise, occasioning the concern of her family and Sir Charles's sister, Charlotte, who observes that "our dear Harriet . . . visibly falls away; and her fine complexion fades" (5:516). Harriet's grandmother, Mrs. Shirley, laments that Harriet's "faded cheeks have shewn the struggles of her heart" (5:539); Mr. Deane, however, "is extremely apprehensive of her declining health" and "believes her in a consumption." Accordingly, he calls in a physician to examine her. Nevertheless, Harriet and her friends, including Charlotte, "all are convinced, that medicine will not reach her case" (5:543). Harriet is not "in a consumption," nor mad, as Clementina is. Her extreme sensibility, nevertheless, requires that she pine and "fade" for love of Sir Charles, that the imprint of her emotions be visible on her body.

Lady Clementina della Porretta, on the other hand, suffers an illness that rivals that of Clarissa Harlowe in its drama and intensity.[51] Unlike Clarissa, however, Clementina is not a narrator; although she appears in a number of dramatic scenes, she is unable to tell her own story in writing. When a "deep melancholy [begins] to lay hold of her heart," as a consequence of her family's pressure to marry the Count of Belvidere despite her love for the unsuitable, because Protestant, Sir Charles Grandison, the family's physicians "all pronounc[e] her malady to be Love" (3:125–26). Clementina at times refuses to speak and at other times engages in rambling, incoherent speech. She is described as "wild" and "half-raving" (3:239), and her family fears "the poor Lady is hastening . . . into a consumptive malady" (3:257). Pious and devout, she declares her unequivocal intention to enter a nunnery.

Clementina's devotion to Roman Catholicism, a further mark of her difference, comes in for its share of blame for her illness. Her confessor has "filled her tender mind with terrors" (3:128), presumably of the dangers of perdition for those who do not embrace the Roman church. Such religious zeal seems to be part of the Italian experience. Her confessor, although described by Grandison as "an honest, a worthy man," has nonetheless "kept up her fears and terrors . . . and betwixt her piety and her gratitude, had raised such a conflict as her tender nature could not bear" (3:128). Later, when Clementina is somewhat recovered from her illness, Father Marescotti hints to her that her "late disorder might be a judgment . . . for suffering [her] heart to be engaged by the *Heretic*," inciting fears that she may suffer a relapse as "punishment of [her] disobedience" (6:61).

Unlike the Italians, the English are no slaves to passion. The della Porretta family declares that Clementina will only be permitted to marry Grandison if he renounces both England and the Anglican church, but Richardson's paragon of English virtue will, of course, hear of no such thing, declaring himself "satisfied in my own faith; Entirely satisfied! . . . A lover of my native country too—Were not my God and my Country to be the sacrifice, if I complied!" (3:129). Despite his admiration and affection for Clementina, and his acknowledgment that the offer of her hand in marriage is an honor, he remains, nevertheless, the defender of both country and faith. There is no lovesickness for Sir Charles, just as there is no overwhelming religious zeal, only a rational, even political, relationship to his church. He is loyal, but reason always prevails: passion and zealotry are the province of women and Italians.[52]

Clementina's passion for Sir Charles and her faith may tip over into what Burton describes as "religious melancholy," but Lady Olivia's passion for Sir Charles, an earthly desire to possess and dominate, unmoderated by the spiritual faith that creates a conflict for Clementina, spills over into violence. By bearing the burden of abjected desires, Olivia, as do Mrs. Sinclair and the prostitutes, becomes a scapegoat in order to secure Clementina's purity; as we shall see, however, Clementina's own physical desire bleeds out repeatedly. Olivia, who has no last name, nor immediate family, is a dangerous figure in more than one way: her very violence and aggressiveness make her gender ambiguous, and she respects no clear-cut boundaries for her behavior. The restraint that makes Sir Charles the well-bred Englishman is totally lacking in Olivia; because she is a woman, her abundance of passion for Sir Charles makes her that much more of an anomaly. Elegant, "nobly born, generous, amiable in her features, genteel in her person, and mistress of a great fortune in possession, which is entirely at her own disposal" (3:117), Olivia would seem to make a desirable wife for any man, yet Sir Charles, who has "not the presumption to look up to her with hope" (3:117), nevertheless rejects her by pleading "difference of religion" (3:117). When Mr. Jervois suggests that Olivia would convert to Anglicanism, Sir Charles questions her sincerity: "But could I be pleased with the change, would she have made it, when passion, not conviction, was likely to be the motive?" (3:117). Sir Charles's objection rings somewhat false, as his explanation continues: "There could be no objection to her person: Nobody questioned her virtue; but she was violent and imperious in her temper. I had never left MIND out of my notions of Love: I could not have been happy with her, had she been queen of the globe" (3:117).

Grandison's real fear, it would seem, is of Olivia's "violent and impe-

rious" nature. Ruled entirely by her passions, willing even to change
her religion to win Sir Charles, Olivia is too disorderly to fit into Sir
Charles's neatly categorized world, where sensibility—under appropriate restraint and tempered by reason—marks the good man or the
delicate female. Olivia is neither "good" nor "delicate"; her forwardness
in pursuing Grandison marks her as transgressive. Olivia follows him
to England and insinuates herself into his household, but despite her
charm, beauty, intelligence, grace, and accomplishment, she cannot fit
in with the Grandison sisters; she is always different, always exotic.

Unlike the suffering Harriet or weeping Emily, Sir Charles's enam-
ored ward, and unlike the melancholy Clementina, Olivia acts on her
desires and frustrations. There is no lovesick pining away for her: en-
raged by Sir Charles's refusal to postpone his return to Italy to see
Clementina, Olivia attempts to stab him with a poniard. Sir Charles
struggles with her, twisting her wrist and admonishing, "Unhappy, violent woman, I return not this instrument of mischief! You will have no
use for it in England" (4:380). Sir Charles has repeatedly declared that
he will not engage in dueling; England, clearly, is not a place where
women can make use of poniards. Sir Charles himself need not make
use of violence to carry his point; his overwhelming munificence—even
in the face of a threat against his life—bullies everyone, including the
wild-tempered Olivia, into compliance. Emily reports to Harriet that
"Lady Olivia is grieved on the remembrance of [the incident]; and ar-
raigns herself, and her wicked passion; and the more, for his noble for-
giveness of her on the spot, and recommending her afterwards to the
civilities of his sisters, and their Lords" (4:380). Olivia displays her injury, binding her twisted wrist with a "broad black ribband," a proud
badge of her struggle and of her loss. While she does not fall ill, her
anger is displayed on her body, just as grief manifests itself in the form
of illness on the bodies of Harriet and Clementina.

Olivia's injury is hidden, just as Jeronymo's "wounds" are never explicitly described. Clementina's illness, however, takes on gruesome
bodily form when the surgeons find it necessary to bleed her, and Clementina takes advantage of this dramatic opportunity to make her body
a spectacle. Despite an initial aversion to being bled, Clementina, as
does Olivia, displays her wound behind a bandage, at the same time
reproaching her mother for allowing the surgeons to proceed: "O my
mamma! And *you* would have run away from me too, would you! . . .
and to leave me with these doctors—See! see! and she held out her
lovely arm a little bloody" (3:190). Clementina, once more displaying

her bandaged arm, then turns her attention to Grandison, who attempts to persuade her to allow the surgeons to "breathe a vein." Clementina seizes the opportunity:

> And do *you* wish it too, Chevalier? — Do *you* wish to see me wounded? — To see my heart bleeding at my arm, I warrant. And as I cannot give you tears for tears, from my eyes, Shall not my arm weep!
>   I will *bid* it flow. (3:193)

Clementina faints and is carried away.

The highly charged eroticism of this scene is hard to ignore. In a novel in which overt displays of sexual desire are missing, Clementina's morbid fascination with the spectacle of her bleeding body, with the idea of being penetrated by the surgeons' lancet, absorbs all of the sexuality that cannot be spoken explicitly. By specifically addressing Sir Charles's desire—"Do *you* wish to see me wounded?"—Clementina succeeds in transposing erotic desire (both Sir Charles's and her own) onto a wounded, suffering body; she has thoroughly internalized Sir Charles's gaze. As Clarissa does, she wishes to exert her will over her body, bidding her own blood to flow when, just shortly before, the surgeons could extract only a few drops from her arm.

Tassie Gwilliam observes that, in the absence of any evidence of Sir Charles's own emotions, the female characters "take over the performance of his feelings"; nevertheless, this scene displays Sir Charles's desire more than it helps to "define" Clementina.[53] The aggressive and erotic passions, as written on the bodies of women, are loose and disorganized; they lack a context that only Sir Charles can provide, as the object of desire. It is as if the women cannot make sense of their own emotions; Sir Charles, with his supreme rationality, gives meaning to their desire, co-opting it to reinforce the argument for the confinement or control of women in and by patriarchy.

Clementina's cousin, Laurana, is a minor character whose body nevertheless participates in the distribution of madness and illness. Laurana is cruel and dangerous; it is in her best financial interest to drive Clementina into a convent, for the estate that Clementina is due to inherit would go to Laurana should Clementina take the veil. Should Clementina marry, Laurana would receive only a "handsome legacy, that she might not be entirely disappointed" (4:456). Clementina's body, as that of Clarissa Harlowe does, represents much more than its materiality: the disposition of a woman's body is directly linked to the possession of a body of land. While Clarissa's estate would link two tracts of land owned by Mr. Solmes, in Clementina's case, her land is "a considerable estate which joins to [the della Porrettas'] own domains." The disposition of this estate is determined by the disposition of Clementina's body—into marriage, thereby "strengthening their house," or into the convent, severely curtailing the lines of inheritance (4:456). When the Count of Belvidere, with whom Laurana is in love, follows Clementina to England, Laurana falls into a fit of melancholy, and she comes to "a miserable end" (7:447). Laurana's suicide marks her as distinctly un-Christian, violent, and impetuous, carried away first by avarice, and then by jealousy and rage. Her death, however, relieves Clementina from the requirement of marriage, leaving her free, at the end of the one-year waiting period she has proposed, to marry or not.

Peter Brooks has observed that we like to imagine a past era of "unified sensibility" when the body, sex, and death were an integrated part of our consciousness.[54] Richardson exhibits nostalgia for just such a unified sensibility; he attempts to recuperate the body in *Grandison*, although he can only do so by partitioning off the body, distributing all its abject and disorderly elements—sex, death, illness—to women and Italians, that is, to everyone who is *not* Sir Charles Grandison, who enjoys the superiority of the unmarked master subject. Although Richardson marks his own health as "precarious" in his introduction, he nevertheless slips easily into the role of the "invisible observer," as he surveys the world from the relatively invisible vantage point of Sir Charles, whose own body becomes the model for an imaginary social body with which Richardson's readers may identify.[55]

Not only do all the suffering characters in *Grandison*—whether physically disabled as Jeronymo is; truly mad, as Clementina is; or simply "fading," as is Harriet—enhance the picture of Sir Charles as a robust young Englishman, they also present him with the opportunity to "heal" them. Sir Charles takes an English physician with him to Italy, as English doctors are reputedly experienced in melancholic disorders, and he offers himself, as well, as a cure for Clementina (although he is refused when he stands by his religion). Harriet, on the other hand, accepts his offer of marriage and is cured; her cheeks bloom once more.

Sir Charles not only cures the ill, he redresses social wrongs as well, straightening out his libertine father's affairs and taking a firm but benevolent hand in the management of the Grandison estates. He takes an interest in the welfare of the community, bestowing his largesse only on the worthy. He is charitable even with strangers, with some reservations: "Beggars born, or those who make begging a trade, if in health, and not lame or blind, have seldom . . . any share in his munificence: But persons fallen from competence, and such as struggle with some instant distress, or have large families, which they have not ability to maintain; these, and such as these, are the objects of his bounty" (6:96).

Sir Charles's social philosophy is idealistic in that it depends on all of society to be as kind and generous as he is himself. He calls on the "merchants of Great Britain," whom he considers to be "the most useful members of the community," to "each, in his several way, according to his ability, and as opportunity may offer, to raise those worthy hearts, that inevitable calamities shall make spiritless" (2:455). He is sure he can encourage charity by "applying properly to the passions of persons, who, tho' they have not been very remarkable for benevolence, may yet be induced to do right things in *some* manner, if not always in the *most graceful*" (5:478).

The prosperity and success of this utopia, however, depend heavily on maintaining a well-structured class system, and it is in this plan that Sir Charles's—and Richardson's—nostalgia reveals itself. If the wealthy merchants should share their bounty with the less fortunate, it is up to the lower ranks to know their place and not aspire too high:

> Of one thing, methinks, I could be glad, that only such children of the poor, as shew a peculiar ingenuity, have any great pains taken with them in their *books*. Husbandry and labour are what are most wanting to be encouraged among the lower class of people. Providence has given to men different genius's and capacities, for different ends; and that all might become useful links of the same great chain. Let us apply those talents to Labour, those to Learning, those to Trade, to Mechanics . . . and then no person will be unuseful; on the contrary, every one may be eminent in some way or other. Learning, of itself, never made any man happy. The ploughman makes fewer mistakes in the conduct of life than the scholar, because the sphere in which he moves is a more contracted one. But if a genius arises, let us encourage it: There will be rustics enough to do the common services for the finer spirits, and to carry on the business of the world, if we do not, by our own indiscriminate good offices, contribute to their misapplication. (5:477–78)

In this passage, Richardson reveals the nostalgic agenda of the sentimental hero as well as his own nostalgia for a social golden age, and it is the bodies of the lower classes that bear the burden of nostalgia. The "great chain" that Sir Charles envisions inevitably depends on the labor—that is, on the bodies—of a sufficient quantity of "rustics" to provide "common services for the finer spirits." In order to progress up the chain or enjoy any social mobility, one would first have to be recognized as a "genius" in order to receive an education—that is, to be freed from physical labor—lest he (or less likely, she) become dissatisfied with the lot assigned by life. The world Sir Charles imagines is fixed, stationary, and predictable, even though Sir Charles himself is a new figure in a new social order, in which aristocracy is reserved for those with natural ability or fine sensibility.

Sir Charles takes account of gender in this world, in response to Mrs. Reeves's observations that many young women marry for lack of better options, since a young man may make his way in the world through trade or a profession, while a woman would be demeaned by the few vocational opportunities available to her. Sir Charles proposes, with the support of Dr. Bartlett, that "Protestant Nunneries" be established in each county, where single women without resources may live voluntarily—rather like the Millenium Hall described in Sarah Scott's later novel. These institutions would have their own hierarchy, thus reinforcing the general class structure of the nation: the matrons would be "women of family" and moral rectitude, while the "attendants . . . should be the hopeful female children of the honest industrious poor" (4:355).

These "nunneries" would not be dedicated to prayer and the glory of God, as Roman Catholic convents are; rather they would serve the "*national* good" by becoming "a seminary for good wives," as "the institution [takes] a stand for virtue, in an age given up to luxury, extravagance, and amusements." In addition to controlling the bodies and consuming habits of women, these nunneries would also resolve the problem of "excess" women, by taking them out of circulation and making them somewhat self-sufficient: they would be required to "employ" themselves and to pool their own resources, "according to their circumstances." Sir Charles's carefully thought out plan counts on the beneficence of "the well-disposed of both sexes; since every family in Britain, in their connexions and relations, near or distant, might be benefited by so reputable and useful an institution" (4:355–56). For those women who have been "betrayed by the perfidy of men [and] find themselves . . . unable to recover the path of virtue," Sir Charles proposes "An Hospital for Female Penitents" (4:356), similar to the Magdalene Hospitals, which would, of course, separate the virtuous women from the fallen.

Sir Charles's "goodness" is fully on display when he reveals the ideas and plans that will benefit the whole of society and solve the problems of contemporary life. His sensibility, pure and uncorrupted by any evil desires, is devoted entirely to creating a fair and just world in which all may flourish, according to their abilities. Is he believable? Even Harriet Byron has doubts: "Can he be so *very* good a man? O yes, yes, yes! wicked Harriet! What is in thy heart, to doubt it? A fine reflexion upon the age; as if there could not be *one* good man in it! and as if a good man could not be a man of vivacity and spirit!" (6:138).

Richardson's plan to create a "good" man in Sir Charles Grandison succeeds, even at the price of believability. In the creation of his novel, Richardson has provided the reading public with a model of the socially minded, educated gentleman who will play his prescribed role to address the ills of society through the right use of his fortune and influence, guided always by his conscience, moral values, and spiritual beliefs. Sir Charles posits a world in which the privileged stratum of society would find its benevolence incited to do the good necessary to benefit the less fortunate and thereby maintain a very tenuous social status quo. It was just as likely, however, that many of Richardson's readers, consumers of the sentimental novel, invested their sensibility in their reading; whether the sentimental novel actually moved the reading public to a significant gesture of social benevolence is uncertain.

Richardson's novels did their share, however, to construct categories that reinforce class, gender, and national identity. By portraying women as prone to physical and mental illness as a result of grief, homesickness, unrequited love, jealousy, or rage, he props up the image of woman as the "weaker vessel," while the sentimental male—who also blushes and sheds tears—is a forceful intellect in a robust body, possessed of a heightened sense of social justice.

The gendered categories of the sentimental body that Richardson constructs intersect with categories of health and illness to reinforce the gendering of space into public and private arenas. Sensible, enlightened males, such as Sir Charles and his friend Dr. Bartlett, assume their rightful role in society, while those female characters whose desires can be brought under control by a successful adjustment to marriage and motherhood, such as Lady L. and Lady G., enjoy good health and domestic bliss. Harriet's "illness" is cured by marriage; yet Clementina, who cannot bring herself to agree to marry the Count of Belvidere, is in constant danger of falling back into madness.

The unruly desires of disobedient daughters, as we have seen in *Clari-*

ssa and *Sir Charles Grandison,* posed a perceived threat to an increasingly fragile social system in the eighteenth century. The passion of women was both feared and envied and was the subject of several works that recall the story of Héloïse and Abelard, a subtext of *Sir Charles Grandi-son,* and the struggle between passion and reason. If Sir Charles's plan for a "Protestant nunnery" could not be realized, the passion of daughters could be contained nonetheless: in Rousseau's *Julie, ou la nouvelle Héloïse,* the prison of the convent described in Pope's "Eloisa to Abelard" becomes the prison of marriage and domesticity.

3

Desire, Body, and Landscape in
Pope's "Eloisa to Abelard" and Rousseau's *Julie*

THE 1616 PUBLICATION IN LATIN OF THE LETTERS OF HÉLOÏSE AND
Abelard revived an interest in the story of these two ill-fated lovers that
resulted in a spate of translations, of varying quality, that extended well
into the latter part of the eighteenth century.[1] The motif of the tutor-
pupil love affair surfaces repeatedly in the long eighteenth century,
hinted at, for example, in the relationship between Sir Charles and
Lady Clementina in Samuel Richardson's *Sir Charles Grandison*. In Alexander Pope's "Eloisa to Abelard" (1717) and Jean-Jacques Rousseau's
Julie, ou la nouvelle Héloïse (1761), however, the story is either explicitly
retold, as it is in Pope's heroic epistle,[2] or reworked into a contemporary
version, as it is in Rousseau's epistolary novel.

What was at stake for these authors in the rewriting of the story of
an ill-fated medieval love affair? Beyond the obvious lure and romance
of the past, and the current of interest in antiquarianism that ran
through the eighteenth century, was there something about the story of
Héloïse and Abelard that appealed to contemporary nostalgia? Pope's
poem and Rousseau's novel exhibit the same desire for a "unified sensibility," to borrow Peter Brooks's term, that is apparent in *Clarissa* and
Sir Charles Grandison. As Richardson does, Pope and Rousseau integrate
passion, sex, and death into their textual bodies by assigning those
drives to the bodies of their female characters; loss, on the other hand,
is the emotion appropriate to the modern male subject. The Héloïse and
Abelard story, in which bodies are *physically* marked and confined—
Abelard marked by castration, Héloïse confined in the Paraclete—is
particularly suited for adaptation as texts that explore questions of gender, space, and the body. While those questions may relate to metaphorical or conceptual differentiation, the original story tells of losses,
restraints, and confinements that are entirely material. Reworking this
tale offers Pope and Rousseau a symbolic structure laden with the

meaning and passion of the original; the nostalgia, the sense of lost unity, and the passion of the eighteenth-century texts carry the full weight of Abelard's castration and Héloïse's desire.

As in other cultural production of the century, anxieties about class differences and social change are deflected onto anxiety about gender; because masculinity is an unmarked category, that anxiety attaches itself to femininity. If woman is located at the site of the unrepresentable other, then by her contiguity, woman can become the subject of nostalgic investment for a multitude of unrepresentable longings. As does illness, gender becomes a category containing a variety of tensions.

Because body and land were considered natural, a bedrock unavailable for analysis, these categories were often invested with nostalgia; as Henri Lefebvre has pointed out, weakening historical or political forces often appropriate images linked to nature, or images associated with maternity or paternity, to naturalize that which is entirely rational. Rousseau, in particular, is nostalgic for the natural relationship of the sexes, for a natural hierarchy: one based on a so-called natural aristocracy in which the self-made man, such as Saint-Preux or Rousseau himself, could claim a place by right of his sex. But in an era of increasing social homogeneity, where "natural" sexual boundaries are becoming blurred, self-definition and self-articulation become increasingly vital; the textual self, for Pope and Rousseau, is founded on loss and longing and is realized and recuperated in nostalgic texts that create a unified identity in which reason (coded male) and the body (coded female) can coexist.

The body, of course, is powerfully written into the original Héloïse and Abelard story: a young woman's intense eroticism, hints of violence, brutal castration, the breaking of vows of chastity—all place the body at the forefront of the text. But along with the presence of the body is the presence of the landscape: that of the Paraclete, a monastery founded by Abelard in 1124, behind the walls of which Héloïse would live out the remainder of her life after being installed as abbess in 1129.[3] Inhabiting an interior landscape in the text is Héloïse's passion, the texture and detail of which are richly illustrated in Pope's "Eloisa" and embodied in Héloïse's voice. Woven into these representations of body and landscape, however, are the authors' attempts to sustain and enhance their authorial subjectivity by constructing a unified body of text; that unity is attained, however, through the abjection of disorderly elements such as sex and death and the distribution of these elements among female or feminized characters. Again we see the author as the master subject, and women and the poor as the bearers of the burdens of nostalgia and tradition.

Pope's and Rousseau's nostalgia for a unified sensibility is deflected onto the fictive domains of body and landscape; by a nostalgic return to the homes of body and landscape, and the recreation of originary stories, Pope and Rousseau attempt to assuage their nostalgia and reinforce their authorial selves. As authors, they alone can tell the stories: Pope's own unrequited love for Martha Blount allows him to speak in Eloisa's voice, while Rousseau, as editor, assembles the letters of Julie and Saint-Preux into a single book, unifying and repairing a body of text in bits and pieces.

The mutilated body behind the texts is that of Abelard, castrated and in need of reparation. In the original story, Abelard finds himself hopelessly and involuntarily estranged from his body, while Héloïse is left to struggle against her passion under the guidance of his cold reason. The story of Abelard and Héloïse captures the dilemma of the Cartesian self in which the body and the mind are separated. By reworking this story, Pope and Rousseau attempt a nostalgic reintegration of reason and passion, constructing authorial selves that partake of and participate in Héloïse's physical passion, while maintaining Abelard's mastery over that passion. The body is integrated into the self by subordinating it to reason; passion and the female voice are tamed and subsumed under the hand of the writer.

The landscape and the body, in these works, are both objects of a masculine gaze; both are most safely viewed at a distance from which the eye can assume mastery. As imaginary spaces, the body and the landscape enhance the subjectivity of the authors by their otherness; the ruination of Abelard's castrated body (and by extension, Héloïse's female body) and the ruination of the landscape symbolically reinforce each other throughout the texts of Pope's "Eloisa" and Rousseau's *Julie*. In Pope's poem, the counterpoint between Eloisa's vibrant young female body and Abelard's sterile and deformed body is accented by the "relentless walls" and "rugged rocks"[4] of her convent, which contain and constrain her body much as his castration and their separation have frustrated her sexual passion. In Rousseau's novel, Julie's "prison" has only metaphorical walls; it is the prison of marriage and domesticity that contains Julie's passion for her former tutor, Saint-Preux. The landscape enclosing Julie has no stone walls or jagged rocks: she is surrounded by the grounds of her father's (now her husband's) country estate, within which she maintains her own private garden, the Elysée.

Julie has internalized restraint; marrying a man her father has chosen for her, she leaves Saint-Preux longing for her body and her presence, but forever condemned to view her at a distance in her new role as wife and mother.

The many social changes of the eighteenth century threatened those aspects of life that traditionally underpinned patriarchy: marriage, domestic ideology, class stability, ownership and control of the land. As in the case of Clarissa Harlowe, the acquisition of a female body through marriage was often directly connected to the acquisition of a parcel of land. As social mobility increased, and both daughters and land began to pass out of the hands of the aristocracy and into those of a newly moneyed middle class, patriarchal institutions were eroding in both real and symbolic terms. It is not surprising, then, that both bodies and land should be invested with a peculiarly eighteenth-century brand of nostalgia that laments a loss that can scarcely be articulated: not just the loss of a imaginary golden age that offered wholeness, unity, plenitude, and constancy, but also that of class privilege and stability.

The longing for that imaginary past is nostalgia, and in this chapter, my focus shifts toward the question of desire: if nostalgia is the desire to desire, is it not also a desire to *be* desired? Such desire runs deep, involving both a sense of one's own body as desirable, a body image intricately involved with the self one presents to others, and the concept of self as defined or limited by the surfaces of the body.[5]

Moreover, the desire to be desired runs back even deeper in the human psyche: it is linked to the desire for the mother and her unconditional love, and the unmediated relationship of the mother-infant dyad—a nostalgic drive to recuperate a lost plenitude, or sense of unity in which bodily boundaries (and sexual difference) are absent. Significantly, mothers are absent or, as is Mrs. Harlowe, inaccessible by virtue of being subsumed within the patriarchal system, in these texts that tell the stories of grieving and suffering women. Clarissa's nostalgia was not just for her home, but also for her mother, who also suffered greatly from the separation but was powerless to intervene in the machinations of her husband and son.

The burden of nostalgia borne by female characters, as I will argue in this chapter, is a necessary displacement of Pope's and Rousseau's own nostalgia for a unified sensibility and a desire to enhance their own authorial subjectivity; their anguish is represented in the nostalgia and suffering of the female characters.[6] Their nostalgia allows the authors to create an imaginary textual self that is free of contradictions, since the contradictions are subsumed within the grieving heroines.

These are stories of disobedient daughters who dare to question authority and act on their desire. Nostalgia is the disease of choice for these female characters, since a desire for home entails a longing for the mother, with a simultaneous recognition of the will and authority of the father. The recognition of paternal law is the oedipal moment for males, yet that paternal law is a problem as well for the female characters in many of the works I examine, since that paternal authority forces a rupture in the happiness and security of the home. Home is the background against which this oedipal drama is played out; home is also the site of an early, remembered, and longed-for sense of unity—the preoedipal. Home, therefore, is the ultimate site of contradiction, encompassing, as it does, both the golden age of the preoedipal and the negotiation of the oedipal conflict. The act of writing entails a renegotiation of the oedipal conflict that surfaces in the desire—and taming of desire—in Pope's Eloisa and Rousseau's Julie.

Contradictions can be found in male sexuality as well. In "Reason, Desire, and Male Sexuality," Victor J. Seidler observes that masculine identity, since the seventeenth century, has been influenced by Cartesian rationality, linking masculine identity to the mind rather than to the body (while the feminine, conversely, is identified with the body). The problem of sexuality for men, Seidler argues, is that it demands "surrender and spontaneity," which men have been taught to avoid. Sex becomes a mental experience, a performance subject to control, divorced from intimacy or dependency. At the same time, masculine gender identity is established on the denial of desire and emotion; masculinity, then, needs to be performed in a "continuous denial of 'femininity' or 'feminine qualities.'"[7] The abjection of feminine qualities, however necessary for subjectivity, nevertheless results in a sense of loss. The nostalgic attempt at reintegration of body and mind that we see in Pope's "Eloisa" and Rousseau's *Julie* is an imaginary resolution of the writers' conflict.

POPE'S "ELOISA"

"Eloisa to Abelard" stands out among Pope's works by being written in the voice of a woman;[8] in "The Argument" that precedes the text of the poem, Pope declares that "the following is partly extracted" from

Héloïse's letters. Pope's use of the word *extracted* is a loose one; while his poem recalls some of Héloïse's laments in her letters, Pope has of course taken the liberty of reworking her thoughts and longings into his own tight couplets. This poem is clearly Pope's, not Héloïse's. What is at stake for Pope in standing behind Héloïse's voice?

Ellen Pollak, in her reading of Pope's 1735 "Epistle II. To a Lady: Of the Characters of Women," emphasizes the ways in which the later poem "collaps[es] the distinction between obedience and desire" in its portrayal of Martha Blount, noting that by locating "power in submission, freedom in necessity, her quintessential 'selfhood' is but a function of her 'belonging' to a desire not her own." Martha is private muse to Pope's public, writing self, "encrypted in the 'living corpus' of his text" and "celebrated as an object/means of masculine fulfillment . . . a male's desire."[9] Martha Blount is not the first woman to appear "encrypted" in one of Pope's texts; if we read the "Epistle to a Lady" alongside "Eloisa," Martha appears to be an evolved and refined Eloisa. Pollak's observations on the "Epistle" and the ways in which Martha Blount's desire is appropriated by the author of the poem suggest a way of reading both "Eloisa" and *Julie* as texts that satisfy their authors' nostalgia for a unified self in which passion and reason can coexist.

Later refinements of Héloïse, such as Rousseau's Julie d'Étange, will find her domesticated, her passion self-policed, her writing more restrained; Julie's passion will write itself on her body in the form of illness. But Pope's Eloisa still struggles with her passion and the process of restraint; by writing her passion, she creates a symbolic substitute for loss, a textual body that will be a monument to her loss. The pleasure in the articulation of loss is also the poet's pleasure, and Pope writes himself into that pleasure and passion, co-opting it in order to construct a textual itself that is "whole" in a way that the post-Cartesian man cannot be.

In Pope's poem, Eloisa's passion is rekindled by a text. As the story goes, reiterated by Pope in the prefatory "Argument," Abelard's letter to a friend, the *Historia calamitatum,* has come to Eloisa by chance. Until this time, her passion has been buried within the "deep solitudes and awful cells" (1) of the convent, the place of contemplation and melancholy, a "last retreat" beyond which her thoughts now "rove" (5) in response to reading his letter. Abelard's text excites the same "tumult" in her "veins" (4) that his body once excited. His letter has become a reconstruction of, and symbolic substitute for, his castrated physical body, which is now a blank, a void.

Without "body"—that is, without a sexed body—the historical Abelard found it necessary to withdraw from public life. Because Abelard's letter does not explicitly appear in Pope's poem—as his body is present only in Eloisa's desire, his text is present only in her response—it is important to draw this text to the surface, in order to analyze what may be suppressed in Pope's recreation of Eloisa's response. Abelard's record of his own response to his castration is revealing:

> Next morning the whole city gathered before my house, and the scene of horror and amazement, mingled with lamentations, cries and groans . . . is difficult, no, impossible, to describe. . . . [My] pupils tormented me with their unbearable weeping and wailing until I suffered more from their sympathy than from the pain of my wound, and felt the misery of my mutilation less than my shame and humiliation. All sorts of thoughts filled my mind— how brightly my reputation had shone, and now how easily in an evil moment it had been dimmed or rather completely blotted out. . . . I thought how my rivals would exult over my fitting punishment . . . and how fast the news of this unheard-of disgrace would spread over the whole world. . . . How could I show my face in public, to be pointed at by every finger, derided by every tongue, a monstrous spectacle to all I met?[10]

Abelard explicitly states that he suffers more from his public humiliation than he does from the pain of his wounded body. He mourns his lost reputation, that is, his public self, and is tormented by the thought of how his "rivals would exult" and "how fast the news . . . would spread over the whole world." Ironically, Abelard envisions himself, even in his pain and misery, as more famous and talked-about than ever. Despite his retirement from public life—which he admits is due, not to any religious conviction, but rather to "shame and confusion in my remorse and misery"—Abelard writes that he was soon in demand once again as a teacher (76–77).

Pope's Eloisa responds to Abelard's text[11] with a letter that, unlike Abelard's *History*, bears the full force of her bodily passion. Eloisa's heart feels "its long-forgotten heat" (6) and her hand involuntarily writes Abelard's name, which she begs her tears to wash away. Eloisa surveys her surroundings:

> Relentless walls! whose darksom round contains
> Repentant sighs, and voluntary pains;
> Ye rugged rocks! which holy knees have worn;
> Ye grots and caverns shagg'd with horrid thorn!

> Shrines! where their vigils pale-ey'd virgins keep,
> And pitying saints, whose statues learn to weep! (17–22)

The images of enclosure within walls, rocks, grottoes, and caverns reinforce Eloisa's containment of her passion. Body and landscape are juxtaposed; she quickly contrasts herself to the rocks and grottoes of this
interior landscape: "Tho' cold like you, unmov'd and silent grown, / I
have not yet forgot my self to stone" (23–24). Eloisa's passion has not
been quenched; nor has she looked upon the Medusa. It takes only a
thought of Abelard to raise her passion to the surface: "rebel nature"
has control of "half [her] heart," and neither prayer nor fasting can "its
stubborn pulse restrain" (26–27). Her body—"rebel nature"—will not
be subdued by any means.

   Despite the absence of Abelard—and his text—from the poem, Abelard is present within Eloisa's desire; he is, in fact, *constituted by* her
physical desire, which continues to burn despite their separation and
despite his castration. Abelard's mutilated body is made whole once
more within Eloisa's memories of her passion and the physical "tumult"
that those memories occasion. Her text is supremely reparative; for this
reason, perhaps, her story was especially intriguing to both Pope and
Rousseau.

   But just as Abelard's "well-known name awakens all [Eloisa's] woes"
(30), sentiments that she conflates with her passions, Eloisa quickly
turns to writing as a symbolic substitution for bodily pleasure

> Yet write, or write me all, that I may join
> Griefs to thy griefs, and eccho sighs to thine.
> Nor foes nor fortune take this pow'r away. (41–43)

Eloisa longs for intercourse realized in writing, a union of grief to grief:
"Then share thy pain," she begs, "allow that sad relief; / Ah more than
share it! give me all thy grief" (49–50). Her longing for his words of
grief is as palpable as her longing for his body. Eloisa celebrates the
power and the sensuousness of writing:

> Heav'n first taught letters for some wretch's aid,
> Some banish'd lover, or some captive maid;
> They live, they speak, they breathe what love inspires. (51–53)

Unable to enjoy Abelard's body, she longs for his words in the material
form of his writing.[12]

The closest we get to Abelard's material body is an unwelcome, intrusive spectacle that suddenly presents itself to Eloisa's imagination: "Alas how chang'd! what sudden horrors rise! / A naked Lover bound and bleeding lies!" (99–100). Eloisa is consumed by guilt that she was unable to prevent the tragedy and imagines an alternative ending, writing herself into the scene:

> Where, where was *Eloise*? her voice, her hand,
> Her ponyard, had oppos'd the dire command.
> Barbarian, stay! that bloody stroke restrain. (101–3)

The self Eloisa imagines is powerful, armed with a "ponyard," capable of defying any "barbarian." The castrated Abelard cannot appear in the poem; a vision of a powerful Eloisa must replace that of the naked and bleeding body of her lover. While a mutilated male body is repressed, a female body is put on display, made visible for the gaze of Abelard and of the reader. Most interesting of all is Eloisa's imaginary act of opposition to Abelard's castration; she laments her *absence* from the scene and imagines that "her voice, her hand, / Her ponyard" could have prevented the "bloody stroke." Only her voice, her hand, and her pen can now reconstruct Abelard's sexuality, but her words are cut off before she can tell the story as it really happened: "I can no more; by shame, by rage supprest, / Let tears, and burning blushes speak the rest" (105–6). Her body—that is, her tears and blushes—must narrate the unspeakable act.

While Eloisa's body takes over her writing, Abelard remains free of the demands of "nature" that cause Eloisa so much suffering. "For thee," Eloisa writes,

> the fates, severely kind, ordain
> A cool suspense from pleasure and from pain;
> Thy life a long, dead calm of fix'd repose
> No pulse that riots, and no blood that glows. (249–52)

Although sexual pleasure is denied Abelard, he is also free of the pain of desire and grief, while his sexualized body survives intact in Eloisa's passion and in her writing. Moreover, Abelard's ability to control his passion—his "cool suspense"—gives him a mastery over his body that Eloisa cannot achieve; nevertheless, the price of that mastery—violent castration—is high. Abelard represents, for both Pope and Rousseau, the modern man: aligned with reason, capable of rhetorical mastery, but separated from the passions of the body. Abelard's rhetorical absence from Pope's poem also lends him a sort of mastery;[13] most importantly, however, that silence opens up a space into which Pope may insert himself.

On a certain level, we could read Pope's own life and his diseased and misshapen body into this poem. Pope himself knew very well the life of "fix'd repose."[14] His own body was scarcely transparent to him: a whole and healthy body, a body that is the object of feminine desire, an earlier, healthier body was something Pope could only long to recuperate. A connection between the bare convent cell that imprisons Eloisa's passion and the sadly deformed body that imprisoned Pope's own physical desire suggests itself.[15]

Pope, nevertheless, is present in this poem in a way that is much more complicated than an identification with Eloisa's cloistered, frustrated desire. Pope is also present in the silent Abelard, who is both the object of female desire and the master of that desire. When Eloisa imagines her death, she longs for the presence of Abelard as spectator: her death is a performance that can only be appreciated by Abelard as grieving lover. She envisions Abelard's weeping over her dying body:

> Thou, *Abelard*! the last sad office pay
> And smooth my passage to the realms of day:
> See my lips tremble, and my eye-balls roll,
> Suck my last breath, and catch my flying soul! (321–24)

But Eloisa's vision takes a sudden turn as Abelard appears to her as a priest rather than as a grieving lover:

> Ah no—in sacred vestments may'st thou stand,
> The hallow'd taper trembling in thy hand,
> Present the Cross before my lifted eye,
> Teach me at once, and learn of me to die. (325–28)

Eloisa, nevertheless, cannot fully forget her body and is unwilling to let Abelard forget: in an attempt to take Abelard back into the realm of the body, she implores him, "See from my cheek the transient roses fly! / See the last sparkle languish in my eye!" (331–32). Eloisa goes on to imagine the remains of their earthly bodies buried in "one kind grave" that will "graft my love immortal on thy fame" (343–44). Her desire, ultimately, is not her own; it is necessarily "grafted" onto Abelard's "fame." The powerful female desire that seems to be struggling to break through the text is finally put under control and revealed as embedded within Abelard's own desire, not for Eloisa, but for fame.

Eloisa imagines a bodily response to her story, even far in the future, when she imagines "two wandring lovers" who have gone to the Paraclete to visit the joint grave, shedding tears over "the pale marble" (347, 349). Bodily sentiment would overpower even religious feeling: in the midst of "the pomp of dreadful sacrifice," the celebration of the Eucharist, if "some relenting eye" should observe their grave, then "Devotion's self shall steal a thought from heav'n, / One human tear shall drop, and be forgiv'n" (354–55, 357–58). Here Pope invokes a popular model of sensibility, one that will become a future model of nostalgia, as both Pope and Eloisa imagine the future "consumers" of sentiment.

Eloisa's immortality will arise not only from Abelard, but also from Pope, whose presence is finally manifested within the lines of the poem as "some future Bard" (359). Pope's qualifications for telling Eloisa's sad story are the "griefs" that he will join to hers. His long, unrequited love for Lady Mary Wortley Montagu, "Condemned whole years in absence to deplore" (361), makes him the poet worthy of recounting the tragic story: "The well-sung woes will sooth my pensive ghost; / He best can paint 'em, who shall feel 'em most" (365–66). Pope's poem will be "well-sung" and legitimated by his own longing and grief. Pope's sudden appearance at the very end of the poem points to his mute presence throughout. Although he shares sentiments of grief and longing with Eloisa, he ultimately assumes the same mastery that Abelard enjoys by virtue of Eloisa's submission, and the grafting of her love onto his fame; Pope, the Bard, will offer Eloisa her own fame, by writing her into what becomes his own poem. By appropriating Eloisa's voice, he also appropriates her grief. As Eloisa has, Pope has loved long and well, but his grief can enter the public sphere under his own name. By containing Eloisa's discourse and putting it under the control of his heroic epistle, Pope assumes the role of Abelard.

Abelard is the "author," after all, of the Paraclete monastery: the nuns are his "flock," his "[p]lants," his "children, who have fled from the "false world" in their "early youth." Abelard has led them to "mountains, wilds, and deserts," where he "rais'd these hallow'd walls; the desert smil'd / And Paradise was open'd in the Wild" (129–34).[16] The monastery was endowed by no patrons; it has only "such plain roofs as piety could raise" (139). Abelard, as Ronald Paulson observes, has become a "georgic farmer" who has reconstructed Paradise[17] (71).

Pope's poem describes in detail the monastery and surrounding land-scape:

> In these lone walls . . .
> These moss-grown domes with spiry turrets crown'd,
> Where awful arches make a noon-day night,
> And the dim windows shed a solemn light, (141–44)

the sisters are expected to dedicate their souls to God. Pope's descrip-tion of the monastery draws on the gloomy elements of a Salvator Rosa painting. The subtext of Pope's dark, solemn, and mysterious landscape is the feminine landscape that Héloïse describes in her letter to Abelard: "And so it is yours, truly your own, this new plantation for God's pur-pose, but it is sown with plants which are still very tender and need watering if they are to thrive. Through its feminine nature this planta-tion would be weak and frail even if it were not new" (111). The way in which Pope's conception of the Paraclete places this community of tender feminine plants in a forbidding, gloomy, and threatening land-scape is curious. The Paraclete, though abandoned, was only five years old at the time it was reopened by Abelard in 1129; the structure itself is relatively new, but is being taken over by nature, as if the land were reverting to a wild, unspoiled state. The landscape itself must bear the burden of time and that of representing the past, hence Pope's invoca-tion early in the poem of the rocks "which holy knees have worn" (19). Ignoring the newness of the monastery, Pope calls on the ancient past of the land to create a nostalgic mood of mystery and wildness, which reinforces Eloisa's own dark passion. While the landscape is dark and forbidding, it is also frankly sensuous:

> The darksom pines that o'er yon' rocks reclin'd
> Wave high, and murmur to the hollow wind,
> The wandring streams that shine between the hills,
> The grots that eccho to the tinkling rills,
> The dying gales that pant upon the trees,
> The lakes that quiver to the curling breeze;
> No more these scenes my meditation aid,
> Or lull to rest the visionary maid. (155–63)

These images, although tinged with baroque references to death and the passage of time, such as the "hollow wind" or the "dying gales," nevertheless retain many positive associations, calling up the scent of pines that "wave high" toward heaven, images of streams that wander and "shine," echoes of "tinkling rills," and visions of lakes that "quiver" and shimmer in a gentle, "curling breeze." There is a peculiar conjunction of pleasure and death in this passage that echoes Eloisa's own ambivalence; her nostalgia for the pleasures she once shared with Abelard is a mix of pleasure and pain.

While these natural features have served as aids to meditation, the scene of nature is now tinted by "Black Melancholy," which imposes a "death-like silence" and a "dread repose." The positive images of nature are suddenly converted to dark, deathlike images:

> But o'er the twilight groves, and dusky caves,
> Long-sounding isles, and intermingled graves,
> Black Melancholy sits, and round her throws
> A death-like silence, and a dread repose:
> Her gloomy presence saddens all the scene,
> Shades ev'ry flower, and darkens ev'ry green,
> Deepens the murmur of the falling floods,
> And breathes a browner horror on the woods.
>
> Yet here for ever, ever must I stay;
> Sad proof how well a lover can obey! (155–72)

"Black Melancholy" is engendered by Eloisa's mourning and has the power to cast a shadow over the entire landscape; this melancholy overpowers the quality of the landscape that should make it appropriate for spiritual meditation. This melancholy is linked also to Abelard's castration by the use of the word *repose* which recurs in line 251 to describe Abelard's life in his castrated body as a "long, dead calm of fix'd repose."

Despite Eloisa's submission to Abelard, and her willingness to show "how well a lover can obey," her mourning for his castrated body nevertheless interferes with her ability to experience the religious conversion Abelard has prescribed for her. Because Eloisa is unable to forget her love for Abelard and, most of all, the bodily pleasures they once shared, she is unable to transcend her body, as Abelard has done so easily. Pope's focus on Eloisa's inability to overcome physical desire is a mark of eighteenth-century gender differentiation, in which women were viewed as fixed in the body. The constant tension in the poem is the result of Eloisa's struggle to surrender, once and for all, her desire for Abelard and to replace it with her dedication to God. Eloisa cannot give up Abelard, because she cannot forget him: "of all affliction taught a lover yet, / 'Tis

sure the hardest science to forget!" (189–90), she laments. Eloisa's pleasure in remembering is one she cannot and will not surrender.

That Eloisa's passion—that is, her melancholy, for the two cannot be
untangled in Pope's view—overpowers even the landscape, stripping it
of its devotional qualities and overlaying it with despair and darkness,
even "a browner horror," suggests a sexual passion that is fluid and
uncontainable, likely to seep into its surroundings: that is, a passion that
is at once eloquent and dangerous. Pope adopts and co-opts Eloisa's
passion and her voice in order to create a sensuous poem. But he suddenly reins in that passion, placing it under his own artistic control.
Pope inserts himself into the last lines of the poem as the "future Bard,"
who is able to represent Eloisa's melancholy and passion by virtue of
the "sad similitude" of his grief to Eloisa's. By the last line of the poem,
"He best can paint 'em, who shall feel 'em most," Eloisa's voice is completely effaced, for this line sounds nothing like her plaintive laments;
rather, this is Pope's own distinctive and easily recognizable brisk tone.
Just as he later contains Martha Blount's desire within his own desire
and within her sense of obedience and submission, he contains Eloisa's
desire—a desire that cannot be surrendered even to God—within his
own desire for fame and immortality. As the poem moves to a close,
Pope retreats into masculinity, erasing ambiguity; he has toyed with
cross-gender identification but finally reasserts borders, as if he has
ventured into a dangerous area by adopting—even temporarily—
Eloisa's passion and voice. Pope's nostalgia for a unified sensibility
allows him the pleasures of desire but is easily abandoned when cross-
gender identification is closed off; in the end, the voice of Eloisa is
silenced and only Pope as poet and public man is left to speak. His nostalgia is a pleasure that the poet may indulge, and abandon, at will.

By recasting a medieval story of power, castration, and passion into
a modern poem, Pope co-opts all the desire and nostalgia packed into
the original text. A wounded male body, a passionate female body, a
dark and forbidding landscape, a moldering monastery, a convent cell
to confine that female passion: all combine to enhance a mood of loss.
By recuperating these elements and rewriting the story as his own,
Pope assumes the mastery of Abelard and the passion of Eloisa.

Rousseau's Julie

The containment of desire and the insertion of the author into the
work as both the object and master of female desire link Pope's "Eloisa

to Abelard" and Rousseau's 1761 novel, *Julie, ou la nouvelle Héloïse;*[18] both are connected to the medieval letters through this device as well. Peggy Kamuf points out that Héloïse is drawn into correspondence with Abelard by her need to revise his misrepresentation of her arguments against marriage and his representation, in the *Historia Calamitatum*, of her as having undergone a conversion. Kamuf writes that, in contrast to "Abelard's rhetoric of a radical break" (a repetition of his sudden and violent castration), Héloïse "repeatedly evokes a continuity and reaches for a language which will leave no doubt about the woman who is writing behind the veil. In a final letter, however, having realized that Abelard will refuse any further protest on her part, Héloïse agrees, in effect, to silence her complaint and address only questions of monastic rule to the patron of the Paraclete. The issue of her conversion is dropped—and Abelard, once again, addresses her *as if* there were nothing behind her veil" (100, emphasis in original). While Héloïse tries to create meaning from her suffering and work through her pain by incorporating it, along with the past, into her identity, Abelard represses his castration by writing over it. In between Héloïse's memory and Abelard's repression is nostalgia—a false memory, but an effective repression. By adopting the voice and desire of Eloisa/Julie, Pope and Rousseau enjoy their memories of passion while effectively repressing any memory of loss or castration. Héloïse's final submission to Abelard's rhetoric is repeated in the erasure of Eloisa's voice from Pope's poem, and the domestication of Julie's desire in Rousseau's novel. In each case, (feminine) body and passion submit to (masculine) reason; ultimately, Abelard, Pope, and Rousseau have the last word.

The submission of the body to reason is an essential part of this triangulation of desire in the medieval *Letters*, a triangulation that is realized in the three-way relationship among Héloïse, Abelard, and God. The central problem in the *Letters* is the question of Héloïse's conversion: Can she be converted? Is she *willing* to be converted? This question is never resolved, since, as Kamuf observes, Héloïse's resistance is rhetorically silenced by Abelard's "writing *as if*" Héloïse has been converted. We do not know whether Abelard, in fact, actually believes in Héloïse's conversion; we know only that, in his writing, he constructs a fiction of her conversion, a fiction that, moreover, covers over his own memory of the physical passion they have shared and of the castration he has suffered as a direct result of that passion. This fiction effectively subdues the passion and pain of the body.

In order for Héloïse to be converted, she must lose her memory of that passion. To forget is difficult for Héloïse, since the memory is not only inscribed in her body, but continually produced by her body through her physical desire. There is a circular relationship between desire and memory: memory creates desire, even as desire uses memory as an object with which to sustain or rekindle itself.

The question of Héloïse's conversion, or the knowability of a woman's desire or repentance, is perhaps what drove the popularity of the Abelard and Héloïse legend. Pope does not explicitly resolve the question, although he marks his text with an ambiguous interruption—the "Ah no" at line 325 in which Eloisa's vision of Abelard as grieving lover is suddenly replaced by one of Abelard as priest, yet another repetition, perhaps, of Abelard's castration. The attention of both Eloisa and the poem itself is then deflected onto a desire for fame and immortality, which finally provides a door through which the poet can walk onto the stage of his work and speak in his own voice.

As is that of Héloïse, Julie's "conversion" is also undecidable. Superficially, Julie succeeds in controlling her desire. She conforms to her father's wishes, marrying Wolmar, the husband of his choice, and lives a virtuous life as wife and mother, terminating her love affair with—if not completely eradicating her desire for—her tutor, Saint-Preux. In Rousseau's scheme, any struggles with desire that Julie may have after her marriage do not count as a stain on her virtue; that she control her body is sufficient. This "silencing" of her body is a fiction similar to that constructed by Abelard about Héloïse's conversion. But her deathbed letter to Saint-Preux—to be read first by her husband, and forwarded to Saint-Preux at his discretion—reveals that her desire for him has never been completely overcome; Julie, like Héloïse, cannot totally forget her passion and Julie just agrees to be quiet. Michael O'Dea has observed that the question of forgetfulness "is often the condition of sexual union in Rousseau's writings, reflecting a characteristic difficulty in integrating sexuality into any larger scheme";[19] once Julie "remembers" her passion, she must die. Julie's death releases her from the same struggles that Héloïse faces with her memories, her conscience, and her spiritual relationship with God.

We know little or nothing about any conflict Héloïse may have faced prior to entering into a relationship with Abelard, but early in Rousseau's novel the reader is made fully aware of Julie's love for Saint-Preux, and her need for a domestic structure that will prevent her from acting on her desire. In letter 6, Julie writes to her cousin, Claire, in order to beg her quick return from the country where Claire has gone to attend her dying governess, Chaillot.

Unexpectedly, after expressing sympathy for Chaillot's death, Julie hints at Chaillot's culpability in Julie's present dilemma. Although she has lovingly raised Claire since the death of Claire's mother, Chaillot has "hardly been prudent with us," Julie writes, observing that Chaillot in effect violated the girls' innocence by unnecessarily revealing "the most indiscreet confidences" and entertaining them with stories recounting "her own youthful adventures [and] romantic intrigues." Moreover, she has instructed the cousins in "at least a thousand things that young girls would be better off not knowing. . . . [H]er lessons were becoming dangerous."[20]

The death of Claire's mother has endangered the virtue of both young women, and now Claire's absence is exacerbating Julie's danger. Nancy K. Miller reads Julie's anxiety as fear of her own desire and the "disruption" that love has caused within her, noting that a split or divided self is evident in Julie's comment to Claire, "It is up to you to restore me to myself" (18). Miller notes Julie's sense of loss here and observes that "Julie is *already* nostalgic for an original and lost innocence."[21]

Julie is also nostalgic for the mother from whom her desire has separated her. Once Julie's sexual desire for Saint-Preux is awakened, her close bond with her mother is broken. She is unable to reveal her need for stricter supervision to her mother; instead she asks Claire to secure her virtue through her constant companionship. There is a suggestion here that any crack in the domestic structure is potentially disruptive: if Claire's mother had not died, the girls would not have been introduced to the many things they would be better off not knowing. Moreover, Claire's mother is replaced, not by Julie's mother, an appropriate substitute, but by a household servant.

The substitution of Claire's mother by Chaillot represents a breakdown in the family that is further complicated by a fissure in the class system; because a servant has stepped into the role of mother, the domestic education of the cousins is compromised and tainted by Chaillot's indiscreet confidences, which young middle-class women should not hear. The family is yet another site where nature and culture intersect: the loss of the "natural" mother and her replacement with a surrogate from a different class spell disaster and threaten a social structure based on the *maison paternelle* and the ultimate authority of the father. Without a "natural" mother to enable and transmit patriarchal ideology,

as Mrs. Harlowe does in *Clarissa*, the family loses its power as an ideological training ground for properly acculturated female subjects. The
seepage of a servant's knowledge into a bourgeois education is dangerous and seems to lead to Julie's unfortunate affair with Saint-Preux,
who is considered, as Peter Abelard was for Héloïse, an unsuitable
match.

Saint-Preux is an elusive, transgressive character whose true name is
never revealed. A modern man who lacks the essential identity of the
natural or savage man, Saint-Preux is constructed by his surroundings.
His most prominent identity is that of the outsider. He is neither noble
nor peasant; rather, he is from an uncertain background and attempts
to transcend the social status into which he has been born. He has no
clear status within Julie's household, being neither a servant nor a
member of the family. Even Saint-Preux's gender is somewhat ambiguous; he can never assume the paternal authority that Julie's father and
Wolmar are entitled to, and his overwhelming bodily passion aligns
him with the female characters in the novel. Yet Saint-Preux is no
Jeronymo della Porretta, whose bodily infirmities suggest castration;
Saint-Preux's masculine passion is very much alive, his body intact.
Rousseau's construction of Saint-Preux is a nostalgic attempt to create
a "whole" man by mediating the fixed gender roles that assign reason
to male characters and passion to female characters; a character such as
Saint-Preux, however, whose gender role has been reinvented, does not
fit easily into the social structure of the novel.

In Rousseau's novel, castration is effected by class, not physical violence, reflecting a movement away from the realm of the body to the
realm of reason and abstraction; the modern world is a social world in
which individuals are increasingly defined through economic and social
position, rather than through what seems to be a stable sexual identity,
or an aristocratic identity established in bloodlines. Class, as E. P.
Thompson reminds us, is a relationship and therefore lacks the reassur-
ing essentialism of an identity anchored in biology.[22] Precisely because
Saint-Preux's class identity is so fluid, he threatens the patriarchal system maintained by the Baron d'Étange and his *maison paternelle*. Saint-
Preux boldly declares his love to Julie, his student, who has been
prepared for such an experience by Chaillot's disclosures, crossing demarcation lines of class and propriety. He also fashions himself a melancholic hero and expresses the desire to see Julie suffering as well,
wasting away for love of him.

Two months after the initial exchange of letters, Saint-Preux writes to Julie:

> How changed you are since two months ago, and you alone have changed! Your languor has disappeared; there is no more vexation or despondency; all your graces are back in place; all your charms are revived; the newly-opened rose is not fresher than you . . . .
>
> [I]s this the nature of a violent, uncontrollable passion? . . . Oh, how much more pleasing you were when you were less beautiful! How I miss that touching pallor, the precious assurance of a lover's happiness, and how I hate the robust health you have recovered at the expense of my tranquility! Yes, I would prefer to see you still ill rather than see this contented air, these brilliant eyes, this blooming complexion that offends me. (21–22)

Saint-Preux's—and Rousseau's—investment in female bodily illness and wasting reveals itself in this passage. Saint-Preux demands to know how Julie's vibrant health and air of contentment can be consistent with a "violent, ungovernable passion"; he sees good health and passion as mutually exclusive. Moreover, he declares that he would prefer to see her "still ill" rather than to see her entirely well, "blooming" in fact. Saint-Preux objects, here, to Julie's use of reason to overcome her passion; he finds the depth of her passion suspect, since it is not, for her, "uncontrollable." The ideal Julie would be unable to escape her body, unable to control her passion. Although Rousseau is able to conceive Saint-Preux as a character who traverses class and gender lines, he is ambivalent toward Julie's gender transgression through her use of reason and has Saint-Preux articulate the prevailing ideology that would make Julie a slave to her passions. Julie's ability to allow reason to dominate passion—that is, her ability to separate the two—threatens the ultimate stability of Saint-Preux's identity; his irrational desire to see Julie "still ill" reflects the need to maintain gender difference by keeping Julie strictly in the realm of the body.

This passage, moreover, highlights the mediating role that Julie's body plays for both Saint-Preux and Rousseau. Saint-Preux's identity—which seems to consist primarily of his own passion and melancholy—must be confirmed by and reflected in Julie's body. We know nothing of Saint-Preux outside his relationship with Julie; he is a modern, self-made man, lacking traditional or aristocratic roots or identity. Rousseau presents a visual image of a healthy, thriving, even "blooming" female body; this is not the body of the languishing Clarissa Harlowe, whose beauty gradually becomes that of an exquisite corpse.

Whereas Clarissa begins as healthy and beautiful, then slowly fades away, Julie falls ill early in the novel and then recovers her health. This return to health and the bodily control it signals are disturbing to Saint-Preux, who desires to see a "pallor" in Julie's cheek. That pallor would assure his own happiness, but Julie's good health is a measure of resistance to Saint-Preux's influence. Her "blooming complexion" and "contented air" frustrate Saint-Preux's desire, leaving it unreciprocated.

Behind Saint-Preux's contradictory desire to see his beloved Julie "still ill" is the insecurity of his social position in relation to Julie: Saint-Preux, despite his transgressive declaration of love for his student and his efforts at self-construction, is nevertheless aware of his status as tutor, occupant of a liminal space, not quite a servant, but not a social equal either. As does that of Chaillot, the governess, Saint-Preux's position vis-à-vis Julie's family represents a threat to the social and family structure; yet, while Chaillot is able to step into the role of Claire's mother, there is no position that Saint-Preux can easily assume within the household. Julie's father's status is fixed, and Saint-Preux's only possibility is to challenge the dominance of Julie's father's by becoming Julie's lover, that is, through the mediation of Julie's body. For that reason, Saint-Preux reads Julie's coolness and composure as marks of their social and economic inequality; only passion can equalize these lovers, and Julie has apparently mastered her passion, leaving Saint-Preux powerless and without resources. Since he cannot hope for a reduction in her social status, he wishes, rather, for a wasting of her body as a mark of his power over her. Julie's control of both her emotion and her rhetoric, in contrast to Saint-Preux's utter lack of control over his desire, and his frantic—and onanistic, as Tony Tanner describes it[23]— writing represents an inversion of roles in this reworking of the Héloïse and Abelard story.

The powerful patriarchal structure of Julie's family, which both reinforces and is reinforced by the d'Étange family's socioeconomic status, allows Julie to be in control of her purse and her passion. Money is Julie's to dispense at will; such largesse, in fact, maintains the status quo by keeping her beneficiaries content. Her passion, meanwhile, is effectively contained within the boundaries of the paternal estate, where it will be allowed some expression (after her marriage) in the artificial and illusory Elysée. Unlike Abelard, Saint-Preux is not freed of the tyranny of the body; rather, he is condemned to live inside a desiring body that is nevertheless forbidden to act on those desires. Saint-Preux can only stand on the edge of modernity because he lacks the

economic resources and class position to go forward. The power of reason—Abelard's consolation—is not Saint-Preux's; that power remains
in the hands of those who can exercise control over other bodies,
namely, Julie's father and husband. In effect, there is no future for
Saint-Preux, whose status is unclear and ill defined.

Julie's recovery of reason and tranquility that so infuriates Saint-
Preux is not represented in the novel. In a tantalizing and puzzling note,
Rousseau—the editor—tells us that "a gap is noticeable here, and will
often be found throughout the remainder of this correspondence. Several letters have been lost, others have been suppressed, still others have
suffered abridgment; but nothing essential is missing which may not be
readily filled in with the help of what remains" (21). Rousseau's editorial intervention, at this very moment in the text, is interesting in its
own assertion of mastery, in this case a mastery over the body of the
text.

By this editorial note, Rousseau writes himself, as "editor," into the
maimed collection of letters ("lost," "suppressed," and "abridged"), ostensibly an authentic collection of "Letters of two lovers, inhabitants of
a small town at the foot of the Alps," much as Pope makes his presence
known within "Eloisa to Abelard." While it could be argued that Rousseau's assumption of the role of editor, like that of Richardson, is a con-
vention of the period, it is worth observing that just as Saint-Preux
begins to feel that Julie is slipping out of his control, Rousseau steps in
to take control of the text. Rousseau's gesture is ambivalent: even as he
asserts his presence, he attempts to render his own "cutting" of the text
invisible.

The reader, at this point, knows nothing of the history of the collection of letters. Only later will it be revealed that Saint-Preux transcribes
Julie's letters to him into a notebook, while his letters to Julie are first
held by Claire, then returned to Julie, discovered by her mother, to
resurface eventually in the possession of Wolmar. Letters may have
been lost at any time and may have been suppressed by anyone through
whose hands they have passed, but the reader can only assume that the
abridgments have been executed by the editor's hand. Rousseau reassures us, however, that "nothing essential" is lost. In other words,
Rousseau, as editor, has modified the raw text of the letters and removed extraneous material, yet he promises the reader a full and coherent text, and he makes this promise in the form of a supplement of his
own words that covers over the gap at the same time that it calls attention to the missing text. Peggy Kamuf calls such editorial interventions

"gestures of closure at the borders of the fictional work, where . . . editorial commentary sets to work sealing cracks in the text" (xvii). Just as Saint-Preux desires to see Julie ill, Rousseau hints at a maiming of the original text as a way of asserting control over a textual body that threatens unruliness through the desire that shimmers throughout the letters. Rousseau's aside implies that the original text needs taming, needs him as editor, in fact.[24]

Julie's response to Saint-Preux's fear that she has governed her passion and no longer really needs him (just as the text may not need an editor) is scarcely designed to relieve Saint-Preux's uneasiness. In letter 9 of part 1, she attempts a rhetorical mastery worthy of Abelard himself, while ascribing to words the same erotic impact that Héloïse does: "Everyone taught me or led me to believe that a sensible girl was ruined at the first tender word that escaped her lips; my troubled imagination confounded the crime with the avowal of passion, and I had such a frightening idea of this first step that I scarcely saw any interval between it and the last" (23). Julie conflates language with the body, or rather sees language and bodily passion on a continuum. There is no separation of reason and desire here: her virtue could be "ruined" by "the first tender word that escaped her lips." During their separation, however, Julie has apparently learned to subdue passion with reason. She insists that her happiness arises from love, but not from sensuality: "two months of experience have taught me that my excessively tender heart needs love, but that my senses have no need of a lover" (24).

In these letters, Julie attempts to rise above physical passion and the body much as Abelard does in the twelfth-century letters. But a struggle for power between the two lovers gradually reveals itself. Unable to assert any power through class privilege, Saint-Preux seeks authority in literary tradition. His letters to Julie are Petrarchan laments about the coldness and cruelty of his beloved and the burning of his own passion. Julie is not blind to the advantages of Saint-Preux's self-fashioning, telling him, "I also know that your situation, troublesome as it is, is not without pleasures. It is sweet for a true lover to make sacrifices, all of which are credited to him. . . . Who knows even if, knowing my sensibility, you are not using a deeper plot to seduce me?" (26–27). Julie maintains the upper hand by awarding Saint-Preux an unexpected kiss in the arbor, and then sending him away as "a test of obedience" (35). Most significantly, however, she sends him money, telling him clearly that she is doing so because she knows her fortune is greater than his. When Saint-Preux returns the money, she doubles the amount and sends it back, challenging him to "prove . . . clearly, incontestably, and without evasiveness" that his honor would be compromised by accepting her gift of money (37).

The question of class again surfaces, emphasizing the social pressures that impinge on their "natural" love for each other. Rousseau is nostalgic for the "natural" relationship of the sexes; the idea of class disrupts any possibility of a "natural" relationship that would be based on biology or sex. Rousseau's nostalgia, then, is for another type of hierarchy: one based on a so-called natural aristocracy in which the self-made man, for example, Saint-Preux or Rousseau himself, could claim a place by right of his sex, and from which he could not be displaced by a woman. Despite the mutual attraction between Saint-Preux and Julie, Saint-Preux is not an acceptable lover for Julie because he lacks the family lineage, social cachet, and fortune that Julie possesses through her father. The idea of the "natural" is actually a leveling device that would erase social and economic privilege. Society, however, allows Julie to carry her father's advantages into the relationship and enjoy a position of relative power; she then extends her power by using her rhetorical prowess to overcome Saint-Preux's objections, challenging him to refute her argument through superior rhetoric—if he can. Moreover, Julie tells Saint-Preux that "you must be humbled for the harm you have caused" (37). Julie plays the part of the cruel mistress here, but unlike Petrarch's Laura, who is silent until after her death, Julie is quite eloquent, challenging her lover to a rhetorical competition. There is little left for Saint-Preux to master—unless it is Julie's body, of which she seems to be in control.

Saint-Preux's dilemma is caused by modernity, Rousseau implies. Modern lovers such as Julie and Saint-Preux, who occasionally transgress gender boundaries, are punished by the failure of their love affair. As Pope does, Rousseau explores cross-gender identification. But Rousseau's project is to show that such violation of gender boundaries does not work: the Baron d'Étange and Wolmar triumph over the ineffectual Saint-Preux, and Julie loses her life. Claire, however, as Lady G. does in *Sir Charles Grandison*, survives because she is able to accommodate herself fully to a feminine, domestic role. Rousseau's nostalgia is evident not only in his evocation of the "natural" as something that has disappeared in modern life, but also in his effort to preserve clearly defined borders between genders.

Rousseau's nostalgia is for an imaginary past; he rejects a modern social structure that has as its foundation patriarchy and primogeniture, inasmuch as that structure supports differences of class. The "natural" past that he mourns, however, is hardly egalitarian; rather, it is a hierarchy in which males enjoy privilege based on their "natural" qualities of physical strength and reason. While Rousseau objects to social inequality between men, he fully accepts "natural" inequality between men and women, locating difference in the body. Rousseau believes in the companionate marriage; that match, however, is cloaked in the ideology of the "natural."

Julie's powerful father is unwilling to tolerate any leaky borders. When he returns to the household, he is taken aback at the impropriety of allowing Saint-Preux to retain his post as tutor without a salary; he is even more indignant when he learns that Saint-Preux is of respectable but not noble birth. Baron d'Étange is all too aware of the dangers posed to his household by the presence of a young male tutor who is willing to work without pay. By insisting that Saint-Preux accept a salary or be dismissed, Baron d'Étange reasserts the primacy of class. Saint-Preux understands completely that accepting a salary would make him a servant of Julie's father, reinforcing the socioeconomic differences between the two lovers. Saint-Preux prefers to view Julie and himself as "two lovers of the same age, both seized with the same passion, united by a mutual attachment," and hence as equals (51). Saint-Preux calls on passion to make the lovers equal and urges Julie to seize the day: "Abandon your plans, and be happy. Come . . . into your lover's arms to reunite the two halves of our single being" (56).

Saint-Preux plays his hand well. He closes his letter with a veiled threat of suicide, which throws Julie, as we learn from the letter that follows, from Claire to Saint-Preux, into a serious illness. Saint-Preux's wish that Julie fall ill is realized: she is "at the brink of death," Claire writes (75). Julie has been ill since Saint-Preux's departure, and conversations with her father have exacerbated her illness. Saint-Preux's letter has caused a violent fever, and Claire begs him to return.

Claire's letter is the only representation of Julie's illness, and we learn that Julie's secret love for Saint-Preux is revealed in her delirious ravings; when her mother understands, she attempts to hide the knowledge from Julie's father. Julie succumbs to passion and grief through illness; her body and voice reveal her desire, despite the control she has attempted to exercise over her body. Unlike Héloïse or Pope's Eloisa, Julie does not write her desire; instead, she falls ill. Julie's "illness" is the mark of her modernity, a social construction that displaces and deflects the "natural" passion of the body that the earlier Héloïse/Eloisa recognizes and articulates; nevertheless, the primacy of Julie's "natural" body reasserts itself in the form of delirium and irrational speech. Rousseau's nostalgia for the "natural" once again reveals itself; "illness" turns out to be merely a fragile framework that cannot adequately explain or contain the passion of Julie's body, a passion that overrides the lovers' social inequality. Julie, moreover, loses her rhetorical power: her language is now out of her control, revealing her passion against her will.

There is a gap after Claire's letter; we learn nothing of Julie's recovery until Claire goes away, and Julie writes her another desperate letter that betrays her fear of being left alone with Saint-Preux: "A passion more terrible than fever and delirium sweeps me away to my ruin. . . . Oh, if you knew what the madman dares propose to me!" (57). Julie seems aware of the connection between her illness and her desire but sees her sexual passion for Saint-Preux as more "terrible" and dangerous even than the serious fever she has suffered.

Her writing here is frantic and fragmented; Julie is demoralized by her illness, and she is being pressured from all sides. Saint-Preux is demanding that she elope with him, while her father has arranged a marriage for her with his friend Wolmar. But the psychological pressure of her situation does not cloud Julie's judgment. She clearly recognizes the injustice of the marriage arrangement: "So, my father has sold me! He considers his daughter as property, as a slave! He repays his debts at my expense! He purchases his life with mine!" (57). Julie's awareness of her status as an object of exchange represents yet another crack in the domestic structure that her father attempts to maintain; this structure, under pressure from within and without, cannot remain intact. The conflicting pressures of her love for Saint-Preux and her duty to her father have weakened her body through illness; her will and resolve lose strength as well.

Julie is at her most vulnerable; without Claire's supervision, she cannot resist her passion for Saint-Preux. As is the departure of Clarissa Harlowe from her father's garden, Julie's fateful encounter with Saint-Preux is a gap in the text. In the very next letter, Julie tells Claire to "never return. You would only come too late . . . .You abandoned me and I was ruined . . . .Your loss is no less irreparable than mine, for it is as difficult for you to find another worthy friend as it is impossible to recover my innocence. . . . I can neither speak nor keep silent" (58). Julie's desire has separated her from both her mother and father, and now Julie writes that Claire's absence has ruptured their friendship.

Julie's nostalgia here is evident; despite her melancholy reproach to Claire, her longing for their past close relationship, now lost, is palpable. Julie longs to efface the boundaries between her and her cousin, a blurring that is echoed in her relationship to language, and her inability to "speak [or] keep silent."

Ruth Ohayon, in her examination of Julie's relationship with her mother, "Rousseau's *Julie*; or the Maternal Odyssey," observes that Claire "assumes the maternal role" after the emergence of Julie's desire places Julie's role as the dutiful daughter in jeopardy.[25] As Nancy Miller does, Ohayon comments on Julie's nostalgia, noting that Julie's longing for the past "echoes Julie's longing for continuity with the mother, prior to the father's emergence as a significant figure."[26]

Julie acknowledges that "it seems that my disastrous passion tried to disguise itself with an all-virtuous mask in order to deceive me": she reveals her reluctance to elope with Saint-Preux for fear of destroying her father or "plunging a knife into her mother's heart" (58–59). On the other hand, she feels a loyalty to Saint-Preux that makes her regret the necessity of concealing from him the impossibility of their marriage. She pities him intensely and regrets that she has deceived "so submissive and tender a lover after having flattered his hopes" (59). All of Julie's emotions, she writes to Claire, "were battering down my courage, all were augmenting my weakness, all were disordering my reason; I had to destroy my parents, my lover, or myself. Without knowing what I was doing, I chose my own destruction; I forgot everything and thought only of love" (59). As Clarissa Harlowe's body does, Julie's body mediates between passion and reason, between a traditional patriarchal system and a changing social structure.

And as Clarissa Harlowe must, Julie must bear the crushing burden of social change that values some aspects of modernity even as it mourns the past. Rousseau's novel differs from Richardson's in that Julie's seduction takes place early on; the real drama is that of Julie's repentance and reconstruction as a virtuous woman. Unlike Clarissa Harlowe, Julie is not raped; she is overcome by love and pity. The self-sacrificing love that Julie experiences is the same love that will allow her recuperation of virtue as wife and mother. Julie will indeed forget everything but love and in her selfless effort to save her child from drowning will precipitate her own death. Michael O'Dea notes that Julie's forgetfulness at this moment "serves to elide the issue of female desire at a vital moment in the novel," a further example of Rousseau's use of forgetfulness as a way to avoid integrating sexuality into the novel.[27]

But although Julie claims that she thought only of love, the fact that she feels guilty for having built up Saint-Preux's hopes of marriage reveals that class difference is a powerful factor. Julie reasserts her superiority by her assumption of loss; her grief for her lost innocence exceeds Saint-Preux's suffering. Julie can now spend the rest of her life atoning for her error, while Saint-Preux must struggle with the frustration of a temporary and illusory sexual satiety. Supported by the social position of her family, Julie remains in control of the love affair and retains the power to send Saint-Preux away at will, a task she ultimately consigns to Claire.

For Saint-Preux, Julie is supremely unattainable. Although he has succeeded in becoming her lover, he can never possess her "natural" and unmediated body. Julie's body exists in culture; her body, in fact, is her father's to dispose of as he sees fit, and Julie, despite her protests to Claire, accedes to her father's plans for her marriage to Wolmar. The natural body that Saint-Preux longs for is a body that exists only as a referent behind the "veil" of the symbolic body; that natural body is best celebrated in its absence.

Waiting for Julie in her dressing room, Saint-Preux writes with rapture that the room is "full of you," and that "all the parts of your scattered dress present to my ardent imagination those of your body that they conceal" (97). Julie's body is dismembered in this version of a blazon.[28] Saint-Preux unifies Julie's body in his imagination by observing the scattered parts of her clothing; moreover, these items stand as substitutes for those body parts that they conceal. Saint-Preux praises "this delicate headdress that complements the lush blond curls that it tries to cover," Julie's "happy shawl," her morning dress and slippers, but Saint-Preux's ecstasy is reserved for Julie's corset, the garment worn closest to her body, and the one that actually takes on the curve of Julie's body: "What an enchanting form! . . . in front, two gentle curves . . . oh, such a voluptuous sight! . . . the whalebone has yielded to the force of the impression . . . delicious imprints, let me kiss you a thousand times!" (97, ellipses in original).

The sight of Julie's corset is overwhelming to Saint-Preux, who experiences Julie's body with all his senses: "Ah, I think I am already feeling that tender heart beating under my happy hand! . . . I see you, I feel you everywhere, I breathe you in with the air that you have breathed; you penetrate my entire being" (97). In this moment of total unity, the essence of Julie's body "penetrates" Saint-Preux. But the body Saint-Preux celebrates is not Julie's material body; rather, it is a reconstructed, nostalgically inflected body created in writing through Saint-Preux's collection and fetishization of Julie's "scattered" garments. Julie's material body, and Saint-Preux's experience of penetrating that body, defy writing, which can take place only in absence. The "real" body, a plenitude, is a nostalgic construction with which Saint-Preux attempts to replace, in fantasy, the material body he cannot possess.

Written in the present tense — "to the moment," as Richardson would say — this letter is a performance of nostalgia that attempts to create, through that performance, the originary moment, or the natural body that cannot be represented. The letter itself draws attention to the contradiction and tension of this effort when, approximately three-quarters of the way into the letter, Saint-Preux writes, "What good fortune to have found ink and paper!" (97). Saint-Preux suddenly shifts tense here and reflects on his experience; at the same time, it is a device that helps the letter explain itself to readers who may wonder how such a record of Saint-Preux's anxious wait in Julie's dressing room can exist. Significantly, Saint Preux observes, "I express my feelings in order to temper their excess; I moderate my ecstasy by describing it" (97). The necessary deferral of the scene of writing is called upon here; to write desire requires absence. And which is more sensual or satisfying, the experience or the writing of the experience?

The following letter, number 55, written by Saint-Preux the next day, exhorts Julie to follow him into death, since they have exhausted all the delights of the body. Saint-Preux's experience of the previous night cannot be captured in words, yet writing temporarily fends off death. Saint-Preux, still enraptured by the moment of sensual pleasure, fears the loss of that pleasure and attempts to deny the permanent condition of loss and longing that characterizes human existence. Yet it is not the sex act itself, those "intoxicating pleasures" that Saint-Preux desires to preserve and relive; rather it is the "intimate union of souls" (98). "Give back," implores Saint-Preux, "that languor so sweet, filled with the overflowings of our hearts: give back that enchanting sleep found in your bosom; give back that still more delightful moment of awakening, and those broken sighs, and those sweet tears, and those kisses that a voluptuous languor made us savor slowly, and those murmurs so tender, during which you pressed to your own that heart which was made to be joined to yours" (98). Saint-Preux's longing is more than a sexual longing; it is, rather, a desire for unity and plenitude. His description of the hours following their lovemaking suggests the relationship of the mother-infant dyad; his is a desire impossible to satisfy, since it is for a time that has *passed*. Saint-Preux's plaintive and repeated request is a clear expression of his loss, and yet he celebrates this loss as something sweet.

Rousseau cannot resist an editorial intervention at this point: "Oh love! If I miss the age at which you are enjoyed, it is not for the hour of sexual pleasure; it is for the hour that follows" (98n). The period of time "that follows"—whether an hour or a moment—is more desirable than the moment of jouissance, which defies representation; the time of reflection, of satisfaction, of stasis, is similar to death, in that it is an obliteration of desire, a movement beyond the pleasure principle. Moreover, it is a return to the mother and the plenitude of the mother's body: there is no speech here, only sighs, tears, murmurings, kisses, sleep.[29]

Julie does not respond to Saint-Preux's letter celebrating this moment and asking her to follow him into death. The letter that immediately follows is from Claire to Julie, warning her of the dangers of continuing any relationship with Saint-Preux. This letter is the paternal, or cultural, intervention in the blissful dyad; Claire's warning is of Baron d'Étange's possible violence should he discover the truth of "some widely whispered rumors" (100) that have resulted from Saint-Preux's imprudent quarrel with Lord Bomston, whose suspicions about the relationship of Saint-Preux and Julie have been confirmed.

Julie's next letters are to Lord Bomston and Saint-Preux. In her letter to Lord Bomston, Julie reveals the truth of her love for Saint-Preux and implores Bomston's discretion and understanding; by this letter, she deflects the peer's anger and helps to preserve Saint-Preux's life and her own secret. In her letter to Saint-Preux, she begs him not to duel with Lord Bomston; she describes her own father's remorse at killing a man in a duel, with graphic depictions of his terrible flashbacks of the violent scene. But Julie closes her letter to Saint-Preux with an invocation even more powerful than the description of the pale and bloody corpse that haunts the baron: "You have sometimes honored me with the tender name of wife; perhaps at this moment I am to bear that of mother" (107).

Whereas Saint-Preux writes his desire, Julie never responds to that letter in kind. Julie's desire, rather, is written into her body: she is, perhaps, to become a mother and, as she says, "she will gain her point . . . by letting [his] heart speak" (107). "One word, a single word," from

Julie will suffice, and that word is *mother*. Furthermore, in a postscript, Julie clearly asserts the authority of her maternal body: "In this letter, I am using an authority that a wise man has never resisted. . . . Remember that I am using, on this occasion, the prerogative that you yourself gave me, and it extends at least to this point" (107). This enigmatic postscript, in which Julie invokes her authority as mother, gives her a transcendental power over a "wise" man. In the single word *mother* is invested an authority and power that exceed those of all the words Saint-Preux could possibly write.

The question of Julie's pregnancy is enigmatic—and phantasmatic—in itself. Her single comment in this letter to Saint-Preux, mentioning only that "perhaps" she is to "bear [the name] of mother," is the main textual evidence of any possible pregnancy. After she falls as a result of being struck by her father, she writes to Claire, "I went into my mother's room, and there became so ill that I was obliged to return to my bed: I even perceived . . . I fear . . . Ah! my dear, I quite fear that my fall yesterday may result in some consequence more disastrous than I had thought. Thus, all is finished for me; all my hopes abandon me at once" (121, ellipses in original). Claire later conceals from Saint-Preux Julie's belief that she has suffered a miscarriage, telling him only that Julie's "expectation had again been mistaken and that there was no longer anything to hope for" (127).[30] The mere possibility of pregnancy, however, accomplishes the irreversible sexualization of Julie's body.

Saint-Preux perceives that there will thus exist no "living memorial of my good fortune, [which] has disappeared like a dream that was never real" (127). In fact, Saint-Preux himself is being made to disappear from town and from Julie's life, more or less "like a dream that was never real." Significantly, Julie refuses Lord Bomston's plan to provide the couple with a home in England, assuring him, "I shall never desert my father's home" (147). Julie will now marry Wolmar, the husband her father has chosen for her, and Saint-Preux will have left no material effect on her life.

When Saint-Preux and Julie meet again, she will have reconstructed her life; she will be a virtuous wife and mother. John Lechte, in "Woman and the Veil—or Rousseau's Fictive Body," extends Starobinski's reading of the veil, observing that modesty functions as a veil, or "a sign that there is always something else beyond it." This referent, the naked or innocent body, "exists only as an object of possible knowledge within a cultural context." The significance, according to Lechte, of this nude body "is symptomatic of the attempt to transcend sexual differ-

ence,"[31] and, I would add, class difference; that is, the imaginary referent, the natural body, represents an attempt to return to an imaginary
blissful moment or place prior to culture, prior to the imposition of paternal law. But the body of the mother that would be located prior to
culture can never be pure or innocent, for to be a mother is to be a
sexualized body that proclaims the reality of sexual difference. The veil
of modesty that the reconstructed Julie wears in her role as virtuous
wife and mother is an attempt to deny or conceal sexual difference.[32]

Julie's Elysée garden is the perfect example of a veil or disguise that
is invisible. This is a garden of Julie's design and execution; self-
contained, it is idyllic, lacking nothing. There is no obvious evidence of
culture here; all appears to spring spontaneously from nature. Unlike
the truly wild landscape surrounding the Paraclete monastery, Julie's
garden is enclosed—not once, but twice. The Elysée is walled, to provide a sense of privacy, separateness, and autonomy, yet it is entirely
contained within the grounds of the paternal estate. The "relentless
walls" of Eloisa's cell, the material enclosure of which she is so painfully
aware, are negated in the structure of Julie's garden. The walls of the
Elysée appear to provide Julie with her own space, but her autonomy
is merely illusion; the garden walls only serve to conceal the walls that
confine Julie within the much larger estate of her husband and father.
The enclosure is not just physical: Julie is apparently satisfied with artifice, complicit in the illusion.[33]

When Saint-Preux first enters the garden he exclaims, "Oh Tinian!
Oh Juan Fernandez! Julie, the end of the world is at your doorstep!"
(127), referring to two deserted islands in the South Seas celebrated in
the voyage of Admiral Anson, as Rousseau's footnote tells us (353).
Saint-Preux immediately connects Julie's Elysée with remote, exotic islands, "virgin" territory.[34] Unspoiled, unenclosed land existing prior to
socialization, such as the islands Saint-Preux imagines, is, for Rousseau,
a site of nostalgic investment: equality is surrendered once land becomes property. In the "Second Discourse," Rousseau observes that
"the first man who, having enclosed a piece of ground, to whom it oc-
curred to say *this is mine* and found people sufficiently simple to believe
him, was the true founder of civil society."[35] Once land is socialized, the
individual no longer enjoys free and communal access to the land and
its bounties; wholeness and unity are lost as the land is divided into
unequal parts, the distribution of which assures inequality within society. Rousseau's thoughts on inequality lead him to contrast what he
calls the "savage" man to the social man who is constructed by others

and who lacks any identity that does not depend on the regard of others or an interdependent economic relationship.[36] Rousseau's nostalgia is for a unified self that is free-standing, and not socially constructed by borders; he connects this nostalgia to the idea of the land itself. Julie's garden is designed to lure Saint-Preux with its promise of unspoiled nature, but the fact that the garden is enclosed at all, that it is owned by Julie and her family, ensures that there is nothing "natural" about it.

Julie quickly corrects Saint-Preux's misapprehension and admonishes him that his reaction is not particularly original, and that many others who have seen the garden react in the same way. Julie immediately redirects his thoughts away from any association of her garden with remote or exotic islands by insisting he guess how much she paid to renovate this garden, which was formerly dry and sparsely planted. The question of money foregrounds the class differences between Julie and Saint-Preux once more. She does not allow him to see her garden as something merely natural; she reminds him that it is a cultivated garden. Saint-Preux guesses incorrectly when he tells Julie that it cost her nothing but neglect: "This place is charming, it is true, but uncultivated and wild. I see no marks of human work. You have locked the door, water has come I know not how, nature alone has done all the rest, and you yourself would never be able to do as well" (353–54). Julie contradicts Saint-Preux, and asserts her mastery over nature, telling him that "It is true . . . that nature has done everything, but under my direction, and there is nothing here which I have not ordered" (354). While Saint-Preux has willingly closed his eyes to artifice—"water has come I know not how"—Julie insists that he recognize that it is she who has provided the water to the garden.

Julie clearly explains that all is artifice, indeed her own artifice, and she and Wolmar go on to reveal all the mysteries of the garden in detail, even describing just how the marks of human cultivation are effaced. By removing all illusion from the garden—by revealing that the veil is indeed present—Julie and Wolmar attempt to force Saint-Preux to recognize that the garden that appears so entirely natural is in fact a cultural construct, a "body" of land existing within culture. Julie's Elysée is not Tinian or Juan Fernandez; Saint-Preux's choice of those islands as a referent is a fiction of his own making.

Julie's Elysée is a false plenitude. Wolmar's plan for Saint-Preux, of course, is to "reeducate" him and to make him think of Julie in a new way that will drive out any thought of his former passion. By revealing to Saint-Preux the constructed nature of Julie's "natural" garden, by showing him that the plenitude he apparently sees is merely artifice with nothing but that artifice hidden (and nothing to promise), Wolmar, by extension, presents Julie's body as another space mediated by culture. He attempts to destroy Saint-Preux's illusion that Julie's is a "natural," because innocent, body. As Lechte observes, the veil covering Julie's body, the veil that seems to promise a plenitude, is that of modesty.

Julie maintains her modesty by devoting her life to becoming an exemplary wife and mother. But Julie's life, as well as her body, is located within culture, and part of that culture is class. Saint-Preux's dream of equality based on passion is false; the Julie that he loves no longer exists now that she has been thoroughly domesticated. In fact, the Julie that Saint-Preux loves has never really existed: the pure and natural body, existing outside culture, is an imaginary referent, as the islands of Tinian and Juan Fernandez are.

When Saint-Preux returns to the Elysée on his own, his attitude toward the space has been so thoroughly shaped by Julie and Wolmar's "education" that he cannot enjoy a private moment in Julie's garden in the same way he enjoyed his moments in her dressing room. Saint-Preux approaches the garden hoping for a repetition of that ecstatic visit to Julie's room: "I shall contemplate her all about me. I shall see nothing that her hand may not have touched. I shall kiss the flowers that her feet have pressed. . . . I shall breathe air that she has breathed" (365). Saint-Preux imagines the garden marked by Julie's body; he sees it as an extension of her body, just as her clothing is an extension of her body in her dressing room. But the body that leaves an imprint on the garden is a social body, one that cannot be retrieved for Saint-Preux's private enjoyment. As he steps into the garden, Saint-Preux is suddenly reminded of the final word that Wolmar has uttered in that very same place, and "the memory of that single word immediately changed the whole state of my mind. I thought I saw the image of virtue where I was seeking that of pleasure" (365). Wolmar's last word is *vertu*, and it hangs over the entrance to the Elysée as does "the inscription above the entrance to Dante's Hell," as Peggy Kamuf observes.[37] Once again, Saint-Preux is subject to the authority of a culturally loaded word, related to that other powerful word, *mother*, through the mediating power of Julie's body: she has reassumed virtue by becoming a mother. Saint-Preux's "reeducation" by Wolmar and Julie has forged the link between the two words.

Although Wolmar is clearly anxious to assert the primacy of culture in Julie's garden, there is another relationship to the land that is repressed by the description of the seamless paternalistic Clarens economy, in which money, the symbol of exchange, is seldom mentioned. The basis of the peace and well-being at Clarens, established on Julie's father's property, is a quasi-feudal economy that in turn depends on the goodwill of both masters and servants. Saint-Preux's letter 10, in part 4, to Lord Bomston extols the harmony of the community of *belles-âmes* whose goodness, fairness, and generosity ensure the eternal cooperation of the servants. Clarens, as Saint-Preux describes it, exceeds even Sir Charles Grandison's paternalistic estate.[38] In his extended discussion of the Clarens economy, Starobinski notes that Wolmar's intention is never to establish equality in the community; rather, he seeks to "win the affection of servants . . . in order to turn them into more docile instruments. The masters retain the privilege of *feeling equal* if it pleases them to do so, but this privilege belongs to them alone, not to their servants. The feeling of equality is therefore still a luxury, whose purpose is to permit the master to enjoy his property without troubling his conscience."[39] The temporary social leveling accomplished by harvest festivals is nothing other than a sentimental—and temporary—construct that offers no threat to the economy of Clarens, "which is based on the domination of masters and the obedience of servants."[40]

CONCLUSION: BEARING THE BURDEN OF NOSTALGIA

The economic system that Rousseau, in the voice of Saint-Preux, extols without question is not, in its conception, vastly different from the other systems in place in *Julie* and in Rousseau's other works: those of gender or of the tutor-pupil relationship. Observes Rousseau in *L'Émile*: "There is no subjection so perfect as that which keeps the appearance of freedom. Thus the will itself is made captive" (120). Referring to Rousseau's system of education, James Donald observes that such "regulation requires the definition of an external authority to which the child/citizen is subject, and yet which authorises him to act as a free agent."[41] In other words, the key to the obedient child, responsible citizen, or virtuous wife is the internalization of restraint, the self-policing of will and desire. Moreover, Donald notes, "the capacities and rules that enable the subject to know, to speak and to act are dramatised in a figure whose mastery and disinterested love are displayed through an incontrovertible competence: the Tutor and the Lawgiver"—or the father, husband, or author. The subject then identifies with these authority figures, and internalizes their points of view, thereby enabling himself or herself to experience restraint "as his or her own desires, aspirations and guilt, [thus evincing] the capacity for self-policing."[42] In Rousseau's *Julie*, as well as in Pope's "Eloisa," the burden of self-denial falls on women; only through the containment of their desire can male virtue and reason be assured.

At the same time the author achieves a nostalgic unity of desire and reason, mind and body. The desire of Héloïse, Martha Blount, Eloisa, and Julie is ultimately co-opted by Abelard, Pope, and Rousseau as a device through which to assure their own fame and immortality. The rewriting of Héloïse's story by Pope and Rousseau reveals their nostalgic desires for an imaginary plenitude that would transcend sexual difference. The construction of sentimental bodies, picturesque landscapes, or idyllic gardens is an attempt to represent a loss that is otherwise unrepresentable; that is, it is a symbolic representation of that which can only be perceived as lost, because it can never be perceived directly. These repeated constructions of bodies and landscapes deflect the anxiety produced by the sense of loss or social change, even as they defer any real acknowledgment of loss.

Body and land are, perhaps, the most heavily invested of all symbolic objects, if only because they retain the aura of that which is "originary," or created by the hand of God as described in the book of Genesis. But body and land are referents always already existing behind a veil that signals their presence, and these referents are necessarily fictional, as we can only imagine them in retrospect, through their signifiers. Repeated constructions of body and landscape are attempts to define and make material these elusive and richly invested concepts. Peter Brooks has called the body "an 'epistemophilic' project"—an attempt to know, and through knowing, to "have" the body.[43] Such a project extends to the land as well.

At stake for Pope and Rousseau is a means of self-articulation through the reconstruction of a medieval tale of passion. In Pope's "Eloisa," as well as in Rousseau's *Julie*, the author attempts to write himself into the text as the teller of the tale, or the one who truly "knows," qualified by virtue of his own passion and sentiment. Simultaneously, passion is displaced onto the female body so that masculinity can be aligned with reason and authorship. These texts, moreover, point to their own creators and the privileged position of the author,

which is described in the epigraph to Rousseau's *Julie*, chosen from Petrarch's *Rime sparse* 338:

> Non la connobe il mondo, mentre l'ebbe:
> Connobil' io ch' a pianger qui rimasi
> [The world did not know her while it had
> her; I knew her, who remain here to
> weep][44]

The self that "remain[s] here to weep" also remains to tell the story and
to assume the identity of author by appropriating the passion and the
voice of a woman, whose dead body must bear the burden of tradition
and nostalgia.

4

The "Secret Pleasure" of the Picturesque

We must therefore use some illusion to render a Pastoral delightful;
and this consists in exposing the best side only of a shepherd's life,
and in concealing its miseries.

— Alexander Pope; "A Discourse on Pastoral Poetry"

I spent part of the last summer in a little village [which] lay entirely
out of the road of commerce, and was inhabited by a race of men
who followed the primeval profession of agriculture for several
generations. . . . I felt a secret pleasure in observing this happy
community.

— Oliver Goldsmith
"The Revolution in Low Life"

WHEN ALEXANDER POPE WRITES OF USING "SOME ILLUSION" IN
order to hide the "miseries" of the shepherd's life, he marks a moment
when culture constructs nature. For Pope, the "nature" of pastoral
poetry is hardly natural at all; it is, essentially, a repetition. Pope seeks
an origin:

The original of Poetry is ascribed to that age which succeeded the creation
of the world: And as the keeping of flocks seems to have been the first employment of mankind, the most ancient sort of poetry was probably pastoral.
'Tis natural to imagine, that the leisure of those ancient shepherds admitting
and inviting some diversion, none was so proper to that solitary and seden-
tary life as singing; and that in their songs they took occasion to celebrate
their own felicity. From hence a Poem was invented, and afterwards im-
prov'd to a perfect image of that happy time; which by giving us an esteem
for the virtues of a former age, might recommend them to the present.[1]

While Pope goes on to point out the necessity of art and illusion in the
creation of the contemporary pastoral, he nevertheless credits an originary moment, at a point in the very distant past—"that age which suc-

ceeded the creation of the world"—with a sense of happiness and tranquility that cannot be found in modern life.

Pope believes in the originary moment and recognizes his conscious attempt to rewrite the past through illusion and repression. His discussion of pastoral examines the art of writing a poem that, although it celebrates nature, is itself artificial: "If we would copy Nature, it may be useful to take this Idea along with us, that pastoral is *an image* of what they call the Golden age. So that we are not to describe our shepherds as shepherds at this day really are, but *as they may be conceiv'd then to have been.*"[2] The pastoral is a construction, a "world which had been deliberately simplified as a contrast to the social complexities of the city."[3] Pope's pastoral is self-conscious, and the figure of the artist — self-fashioned and self-promoted—is always present in his writing.

Despite Pope's awareness of the artifice of pastoral, he nevertheless reveals nostalgia for the origins of the genre, imagining the "ancient shepherds" amusing themselves through song. This nostalgia for an originary moment, "the repetition which is not a repetition," as Susan Stewart calls it,[4] is at the heart of the longing for the land and the desire to recuperate an idyllic past that develop into a passion for the picturesque during the course of the eighteenth century. Pope's discourse on pastoral, written in 1704, and his pastoral-political poem "Windsor Forest," begun in 1704 and completed in 1713, are not generally considered picturesque literature, the main body of which dates from the second half of the century. But the nostalgia present in the writings of Alexander Pope and Oliver Goldsmith, the particular focus of this chapter, participates in the "secret pleasure" that Goldsmith's essay describes. That secret pleasure derives from a fantasy of restoration, not just of a simpler, pastoral lifestyle, but of a prelapsarian world that is orderly and controlled, a paradise uncontaminated by unruly elements that seemed to pervade contemporary life.

The pastoral has traditionally been linked to a longing for the past, especially for lost youth, an element of Theocritus's *Idylls*. This longing was woven into the idea of the countryside, recreated through memory and imagination, as a place of simplicity and innocence. Virgil's *Eclogues* also paint an attractive picture of rural life but include the tension of dispossession; over time, the actual history present in the *Eclogues*, that of the defeat of Brutus and Caesar in 42 BC, after which land was taken from landowners to be awarded to returning soldiers, disappears. Only the beauties of the rural life are left, but lacking context, "ideologies become myths."[5]

One aspect of pastoral mythology dictates that rural life is more wholesome and "natural," giving rise to figures such as the "happy swain" or the contented villagers whose peaceful lives proceed according to the rhythms of the seasons. The rural life is also a counterpoint to city life, specifically London life. The simplicity of country life exists as a constant contrast to the congestion and anonymity of the city, the unhealthful air and grime of crowded living conditions, or the cruelty of a market economy. Pastoral's most potent element, however, is its availability to a wide variety of interpretative schemes; there is a version of pastoral accessible to every group. The wealthy, for example, have had access to a pastoral fantasy of the fruitful and abundant Earth, which mystifies social relations by erasing the actual labor of the workers who sow, tend, and reap the harvests. The workers themselves, or other less affluent groups, can look back to a "better" time when, it seems, individuals enjoyed more influence and recognition; this version of nostalgia, however much it may acknowledge class, erases gender, race, and ability. Even utopians have access to a version of a golden age supposedly prior to the development of social hierarchies and inequalities.[6] Most significantly, I think, the "shifting intermediate groups," as Raymond Williams has called them, are heavily invested in nostalgia for a golden age. These groups, having only recently "arrived" at any kind of status or security, repress their anxieties about the tenuousness of their social positions through indulgence in fantasies of lost innocence or a simpler past. Those who have benefited from social mobility are often the first to be threatened by social change that jeopardizes their own status.[7]

Eighteenth-century cultural nostalgia, as did the pastoral, celebrated an idealized way of life that could only exist in the past. The contradictions created by the growth of industrialization and capitalism, and the disappearance of traditional ways of life, nevertheless demanded attention. Poverty, unemployment, homelessness, and enclosure all threatened the seamless progress that the Enlightenment had promised; social change would accelerate, and social instability would increase as the century continued. Most, if not all, of these problems would have a direct effect on the landscape. As the land was enclosed for private use, the appearance of the land changed, and a sense of entitlement—both to the use of the commons and to an unspoiled vista—was lost. The landscape was undergoing drastic modification; in response to those changes, the land became a primary locus for cultural nostalgia.

THE PICTURESQUE, IDEOLOGY, AND THE LAND

Toward the end of the century, the picturesque emerged as an aesthetic theory that co-opted and assimilated these social problems, containing them within its own curious boundaries. The trajectory from the Augustan pastoral of the beginning of the century, as practiced by Pope, to the picturesque of the late eighteenth century allowed some elements of the pastoral to be discarded, while others were maintained. These exclusions and inclusions reflect the social changes taking place in England at the time.[8] The picturesque also celebrated the irregular, the rough, the quaint, and the imperfect, elevating the ruined cottage or a ragged peasant to the subject of a painting or poem. By aestheticizing decay and poverty, the picturesque succeeded in keeping real social problems at a safe distance.[9]

Most of the critical work done on the picturesque understandably focuses on William Gilpin, Sir Uvedale Price, and Richard Payne Knight, the major theorists of the picturesque. But certain elements of picturesque theory appeared as early as 1624 in Henry Wotton's *Elements of Architecture*: "For as Fabriques should bee *regular*, so gardens should bee *irregular*, or at least cast into a very Wilde *Regularitie*."[10] The landscape Wotton describes—one created to appear natural, ancient, or untamed—reveals a cultural investment in the idea of landscape underlying the passion for landscape gardening of the seventeenth and eighteenth centuries.

The picturesque eventually extended beyond landscape gardening into many other arts. With its depiction of an English countryside and way of life that were rapidly disappearing, the picturesque, as it was practiced in painting and poetry, was an ideal vehicle for the cultural nostalgia of the period. That nostalgia and desire would be codified by the end of the century by Gilpin, Price, and Knight, but, as in gardening theory, picturesque elements began to appear in art and literature earlier in the century in works such as Pope's "Eloisa to Abelard" and "Windsor Forest" or in Goldsmith's *Deserted Village*. The nostalgia of these poems, and of the picturesque, offers aesthetic resolution to and consolation for the contradictions of capitalism by extolling a lost past in which the land was "natural" and unspoiled, much like a virginal body, pure and untouched.

The picturesque draws on its ability to appear "natural" for its success. As is the body, the land is often taken for granted, "natural," or transparent and, perhaps more importantly, as "precisely that which cannot be produced," according to Neil Smith.[11] As is the body, nature is seen as essence, mysterious yet transparent, a bedrock unable to be produced and resistant to analysis.[12] Nature carries with it the illusion that it exists outside, or even prior to, the symbolic; it seems to be located within "the realm of use-values rather than exchange-values," Smith observes, just as the idea of the natural body seems to be located outside culture and exchange.[13]

Smith notes the frequency with which nature is conceived as female, observing that the practice of aligning femininity with nature is "prevalent" and "deep-seated" and further remarking that

> it is striking that the treatment of women in capitalist society parallels the treatment of nature. As external nature, women are objects which mankind attempts to dominate and oppress, ravage and romanticize; they are objects of conquest and penetration as well as idolatry and worship. . . . Women are put on pedestals, but only once their social domination is secure; precisely as with nature, romanticization is then a form of control. But women can never be wholly external since in them resides fertility and the means of biological reproduction. In this sense they are made elements of universal nature, mothers and nurturers, possessors of a mysterious "female intuition," and so on.[14]

Smith touches on something here that is often noted, but not always analyzed, and even Smith's attempt to make sense of the feminization of nature seems to fall short. As nature is, the body is sometimes seen as "that which cannot be produced," something, therefore, that is outside the realm of the social, or prior to human activity. Bodies, however, are produced, although that *re*-production is naturalized, and not viewed as a material process as other productive activities are. Instead, we consider human reproduction "natural," attributing use value, but not exchange value, to it. The implications of such naturalization have far-reaching effects on the ideology of the family and the position of women in society.

On the land itself, Smith notes that "with the progress of capital accumulation and the expansion of economic development," the essential, "material substratum" that nature appears to be is increasingly the result of social production. But Smith's most interesting conclusion is that as nature is produced, "use-value and exchange-value, and space and society, are fused together."[15] As use value and exchange value are embedded within nature, it becomes increasingly difficult to differentiate

between these two types of value; the stamp of the social on space becomes increasingly difficult to detect at all.

POPE'S LANDSCAPE: "WINDSOR FOREST"

The landscape that appears in Pope's "Eloisa to Abelard" is barren
and forbidding, marked by Eloisa's solitude and longing. But, as is the
landscape in Pope's "Windsor Forest," that of "Eloisa" is socially constructed, only apparently natural, and designed to contain Eloisa's passion in a safe and secluded space. Pope's interest in landscape is evident
in his earlier poetry as well, and unlike the seclusion prescribed to contain Eloisa's desire, the idealization of retirement—for the poet or the
sensitive man—appears in the "Ode to Solitude" (c. 1700), while the
rewards of simple country living are extolled in "The Happy Life of a
Country Parson" (1713), a poem that describes the very life Goldsmith's Dr. Primrose seeks in *The Vicar of Wakefield*.

Pope's "Windsor Forest" attempts to contain the contradictions between progress and conservation. Pope began the poem in 1704 as one
of the pastorals; after the Peace of Utrecht in 1713, he modified it into
a political poem that looks forward to an era of peace and prosperity
under the reign of Queen Anne. The Windsor Forest of the poem is not
a simple piece of land, but a highly politicized one. The forest Pope extols is a mixed landscape; originally enclosed by William I for royal
hunting, the land was *foris*, or outside, common lands. The historical
Windsor Forest is thoroughly imbued with social and political implications;[16] the natural geography of the landscape has been overdrawn by
the political boundaries established under the Normans, making the
land comprising Windsor Forest a contested space: once as pristine as
the "Groves of Eden,"[17] the land became a lonely wasteland under Norman rule but promises to be fruitful and resplendent once again under
Queen Anne. Windsor Forest seems to promise to satisfy, through political means, a nostalgic longing for a paradise lost. Pope "fuses," to
use Smith's concept, "space and society" and interrogates the imprint
of the social and legal systems on the land itself.

Pope begins the poem with a reference to "The Groves of *Eden*" (7)
as described in Milton's *Paradise Lost*. Pope writes himself and his desire
for fame (the same desire for fame that is held back until the very end
in "Eloisa to Abelard") into the beginning of "Windsor Forest," when
he draws a connection, not only between the Forest and Eden, but be-

tween Milton's rendering of Eden and his own poem: "*These* [groves], were my Breast inspir'd with equal Flame, / Like them in Beauty, should be like in Fame" (9–10). The landscape, whatever else it may represent, is already invested with Pope's longing for fame through his own creative reproduction of that landscape; the land that Pope describes is already mediated through his own desire.

That mediation results in an aesthetic imposition of harmony and coherence:

> Here Hills and Vales, the Woodland and the Plain,
> Here Earth and Water seem to strive again,
> Not *Chaos*-like together crush'd and bruis'd,
> But as the World, harmoniously confus'd:
> Where Order in Variety we see,
> And where, tho' all things differ, all agree.
>
> (11–16)

The imposition of order upon nature is the mark of culture; in fact, it is the mark of the aesthetic act that creates a poem around a forest. Without the filter of the poet, nature would be chaotic, with all its elements "crush'd and bruis'd"; yet, through Pope's poem, we are able to "see" the order in the mixture, the common thread that links the differing elements to each other, and the past to the present. Only this artistic mediation allows us to interpret nature, to understand the otherwise jumbled elements of the landscape, and it is Pope, the poet, who provides us with the key to understanding through his aesthetic production.

Political concerns are woven into Pope's celebration of the landscape's beauty: "Let *India* boast her plants, nor envy we / The weeping Amber or the Balmy Tree / While by our Oaks the precious Loads are born, / And Realms commanded which those Trees adorn" (29–32). This allusion to exploration and colonization provides yet another layer of meaning for the poem and takes it beyond a pastoral celebration of an unspoiled landscape; the beauty of Windsor Forest is immediately compared to that of other, foreign lands, and the poet's and readers' thoughts turn, not to the past, but to the future. Pope is quick to point out, however, that English oaks dominate the trees of subjugated lands — India and the West Indies, with which trading rights were acquired through the Peace of Utrecht — by being made into ships that will carry away goods and spices, thereby allowing England to consolidate its power through trade. The reconstruction of nature (oaks) into tools of domination (ships) echoes the function of the poem, which re-writes nature into an artificially coherent product with an ideological purpose.

The Peace of Utrecht, the result of Tory compromise, contained its own contradictions. The Whigs preferred a military victory, but the To-ries surrendered some territorial control in order to gain trading rights with the West Indies.[18] Through the *asiento*, an exclusive contract to supply slaves to its American colonies, Spain granted England a mo-nopoly on the slave trade with Spanish America.[19] The "peace" ob-tained through the Peace of Utrecht contained within itself the violence of increased slavery and the promise of expanding mercantile success: an exchange of one kind of violence for another, or a displacement of violence onto distant, subjugated lands.

The fruitfulness of the land represented in the poem, which Pope compares to that of ancient Greece and Rome, and the "Peace and Plenty" that abound are attributed to the fact that "a STUART reigns" (42), a reign that promises to restore an idyllic past and satisfy nostal-gia. The positive comparison between Queen Anne's current govern-ment and the golden age of Greece and Rome is quickly interrupted by a negative contrast to the days of the Normans. Pope tells us:

> Not thus the Land appear'd in Ages past,
> A dreary Desart and a gloomy Waste,
> To savage Beasts and Savage Laws a Prey,
> And Kings more furious and severe than they:
> Who claim'd the Skies, dispeopled Air and Floods,
> The lonely Lords of empty Wilds and Woods. (44–48)

The Norman conquest marks, for Pope, a rupture in the natural peace and plenitude of the island; this rupture, moreover, scars the land with the enclosure of the New Forest, and the imposition of "Savage Laws," that is, the Norman forest laws and courts. The natural har-mony between the bountiful land and the gentle seasons has been lost in the face of human greed and the desire for power:

> In vain kind Season swell'd the teeming Grain,
> Soft Show'rs distill'd, and Suns grew warm in vain;
> The Swain with Tears his frustrate Labour yields,
> And famish'd dies amidst his ripen'd Fields. (53–56)

The Swain, who works in cooperation with nature, can no longer reap the fruits of his labor and dies of hunger; during the Norman period, Pope points out, a lack of harmony existed in the human relationship to the land. Pope's Swain, watering his crops with his tears, yet perishing from hunger in the very midst of plenty, is an emblematic figure, placed in the poem for dramatic display. The Swain is feminized and nostalgic; he weeps instead of speaking, and he is the subject of the poet's and reader's gaze, not unlike the female figures who people Goldsmith's *Deserted Village*. Pope's depictions of the fruitful, harmonious pre-Norman landscape and the nostalgic swain are displacements that belie the social realities of Pope's own time. The real economic and social relations between the workers and the landowners are absorbed into what Raymond Williams calls "the natural vision," in which the land, as did the Garden of Eden before the fall, magically provides its plentiful bounty for all (24).

The death of the Swain's body is echoed in the ruination of the land. Pope goes on to paint a desolate scene in which

> The levell'd Towns with Weeds lie cover'd o'er,
> The hollow Winds thro' naked Temples roar;
> Round broken Columns clasping Ivy twin'd. (67–69)

Pope's vision is of a lost, classical period of beauty and harmony, a prelapsarian paradise that the Normans destroyed. This desolate landscape with its "hollow Winds" and "clasping Ivy" is a proleptic version of the landscape of the Paraclete, but the seclusion forced upon Eloisa in Pope's later poem becomes a desirable retirement for the male poet. Intricately woven into Pope's regret at the wasted and enclosed landscape is a longing for just such a retirement. His desire links him, not only to Horace, whose poetry celebrated the ideal of retirement, but also to political figures such as Scipio and Atticus, invoked by Pope in lines 257–58. While the contrast of Eloisa's seclusion to the voluntary retirement of the poet or political man is unspoken, there exists a more obvious contrast to yet another image of female retirement, that of Pope's own imaginative creation, the nymph Lodona.

With his invention of Lodona, Pope writes a creation story that recovers the origins of the river Loddon. While the idea of retirement for Pope and Horace leads to personal fame through the creation of literature, the retirement desired by Lodona, Diana's mythical nymph, leads to the creation of a river, an essential element of the landscape. The

landscape itself is aligned with Lodona, and specifically encoded as feminine in Pope's description:

> Here waving Groves a chequer'd Scene display,
> And part admit and part exclude the Day;
> As some coy Nymph her Lover's warm Address
> Not quite indulges, nor can quite repress. (17–20)[20]

Lodona's body is literally dissolved and absorbed into the Earth itself, almost as if she were returning to the source of her existence.
Chased by Pan, who is fervently in love with her, Lodona calls on
"Father *Thames*" for aid. She also appeals to the goddess: "'Ah *Cynthia*!
ah—tho' banish'd from thy Train, / Let me, O let me, to the Shades
repair, / My native Shades—there weep, and murmur there'" (200–
203). Lodona's grief and desire to return to her "native Shades" cause
her body to dissolve:

> melting as in Tears she lay,
> In a soft, silver Stream dissolv'd away.
> The silver Stream her Virgin Coldness keeps,
> For ever murmurs, and for ever weeps;
> Still bears the Name the hapless Virgin bore,
> And bathes the Forest where she rang'd before. (204–8)

A curious shift occurs between Lodona's escape from Pan and Eloisa's
seclusion in the Paraclete. While Eloisa will struggle with her passion,
recreating her sexuality through her writing, Lodona retreats from her
sexuality altogether and simply disappears into the landscape, becoming one with the Earth.[21]

The river Loddon flows through the forest and into the Thames,
where it enriches and supports the river that, monarchlike, "survey'st
our lofty Woods, / Where tow'ring Oaks their growing Honours rear, /
And future Navies on thy Shores appear" (230–32). Nationalism surfaces once more in Pope's poem, tied to the richness of the land, specifically the "Oaks" that will become the ships of England's imperial
"Navies." The idea of tradition and continuity is represented by bodies
of water all flowing into the Thames, eventually extending out into the
sea, and hence into the world.

The source of this unity and power, in Pope's mythology, is the body
of a woman, which—once returned to the Earth, its source—waters the
landscape and the mighty oaks. But this imaginary woman's body is

powerful only once it has retreated from sexuality and embedded itself in the land. The origin Pope seeks is female; despite the inherent power of an origin, the land, as female, is subject to domination. Such a contradictory and ambivalent response is displaced onto the sentiment that longs for a pure, unspoiled landscape and yet justifies the exploration and domination of foreign lands. It is an ambivalent reaction toward the overwhelming power of the (feminine) land, and a way of attempting to dominate, through nationalism, other landscapes that are encoded feminine, specifically India, the West Indies, or other areas subject to imperial subjection.

"Windsor Forest" closes with a celebration of British imperial domination: "Thy Trees, fair *Windsor!* now shall leave their Woods, / And half thy Forests rush into my Floods, / Bear *Britain*'s Thunder, and her Cross display, / To the bright Regions of the rising Day" (385–88). As Laura Brown observes, the British navy is obscured here by a "picturesque pastoral image of the oak."[22] British colonialism is linked—in a peculiar contradiction—to an image of world harmony:

> The Time shall come, when free as Seas of Wind
> Unbounded *Thames* shall flow for all Mankind,
> Whole Nations enter with each swelling Tyde,
> And Seas but join the Regions they divide;
> Earth's distant Ends our Glory shall behold,
> And the new World launch forth to seek the Old. (397–402)

Not only will the world be unified and peaceful, but the movement outward from Britain to the New World will be reversed, as the people of that world will be magically empowered to visit Britain on a reciprocal basis:

> Then Ships of uncouth Form shall stem the Tyde;
> And Feather'd People crowd my wealthy Side,
> And naked Youths and painted Chiefs admire
> Our Speech, our Colour, and our strange Attire!
> Oh stretch thy Reign, fair *Peace!* from Shore to Shore,
> Till Conquest cease, and Slav'ry be no more:
> Till the freed *Indians* in their native Groves
> Reap their own Fruits, and woo their Sable Loves. (403–10)

The vision here is not only of Britain's economic and political domination of the New World, but of an ideological and moral domination so total that the colonized "Feather'd people," "naked Youths," and "painted Chiefs" literally travel to Britain's shores in abject admiration. Such a mystification of the violence of colonization renders the colonized subjects as "grateful beneficiaries," and even "celebrants of English imperialism," as Brown observes.[23]

Pope once more celebrates the peace and concord that justify and obscure the realities of Britain's mercantile imperialism:

> Exil'd by Thee from Earth to deepest Hell,
> In Brazen Bonds shall barb'rous *Discord* dwell:
> Gigantick *Pride*, pale *Terror*, gloomy *Care*,
> And mad *Ambition*, shall attend her there. (413–16)

Pope's use of pastoral in "Windsor Forest" serves to repress the violence of imperial expansion and mystify the contradictions implicit in the poem's final vision of harmonious equality. Pope utilizes a "rhetoric of reversal to avoid his own implication in imperialist brutality and capitalist acquisition."[24]

The contradictions and ambivalence contained in Pope's pastoral will resurface in the picturesque, although the route from the pastoral to the picturesque is not straightforward; travel narratives, the graveyard school and other elegiac poetry, and, to a certain degree, the sentimental novel all contribute to the picturesque. We find, however, the same ambivalent and contradictory response throughout this literary trajectory: an idealization of a nostalgic, feminized past, with a concurrent admiration—however subdued—of masculine progress and domination. The sentiment linked to a traditional, agrarian way of life that kept the land under cultivation, free of enclosures, and hence, "natural," is linked, inevitably, to the people who live on and work the land: the peasants and cottagers typified by the colorful, broken-down Edwards, who moves Harley to tears with his story of economic ruin and loss of his home in Mackenzie's *Man of Feeling*.

Picturesque figures such as Edwards captivated contemporary readers, who relished their own flutters of sentiment and indulged in the pleasures of nostalgia. But the charm of picturesque characters and crumbling cottages concealed the harsh reality of changes in England's social and economic structures, just as Pope's use of pastoral and picturesque elements concealed the brutality of mercantile imperialism. The picturesque had a price, and the burden of nostalgia was borne by the peasants and cottagers who are so carefully rendered in the works of Oliver Goldsmith.

GOLDSMITH'S NOSTALGIA

Although *The Vicar of Wakefield* (1766) predates *The Deserted Village* (1770), the nostalgia Oliver Goldsmith reveals in his celebrated poem was not new; "The Revolution in Low Life," which appeared in *Lloyd's Evening Post*, June 14–16, 1762, approximately the same period in which Goldsmith is believed to have written *The Vicar*, contains similar sentiments. A reciprocal reading of these three works will allow a new reading of *The Vicar* as a nostalgic and picturesque novel and perhaps illuminate the contradictions of a novel that has traditionally puzzled many readers.

Goldsmith's contradictions and ambivalence can also be found in his politics, which have often been the subject of inquiry. Goldsmith supported a strong monarch, yet, in works such as *The Deserted Village* or *The Traveller* (1764), he calls for reform, and he clearly feels regret and tenderness for the dispossessed poor. His positions and politics have been seen as inconsistent; I would like to suggest, however, that Goldsmith's particular nostalgia includes not only a longing for home, but also a longing for the protective, paternalistic father figure of a monarch. Goldsmith, who observes the world through the glass of his own personal indigence and his family's experience of downward mobility,[25] often managed these conflicts through the use of a persona in his writings. The adoption of various narrative perspectives was an attempt to resolve the contradiction between the advocacy of a strong monarchy and the reform needed for assistance to and protection of poor agricultural workers.[26]

While the narrative voice is the material evidence of Goldsmith's ambivalence, I believe that what drives Goldsmith's desire for both the strong structure of a powerful monarchy and the need to preserve traditional ways is his nostalgia. More than anything else, Goldsmith longs for life "the way it used to be," and I believe that tracing the thread of Goldsmith's nostalgia through "Revolution," *The Deserted Village*, and *The Vicar of Wakefield* will suggest a way to read his novel, a work that has traditionally been difficult to classify or even to work into any coherent overview of the development of the novel.[27]

Some eighteenth-century novels, in the picaresque tradition, treat the

topic of leaving home and finding one's way in the world through a series of misadventures—*Moll Flanders* or *Tom Jones*, for example. Others,
such as *Evelina*, negotiate the more sophisticated (if less picaresque)
problems of young women entering the wider social sphere outside
their immediate families. Significantly, these novels are founded on a
break or rupture that potentially creates desire, the desire for home,
which is at the core of nostalgia. Unlike these protagonists seeking their
way in the world, Oliver Goldsmith's Dr. Primrose keeps trying to *create*, or at least maintain, a home; his movement, as protagonist, is in
the opposite direction. The idea of retirement, so prominent in Pope's
writings, surfaces in Dr. Primrose's attempt to retreat from the world
and create a safe and predictable household, his own little kingdom in
which he will function as a paternalistic monarch. His attempts to consolidate his household are continually frustrated, however—not just by
the unpredictable events of the world at large, but even by the actions
of the very family members he wishes to protect. Within his retreat into
domesticity, we see Dr. Primrose's attempt to "make his mark" on the
world through his writing, much as Pope does, and his mark on the
home through the kind and tender care of his family, which necessarily
includes the management of feminine desire. Moreover, he seeks a spiritual identity as a Job-like figure whose patience and suffering will gain
him redemption and create meaning from the bewildering and improbable train of misfortunes that befalls him.

A poem like *The Deserted Village* confirms the failure of Dr. Primrose's
quest for domestic bliss. *The Vicar of Wakefield*'s disconcerting veneer of
good-natured humor overlaying a potentially tragic story is an attempt
to impose coherence on the Primrose family's story, somewhat like the
vicar's attempt to tame his unruly family into a harmonious domestic
group. As does Dr. Primrose, who seeks comfort through his retreat
into domesticity, the narrator of Goldsmith's *Deserted Village* (not a novel
of discovery and voyage, but a nostalgic "village" poem that seeks comfort and stability through homecoming) has been chastened by his experiences in the outside world and longs only for the safety and security
of home. But the blissful sense of security that the poem's returning
traveler wishes to recover can never be found again: the village, as has
the narrator, has been irrevocably changed. Bliss is to be found only in
memories, in the imagined happiness and ignorance of danger that are
part of childhood.

Significantly, the point of view of the narrator in both "The Revolution in Low Life" and *The Deserted Village* is that of a consumer of land-

scape; the experience recorded is that of the traveler or visitor. In his 1762 essay, Goldsmith's narrator reports that he "spent part of the last summer in a little village, distant about fifty miles from town, consisting of near an hundred houses. It lay entirely out of the road of commerce, and was inhabited by a race of men who followed the primeval profession of agriculture for several generations. Though strangers to opulence, they were unacquainted with distress" (1052). Why the narrator has gone to this village to spend a few summer weeks is never explained. But he clearly sets himself apart from the villagers: they are a "race" who have engaged in the "primeval profession of agriculture for several generations." Their standard of living is not enhanced by the luxuries of imported goods that those living in the cities enjoy; nevertheless, their needs are satisfied. Presumably, they are living in self-sufficient, domestic economies that exist independently of trade and commerce. Is it too much to presume that the essayist has gone to this village precisely because it seems to be unspoiled and "entirely out of the road of commerce," because he desires to consume a pastoral experience in the countryside? At no time does the narrator indicate that he participates in the labor of the community. Instead, he is simply a visitor, who enjoys "a secret pleasure in observing this happy community. The cheerfulness of the old, and the blooming beauty of the young, was no disagreeable change to one like me, whose whole life had been spent in cities" (1052).

The source of the writer's "secret pleasure" is the same desire for origins that Pope expresses in "Windsor Forest" and that the picturesque tourist seeks to satisfy. Having spent his life in cities, the narrator enjoys the "otherness" of the villagers and participates in their lives vicariously, through his own nostalgia, well outside the danger that we soon learn is about to befall them—that of displacement from their bucolic village—for the writer reports that his "satisfaction was soon repressed, when I understood that they were shortly to leave this abode of felicity, of which they and their ancestors had been in possession time immemorial" (1052).

The writer latches on to the villagers' loss and makes it his own through his essay of lamentation; his nostalgia is actually enhanced by, or even predicated upon, the imminent loss of the villagers' way of life. The loss that Goldsmith describes is that of family, community, and tradition: the villagers have intermarried and are all "in a manner one family" into which the "poor traveller and stranger" is welcomed. Moreover, they celebrate traditional holidays "with the strictest obser-

vance: They were merry at Christmas and mournful in Lent, got drunk
on St. George's-day, and religiously cracked nuts on Michaelmas-eve"
(1052). Their lives pass according to the seasons and the church year;
theirs is not a city lifestyle that responds to the needs of commerce.

The writer links the security of family and tradition to residence on
the land; in short, to the idea of home. Now that the land on which these
agricultural workers live has been purchased by a wealthy London merchant, who intends to "lay out the whole in a seat of pleasure for himself" (1052–53), the villagers have been uprooted from the land and
have lost the limited autonomy of subsistence living; they are now to be
driven out into a wage economy in which their only property will be
their own labor. They will be forced to "toil as hirelings under some
rigid Master, to flatter the opulent for a precarious meal, and to leave
their children the inheritance of want and slavery" (1053).

The narrator blames the money economy for these new social problems, specifically the wealth derived from foreign trade, which, unlike a
local, domestic economy in which all may participate, is restricted to
only a few who possess the resources to pursue still greater wealth. By
the time Goldsmith elaborates on this theme in *The Deserted Village*, his
narrator will have become one of the dispossessed, lamenting not a village from which he has been driven away, but a village that he has left
voluntarily and can no longer hope to return to in his old age.

The Vicar of Wakefield, which appeared between the publications of
"Revolution" and *The Deserted Village*, plays an interesting mediating
role between these two works that narrate the experiences of consumers of the picturesque. *The Vicar* tells the story of Dr. George Primrose's
desire for a happy home. At the beginning of the novel, we find the
Primrose family at the height of contentment: Dr. Primrose has chosen
a wife "as she did her wedding gown, not for a fine glossy surface, but
such qualities as would wear well."[28] From the first paragraph, the material and economic concerns that will dominate the novel are apparent:
the Vicar's wife and family are needed not only to provide happiness
and contentment, but also to support—in both material and emotional
ways—his own self-construction as patriarch. While the Vicar fancies
himself a writer, Deborah shines in the kitchen: "for pickling, preserving, and cookery, none could excel her." Deborah also takes pride in
"being an excellent contriver in house-keeping" although the Vicar
makes a point of noting that he "could never find that we grew richer
with all her contrivances" (37), an ironic observation in light of his own
subsequent financial mismanagement.[29]

The Vicar of Wakefield, traditionally considered a sentimental novel, participates in the developing genre of the picturesque. As is the picturesque, the life the Vicar seeks for himself and his family is an attempt to construct an idealized version of life untouched by modernity and to achieve a way of life that conserves an imagined past, covering over, in the process, the contradictions that underlie these nostalgic constructions. In *The World We Have Lost*, Christopher Laslett suggests that our nostalgia for "a world we once all possessed, a world now passed away," is not so much for a pastoral or preindustrial world, but for a world constructed around the family, which has been irrevocably transformed by industrialism.[30] The pressures on the family in the eighteenth century are written into sentimental novels such as *Clarissa* and *Julie* and are located at the heart of *The Vicar of Wakefield*, as well as "The Revolution in Low Life" and *The Deserted Village*.

Laslett's concept of "subsumption" illuminates the connection between the family and the picturesque. Laslett notes that there was a large group of people—including women, servants, and unmarried persons—who were "subsumed" into the identities of their fathers or their masters. Beyond these household groupings, there was yet a larger "family" structure that extended from the manor house outward to include the cottages.[31] Yet there was another large body of individuals who, according to Laslett, "must be looked upon as null, as having no function, not even as subsumed into units which did have a function. These were the paupers, anyone who was in receipt of charity for his upkeep, or who had ever been in such a position. . . . Growing in the sixteenth and seventeenth centuries, a great mass by the year 1800, such persons had nevertheless existed at all previous times."[32]

In the aesthetic production of the eighteenth and nineteenth centuries we see literature and art that respond to the struggle of the subsumed persons (women, servants, the unmarried) to individuate themselves. The novel, particularly, was an arena in which the lives of these individuals could be narrated, as they are in *Moll Flanders*, *Roxana*, *Pamela*, or *Tom Jones*. Moreover, the ever-increasing body of dispossessed persons, paupers, Gypsies, or other homeless, landless individuals resulted in an aestheticization of their plight, which served to keep their distress at a distance; while the sublime celebrated vast mountains, splendid vistas, and wildly crashing waterfalls, the picturesque glorified decay. That decay—crumbling cottages, broken-down carts—was not based on nature, as the sublime was, but on the human element of the landscape. The people displaced from the ruined cottages, or required to work with an old and unreliable cart, regularly appear in picturesque paintings, novels, and poems.

Appear is the operative word, for the Gypsies, paupers, and other displaced groups are seen, but seldom heard. Unlike the wives, daughters, and servants who are emerging from the subsumption of the extended family, the subjects of the picturesque will not develop their own voices. What we witness in *The Vicar* is precisely Dr. Primrose's attempt to preserve his voice—and the mastery of his family and his own narrative—as his assets dwindle and his social position becomes increasingly precarious.

Careful reading reveals that the happiness the Primrose family enjoys at the start of the novel is based on financial stability and solvency. Despite his celebration of the simple pleasures of family life, Dr. Primrose acknowledges that the "harmony" in which his family lives with the Wilmots, whose daughter, Arabella, is engaged to George Primrose, depends on Mr. Wilmot's knowledge that the Vicar "could make a very handsome settlement" on the couple (41). When it is revealed that Dr. Primrose has lost his modest fortune, the marriage is called off, and the Primrose family's misadventures begin.

Financial independence is not the only assumption undergirding the Primrose family, however. Early on, as he describes his family, Dr. Primrose is proud to point out that he has written an epitaph for Deborah—despite the fact that she is still alive—in which he commends "her prudence, oeconomy, and obedience till death." Moreover, he has "got it copied fair, with an elegant frame, [and] placed it over the chimneypiece, where it answered several very useful purposes. It admonished my wife of her duty to me, and my fidelity to her; it inspired her with a passion for fame, and constantly put her in mind of her end" (41).[33] Deborah's goodness and "obedience" are already projected until her death, leaving her very few options if she wishes to attain the "fame" that Dr. Primrose's epitaph seems to promise—and that the Vicar assumes she desires. We might even say that the happiness and stability of the Primrose family are predicated on a dead female body.

What does it mean to have a "souvenir" of Deborah's life on display, even while she is still alive? Susan Stewart notes that the function of a "souvenir" is "to create a continuous and personal narrative of the past" (140). To have a souvenir of Deborah, then, is to place her within an idealized narrative that allows her no agency. Dr. Primrose writes not only her epitaph, but also her life as she lives it. By attempting to lock

Deborah into his own narrative, he controls her present and future behavior by keeping the human Deborah at a distance.

The Vicar's representation of Deborah, as is Goldsmith's representation of "sweet Auburn" in *The Deserted Village*, is an attempt to prop up
the writer's increasingly fragile controlling viewpoint, while suppress-
ing any unruly or alternative interpretations. Dr. Primrose is able to
set off his own identity against the ground of Deborah's epitaph: with
Deborah as the exemplary wife and mother—passive, domestic, and the
bearer of tradition—the Vicar asserts himself as active, independent,
and creative. The narrator of *The Deserted Village* is also very much a
man of the world, who constructs his own identity against the background of a passive, organic, and feminized rural village. The distance
created by these reinforced and gendered boundaries is crucial to maintaining the identity of the nostalgic writer. Susan Stewart observes that
"the nostalgic is enamoured of distance, not of the referent itself. Nostalgia cannot be sustained without loss. For the nostalgic to reach his
or her goal of closing the gap between resemblance and identity, *lived*
experience would have to take place, an erasure of the gap between sign
and signified, an experience which would cancel out the desire that is
nostalgia's reason for existence."[34] But, notes Stewart, the place of the
souvenir is the attic or cellar, outside the "the temporality of everyday
life," which is conducted in kitchens and parlors.[35] By placing Deborah's epitaph, "copied fair" and in "an elegant frame," directly over the
fireplace—that is, at the hearth, the heart of the home—the Vicar creates nostalgia for the present at Deborah's expense. She is objectified,
her living body substituted by a framed fair copy of her epitaph; she is,
to be precise, replaced by a narrative written by Dr. Primrose, a visual,
material *display* of his construction of her life. As the rustics or Gypsies
are in a picturesque painting, Deborah is regarded from a distance, aestheticized into a quaint memory of herself. Her own desire—her vanity,
her love of luxury, her ambition to marry her daughters well—along
with her sexuality is erased and replaced by the Vicar's nostalgia, which
is created and maintained by his fictitious construction of Deborah. In
every sense, Deborah's epitaph confirms the Vicar's identity as patriarch and writer.[36]

In Dr. Primrose's household, eighteenth-century society is produced
in microcosm: his superiority is held in place partly by his superior liter-
acy. As a clergyman, Dr. Primrose occupies a liminal position in the
social hierarchy; his education and calling qualify him as a gentleman,
even if his real economic circumstances are at odds with his social

status. Within the "little republic" (50) of his family, Dr. Primrose assumes the role of patriarch and models his household on the monarchy that Oliver Goldsmith himself revered. The Vicar announces, in his debate with Mr. Wilkinson, that he "would have all men kings" in a society in which "some are born to command, and others to obey" (114). In the Vicar's own "republic," however, those born to obey are women, specifically his wife and daughters.

What is the economy of the "little republic" ruled by the Vicar? By his own description, labor is strictly divided, and domestic labor is rendered invisible. The walls of the snug little cottage the Vicar describes are "nicely whitewashed," and the cottage itself is "kept with the utmost neatness, the dishes, plates, and coppers, being well scoured, and all disposed in bright rows on the shelves"; he fails to mention, however, just who has done all this whitewashing, tidying, scouring, and arranging. While a servant is given credit for preparing a morning fire, the labor of his daughters is depicted as merely decorative: they have "adorn[ed] the walls with pictures of their own designing" (50).

While the Vicar and his son "pursue [their] usual industry abroad," the women of the Primrose family busy themselves "in providing breakfast, which was always ready at a certain time." The gentle irony of this statement — on the one hand, the women's labor is less important than the "industry" of the men, but on the other hand, they are always on a tight schedule — is enhanced by the sentence that follows, which clearly points to the Vicar as family timekeeper.[37] He reports that he allows a half-hour for breakfast, and an hour for dinner, "which time was taken up with innocent mirth between my wife and daughters," but "in philosophical arguments between my son and me" (50). At every turn, the concept of separate spheres for men and women is reinforced, but as the Primrose family's social position begins to change, the Vicar will find it increasingly difficult to control the desires of his wife and daughters. As David Durant notes, the Vicar is finally defeated by "the unruly actuality of experience;"[38] I would add that the unruliness of the body also contributes to his failure as patriarch.

After his initial financial downturn, Dr. Primrose and his family retreat to a humble curacy of £15 per year in a village seventy miles away from their home, where the Vicar hopes to supplement his income by managing a small farm.[39] As do the narrators of "The Revolution in Low Life" and *The Deserted Village*, Dr. Primrose speaks of the village from a distance, as a tourist might. His description of his new home is, in fact, an echo of the description of the village in "Revolution":

The place of our retreat was in a little neighbourhood, consisting of farmers, who tilled their own grounds, and were equal strangers to opulence and poverty. As they had almost all the conveniencies of life within themselves, they seldom visited towns or cities in search of superfluity. Remote from the polite, they still retained the primaeval simplicity of manners, and frugal by habit, they scarce knew that temperance was a virtue. They wrought with chearfulness on days of labour; but observed festivals as intervals of idleness and pleasure. They kept up the Christmas carol, sent truc love-knots on Valentine morning, eat pancakes on Shrove-tide, shewed their wit on the first of April, and religiously cracked nuts on Michaelmas eve. (49)

Parts of this passage repeat Goldsmith's essay nearly verbatim. What does it mean that Dr. Primrose speaks in the same voice as the narrator of "The Revolution in Low Life"? It is clear that Dr. Primrose observes the villagers from an outsider's point of view, just as the narrator of "Revolution" participates only vicariously in the pleasures of rural life during the few summer weeks he spends in the country. Such vicarious pleasures are precisely those of the readers of Goldsmith's texts; the success of the sentimental narrative depended entirely on its ability to produce tender feelings—at a distance. In both narratives, the rural folk represent simplicity and virtue that can only be found in a village still untouched by modernity, a perfect focus for the city dweller's nostalgia. And in both narratives, the visitors to the village remain just that: tourists, observing the village and its inhabitants from a certain distance, as something quaint that offers pleasure to the observer. Writing about the village—as does writing Deborah's epitaph—freezes it in time and keeps it at a distance and under control; reading about the village afforded readers an illusion of their own virtue at being able to feel sentiment.

The nostalgia evoked by the image of the villagers and their simple pleasures results in a picturesque description of their lives, a description that denies hardship or suffering; indeed, these villagers work "with chearfulness" and need not cultivate the virtue of temperance, since they have no desires that need curbing. In contrast, however, Dr. Primrose's family might be said to suffer from a lack of simplicity. Modern life has sown seeds of dissatisfaction and created new desires: a desire to consume material goods, a desire for upward mobility.

The Vicar struggles with his wife and daughters to make them accommodate themselves to their reduced station in life: "My chief attention therefore," he observes, "was now to bring down the pride of my family to their circumstances, for I well knew that aspiring beggary is wretchedness itself." He advises his family that "'the poor live pleasantly without our help [so] let us from this moment give up all pretensions to gentility . . . and draw upon content for the deficiencies of fortune'" (44). It falls to the female members of the Primrose family— the bearers of tradition and the link to a romanticized pastoral or picturesque past—to accept their lot "with chearfulness." The growth of domestic ideology assigned women a redemptive function in the family, requiring them to maintain, within the household, traditions that were disappearing from an increasingly alienating social world. Nonetheless, Dr. Primrose finds it necessary to deliver a subtle admonishment to his wife and daughters on the first Sunday in their new parish when they appear dressed "in all their former splendour: their hair plaistered up with pomatum, their faces patched to taste, their trains bundled up into an heap behind." Despite his chagrin, the Vicar is amused by their "vanity," especially that of Deborah, "from whom [he] expected more discretion" (51). Dr. Primrose's amusement at the vanity of his wife and daughters—apparently, his sons exhibit no such silliness—marks him as a benevolent patriarch, and the female members of his family as weak, subject to frivolous desires, and unable to control their inclination toward comfort, luxury, and the consumption of material goods.

As do Mr. Harlowe and M. d'Étange, however, the benevolent Dr. Primrose learns that feminine desire—particularly that of daughters—is not easily controlled and can threaten the stability of a family structure built on an assumption of "natural" hierarchy based on gender. As Timothy Dykstal points out in "The Story of O: Pleasure and Politics in *The Vicar of Wakefield*," Dr. Primrose and Squire Thornhill find themselves at odds over Olivia: the Vicar "wants to preserve his daughter's virtue" while the Squire "wants to take it away"(333).[40]

As Clarissa Harlowe does, Olivia leaves her father's home as a result of pressure to marry someone she does not love. Olivia is not the divine Clarissa, however: her desire is more transparent. While it might be argued that Robert Lovelace tricks Clarissa into stepping outside her father's garden door, Olivia needs only minimal encouragement to run off with Squire Thornhill and marry under what she knows to be questionable circumstances—"privately . . . by a popish priest" (138). Just as Clarissa rejects an arranged marriage with the repulsive Mr. Solmes, Olivia rejects an arranged marriage with the plodding Farmer Williams, thereby refusing the role of property to be exchanged between men, in favor of following her own desire; Dykstal believes that "blinded by his familiarity with [what Foucault calls the system of] alliance, Goldsmith's Vicar fatally neglects that rising system of sexuality"[41] that drives Olivia (and possibly Clarissa Harlowe) to run off with a man who is desirable, if dangerous.

The Vicar's problem, like that of Mr. Harlowe, is excessive faith in his own power as patriarch. But while Mr. Harlowe retains the power to intimidate his wife and daughters with his physical and psychological cruelty, the good-natured Vicar has seemingly lost the battle with feminine desire. Deborah and her daughters cannot overcome their desire for luxury and material goods—such as complexion washes, fine clothes, or proper horses—that will increase Sophia's and Olivia's desirability on the marriage market; Dr. Primrose cannot confront these desires directly and is reduced to knocking over and spilling the complexion washes as if by accident. Simply, the Vicar's reign over his "little republic" is not strong enough to withstand Olivia's desire for Squire Thornhill. When Dr. Primrose observes to his penitent daughter that "surely it was no small temptation that could thus obliterate all the impressions of such an education, and so virtuous a disposition as thine," Olivia points out that Thornhill "owes all his triumph to *the desire I had* of making him, and not myself, happy" (138, emphasis mine). Olivia attempts to displace the sexual aspect of her desire onto Squire Thornhill—by claiming she wants to make "him, and not myself, happy"; despite her internalization of his desire, she nevertheless claims this desire as her own.

Unlike Clarissa, Olivia does not struggle with her desire; instead, she gives in to it, even enjoys it, admitting that after realizing her mistake in eloping with Thornhill, she nevertheless continued to love him so "tenderly" that she "strove to forget [her] infamy in a tumult of pleasures" (139). Olivia's elopement, like Clarissa's departure from Harlowe Place, is a radical attempt at claiming subjectivity and agency. But while Clarissa retains and develops her subjectivity through her continued resistance, suffering, and saintly death, Olivia has her only access to subjectivity through her desire; as Timothy Dykstal points out, she is readily absorbed back into the "alliance" of men when her marriage to Squire Thornhill is revealed to be valid, and her subjectivity subsequently disappears.[42] The only evidence that remains of her attempt at agency is her short and pitiful song, which asserts that a ruined woman's only recourse, the "only art" that can hide her guilt and "give repentance to her lover," is "to die" (148). Unlike Clarissa's protracted death, which takes up much of Richardson's mammoth novel, Olivia's song is only two stanzas long, a faint echo of her attempt to claim her desire for her own.[43] Ultimately, Olivia Primrose has more in common with Lydia Bennett than with Clarissa Harlowe.

Unlike his wife and daughters, who are "infected" with modernity, the Vicar shows no reluctance to move to a more humble village and modest lifestyle. His nostalgia allows him to enjoy the move and to see it as a test of character. Dr. Primrose and his family, however, will not be the only ones to suffer as a result of his diminished finances. What of the widows and orphans of the diocesan clergy who have been the beneficiaries of his £35 living at Wakefield? Dr. Primrose's inability to dispense largesse to the community will have a trickle-down effect, contributing to the overall impoverishment of the village once he has departed; this fact, however, is not articulated and is one of the contradictions that the contrived happy ending of the novel suppresses. The idea of trickle-down economics does not go away and reappears in *The Deserted Village*, where a village is destroyed by a larger economy that partakes of international trade, a colonial system, and a large-scale redistribution of wealth that renders impossible the insular self-sufficiency of a rural village based on agriculture.

The narratives that Goldsmith creates in *The Vicar of Wakefield* and "The Revolution in Low Life" represent his attempt to construct an identity posited on loss; most especially, an identity as the writer of loss. In his essay, "'A Garden, and a Grave': The Poetry of Oliver Goldsmith," Roger Lonsdale notes that "by the mid-century a number of poets were fumbling in various ways to discover a personal voice which could not be reduced simply to the anonymous, traditional, or rhetorical."[44] Goldsmith's own personal voice, a nostalgic voice, would assert itself boldly in his most memorable work, *The Deserted Village*, which articulates the social nostalgia surrounding the changes in the landscape that resulted from widespread enclosure.

Ann Bermingham observes in *Landscape and Ideology* that the eighteenth century was the great era of land enclosure, as well as the great era of British landscape painting. Bermingham notes that "this coincidence of a social transformation of the countryside with the rise of a cultural-aesthetic ideal of the countryside repeats a familiar pattern of actual loss and imaginative recovery. Precisely when the countryside—or at least large portions of it—was becoming unrecognizable, and dramatically marked by historical change, it was offered as the image of the homely, the stable, the ahistorical."[45] Bermingham, of course, speaks of painting, the visual images that have defined, to a great extent, our image of the English countryside. But prior to the landscapes painted by Constable, which are the main focus of Bermingham's study, Oliver Goldsmith was lamenting the passing of a simple, rural way of life: that of a "deserted village," and that of a family touched by modernity. The "image of the homely, the stable, and the ahistorical" that Bermingham mentions applies equally to the family—particularly the women of the family, whose bodies are heavily invested with notions of stability and tradition—and to the land, the body of which is also invested with the responsibility of tradition and continuity. Bermingham locates contradiction in landscape painting's attempt to offer a stable, ahistorical image of an unenclosed countryside in the face of radical change in the land and in a rural way of life.

In *The Deserted Village*, Goldsmith negotiates the changes in the countryside, not by offering a stable or an ahistorical image that denies loss or attempts to "freeze" time, but by latching on to loss and adopting the affect of loss, nostalgia, as his own, thereby asserting his own narrative or poetic voice. He writes his nostalgia through co-opting the villagers' loss and creating a piece of writing that stands as a monument to that loss. In order to reconstruct the imaginary body of a village, aesthetic distance is essential; the lament cannot come from those within the lived experience of the village. The position of poet, tourist, or returning native provides the distance necessary for Goldsmith to speak of nostalgia, and that nostalgia, in turn, gives Goldsmith a voice that distinguishes him as a poet and man of letters. Goldsmith creates a unique voice that will assure him of literary fame and deny change or death; unlike the village, his voice and his writing will remain intact, a permanent body of cultural work that resists change by maintaining an aesthetic distance from real historical loss.

Goldsmith's creation of "sweet Auburn" is an attempt to make nostalgia material by locating it in a place—a space that has been named and invested with meaning.[46] That his effort has been hugely successful is witnessed by the enduring popularity of Goldsmith's long poem. In their essay "On the Use of Contradiction in the Eighteenth-Century Long Poem," John Barrell and Harriet Guest examine competing discourses in Young's *Night Thoughts* and Pope's "Epistle to Bathurst," which they conclude allow the contradictions of capitalism to be enunciated as long as they are "prevented from coming into contact with each other."[47] *The Deserted Village*, on the other hand, note Barrell and Guest, condemns luxury without any contradicting claims for the benefits of capitalism; nevertheless, Goldsmith's poem became popular on a wave of sentiment. Contemporary reviewers found the poem charming, and when they reproduced sections of the poem, they usually chose the extended descriptions of the schoolmaster, the clergyman, and the ale-house. The effects of this truncation were to render invisible Gold-smith's political statement and turn the poem into an exercise in the creation of images; indeed, these three images have become "classic," as Barrell and Guest observe.[48]

While I agree that editorial intervention by eighteenth-century re-viewers has handed down an imaginary poem—that is, an idea of Gold-smith's poem that is not entirely supported by the actual poem itself—I cannot fully agree that Goldsmith's lament for the devastation of the village and his condemnation of capitalism are not at all "counterbal-anced by any assertion of the political and economic advantages it se-cured."[49] Rather, I would like to suggest that the counterbalance or contradiction is merely invisible, embedded in the voice of the narrator, who speaks from the privileged position of the poet, assuming the moral high ground and observing the village from an aesthetic distance with-out suffering the economic hardships of the villagers, in much the same way as the narrator of "The Revolution in Low Life."

It is likely true, as Barrell and Guest assert, that the growth of liter-ary periodicals, whose reviewers selected and reproduced "remarkable passages" from poems and prose works, contributed to a growing ten-dency to read poetry for image and feeling, rather than content or meaning.[50] Certainly contemporary critics, using their own preferences, managed to canonize certain images of the poem (the parish priest, the schoolmaster, and the alehouse); nevertheless, the poet has already cho-sen these images to illustrate his concept of a ruined village. The struc-ture of *The Deserted Village* readily lends itself to the reviewers' truncation: the three often-quoted selections easily stand alone, while other places or persons in the poem receive either very brief treatment or are so tightly woven into the fabric of the poem that it is impossible to extricate them neatly.

It is illuminating to examine these images that have not been fre-quently quoted or canonized. If the parish priest, the schoolmaster, and the alehouse were selected by contemporary critics as memorable im-ages, what of those images neglected in Goldsmith's long poem, left un-read or unanalyzed, perhaps even unremembered? Many of these images are of women, and often sexualized. In the midst of Goldsmith's description of the cheerful diversions of the village appear the "bashful virgin," casting surreptitious "looks of love" at a young man, and the matron who disapproves of the young woman's desire;[51] less innocent is "the coy maid, half willing to be pressed," whose image is actually embedded within that of the alehouse (251).

While these two images are brief, Goldsmith offers a longer description of a poor and elderly woman, a "sad historian." The poem's narrator observes her at a distance:

> yon, widowed, solitary thing,
> That feebly bends beside the plashy spring;
> She, wretched matron, forced in age for bread,
>   To strip the brook with mantling cresses spread,
> To pick her wintry faggot from the thorn,
> To seek her nightly shed, and weep till morn;
> She only left of all the harmless train,
> The sad historian of the pensive plain. (131–37)

Although Goldsmith designates her the "historian," she is a historian who does not write or speak; she simply weeps. As are all the female images in *The Deserted Village*, this woman is merely a spectacle, something to be seen but not heard. Her agency is limited to searching for food, fuel, and shelter; history is not written by her hand, but through her body. The presence of her frail, bent body scavaging the land attests to the sad history of the village; she is, nevertheless, merely an image of history, a "bearer of meaning," not a "maker of meaning," to borrow Laura Mulvey's expression.[52] Goldsmith's concern for the landscape is projected onto the woman's body; the physical changes in the landscape have been mapped onto the elderly woman's body, which is aged, damaged, nonproductive.

The other extended description of a woman is that of a homeless woman, likely young, who has sought her fortune in the city, only to return to the village in disgrace. She is also a spectacle and the poem's narrator bids the reader look at her: " — Ah, turn thine eyes," he writes,

> Where the poor houseless shiv'ring female lies.
> She once, perhaps, in village plenty blest,
> Has wept at tales of innocence distressed;
> Her modest looks the cottage might adorn
> Sweet as the primrose peeps beneath the thorn:[53]
> Now lost to all — her friends, her virtue fled,
> Near her betrayer's door she lays her head,
> And, pinched with cold, and shrinking from the shower,

> With heavy heart deplores that luckless hour,
> When idly first, ambitious of the town,
> She left her wheel and robes of country brown. (327–38)

"Ambitious of the town," this ruined maid has been seduced as much by the lure of the city as by a man; she is a victim of modernity and of her own desire. But the town itself is a dangerous and even sexualized space, Goldsmith points out, and aspiring to leave the safety and innocence of the village can corrupt a chaste young woman.

But while this young woman and the elderly widow are tied to the land, unable to leave the village, Auburn's "fair tribes" depart for "distant climes," the wilds of America (340, 343). As the villagers prepare to leave Auburn forever, the daughters are silent and tearful, while the mothers complain and attempt to comfort fretting babies. Set in contrast to the domestic charms of the village, with its "cooling brook," "grassy-vested green," and "warbling grove" (362–63), America is painted as a sinister place. In fact, Goldsmith's description of the British colony of Georgia sounds much like the description of other colonies in Africa, India, or South America: dark, dangerous, unpredictable, untamed—everything that Auburn is not. The former villagers in this new land make their way "through torrid tracts with fainting steps"; suffer under "blazing suns"; venture into "matted woods, where birds forget to sing" (345, 349, 351); and traverse "pois'nous fields"

> Where the dark scorpion gathers death around;
> Where at each step the stranger fears to wake
> The rattling terrors of the vengeful snake;
> Where crouching tigers wait their hapless prey,
> And savage men more murd'rous still than they;
> While oft in whirls the mad tornado flies,
> Mingling the ravaged landscape with the skies. (354–60)

In contrast to the dark and negative image of the colonies, Goldsmith presents Auburn as pristine. His image of the land is femininized; it is beautiful while new and unspoiled, but sadly worn when well used, forced to count on artifice and adornment to enhance its appearance:

> As some fair female unadorned and plain,
> Secure to please while youth confirms her reign,
> Slights every borrowed charm that dress supplies,
> Nor shares with art the triumph of her eyes;

But when those charms are past, for charms are frail,
When time advances, and when lovers fail,
She then shines forth, solicitous to bless,
In all the glaring impotence of dress. (288–96)

Goldsmith refers here to the improvement of land by men of "wealth
and pride" who occupy more than their fair portion of it (277). The
country estates they occupy, formed by the enclosure of commons, require space for their own private version of nature: lakes, parks, horses,
hunting—but not farming. The land has been taken out of productive
use that benefited the entire community and turned into a seat of pleasure that only the landowner and his friends may enjoy for idle diversions and the pleasure of the view.

As has the young homeless woman, the land has been ruined, because
it has been "by luxury betrayed." It has lost the innocent beauty of "nature's simplest charms" and is instead adorned with splendid vistas and
ornate buildings that are merely artificial (297–98). Meanwhile, the villagers go hungry; the land becomes at once "a garden and a grave"
(304).

The poet attempts to find a place for himself on the continuum between the villager and the city dweller by claiming his own personal
poverty and assuming the voice of the struggling artist—"sweet Poetry"
(409), he claims, finds him poor and keeps him that way. His poverty,
however, is ennobling, and his poetry, a "charming Nymph" (413), is
also the "source of all [his] bliss" (415) and a "nurse of every virtue"
(418). While the peasants are being forced out of their cottages and off
the land, the poet has long lived in the city and has chosen the life he
leads. In a sense, he too has been seduced by the city. The spoliation of
the village does not affect him in any material way; what is lost for the
poet is the luxury of a memory, the luxury of a charming place to which
he may retire or retreat when he feels ready to do so.

The narrator, as a former villager, feels entitled to assume residence
in the village; unlike the newly arrived London merchants, he does not
claim any right to live in the village by virtue of ownership of property,
but by virtue of birthright. His attitude is aristocratic in that he claims
a connection to the land that money cannot buy; his aristocracy is one
of blood and tradition, and his nostalgia celebrates the old, the original,
and the status quo. Goldsmith's celebration of the original and the old,
however, is purely aesthetic. His poetry will not have a material impact
on the lives of the most sorely affected; his poetry may, however, gain
him fame, and possibly money.

Goldsmith has lost his home, but the nostalgia that arises from this loss feeds his art; his nostalgia for a disappearing landscape and way of life is made material in the art and literature of the picturesque. The images in *The Deserted Village* that have been handed down—the schoolmaster, the clergyman, and the alehouse—participate fully in the ideology of the picturesque, which celebrated the visual—and distanced—representation of the curious, the crumbling, and the colorful.

Although *The Deserted Village* is ostensibly about the depopulation of the land, the poem does not really speak of the land, but of the people in the village and certain structures on the land, such as the alehouse. Goldsmith's alehouse, for example, is depicted as neat and tidy, with its walls whitewashed and its floors "nicely-sanded" (229). Its traditional sign post is now missing, but it is filled with picturesque objects: much as the colorful people of the village do, these objects retain a luster of quality. The varnished clock, the chest that is a "bed by night" and "a chest of drawers by day" (232), the pictures carefully "placed for ornament and use," the hearth either warming the house or filled with decorative flowers and greenery, all contribute to a cozy scene. The most picturesque touch of all—the "broken tea-cups"—crowns the description of this memorable building. As are all things picturesque, the broken cups are no longer viable working objects: they are a spectacle, for visual pleasure only, retained as a quaint decoration, a reminder of the past that the keeper of the alehouse could not bear to discard and decided to put to decorative use.

The descriptions of the clergyman and the schoolmaster are placed directly between those of the old woman and the alehouse. In contrast to the silent images of the women and the picturesque rendering of the alehouse, these descriptive pieces highlight the activity and agency of the parson and the schoolmaster: these are men who make things happen in the village. Unlike the broken tea cups, the ruined maid, or the impoverished old woman, they have not outlived their usefulness. While the narrator seems to empathize with the plight of the women, he does not foresee any possibility of their rehabilitation. The clergyman and the schoolmaster, on the other hand, will not disappear from society, although they may change. As individual men, they will die, as does Goldsmith's father, the country parson; the importance of their contribution to the social good, however, ensures that their work will be carried forward into the future, and that their positions in the village will be long remembered.

It is hardly a coincidence, then, that Goldsmith's sketches of the schoolmaster and the clergyman are so memorable. Unlike the female characters in *The Deserted Village*, who merge with the landscape, the cottage, or the alehouse, the clergyman and the schoolmaster assume a place in the history of this village, and in the history of Britain in general. Goldsmith himself longs for posterity as a writer. He strives, through his writing, to construct a self that will distinguish him from the ordinary man; in this quest, he identifies with the parson and the schoolmaster, whose mobility and agency distance them from the fading village. Just as their descriptions are detachable from the poem as a whole, these male figures possess an autonomy that ensures their survival.

Raymond Williams notes Goldsmith's personal investment in the "nostalgic portraits" of the parson and the schoolmaster; these men, Williams writes in *The Country and the City*, were both independent and revered in their own village; it is precisely such financial independence and public honor that Goldsmith, as a poet, desires. Goldsmith has written himself and his own desire for fame (not unlike that of Pope) so fully into the poem that his own condition as impoverished poet is mapped onto the land itself: "This creation of a 'desart' landscape," Williams observes, "is an imaginative rather than a social process; it is what the new order does to the poet, not to the land."[54] The actual social history of the village and its laborers is obscured in the interest of the writer's own longing for immortality and fame, his nostalgia for a plenitude that is imagined and displaced onto the land, the village, and a mythical way of life.

The distance from the village that the clergyman, the schoolmaster, and the writer share allows them to observe the village and its people with a "secret pleasure" that only they—or a consumer of landscape, pastoral, or picturesque, such as a tourist or reader—can enjoy. The rendering of the picturesque landscape or the pastoral poem is accomplished, as Pope reminds us in "A Discourse on Pastoral Poetry," through careful "illusion" and "concealing [of] miseries" (120). The act of concealing asserts the power of the writer and marks the construction of nature by culture; in the case of Pope and Goldsmith, those constructions of nature will be consumed by the reading public.

THE BURDEN OF NOSTALGIA

The construction of nature through the pastoral and the picturesque seeks to determine an origin in an unspecified past time, located within the land—a past that is encoded as female, while the future is encoded as male. The recovery of that female origin and the creation of an imaginary landscape invested with masculine nostalgia are assumed by writers such as Pope, Goldsmith, or Rousseau, whose subjectivity as men and as writers is constituted by their nostalgic stance, a Janus-like position that looks forward and backward at the same time.

Such nostalgia allowed Pope and Goldsmith to redefine masculinity at a time when gender roles were perceived as unstable; as notions of femininity were being fixed, these writers were able to assume a position that spoke with authority to both genders. The association of the past and the landscape with the feminine allowed a celebration of femininity that was desexualized. Concern about unregulated feminine sexuality that would, in the landowning classes, disrupt social boundaries and leave lines of inheritance in disarray and, in the lower classes, produce more bodies to fill an increasingly crowded landscape resulted in a nostalgic longing for the tradition and security that a desexualized mother represents.

But the role of the mother, as we see in *The Vicar of Wakefield*, also threatens to be unstable and needs fixing, just as Dr. Primrose attempts to fix Deborah in the past by writing her epitaph and placing it in a prominent position over their hearth. The dangers of social change seem to reach into the heart of the home and into the family, a "natural" entity, as is the land, worthy of idealization and in need of careful preservation.

Pope and Goldsmith, as Dr. Primrose does, seek to allay a threatening modernity by coopting feminine agency. They attempt to keep the world "in order," speaking for a nostalgic masculinity under siege by social and economic change, struggling to maintain a weakening status quo. Cultural nostalgia will eventually be adopted by the socially mobile—the growing middle class, which enjoys the benefits of economic expansion—and will be turned into an object of consumption: objects available for consumption include the countryside, via travel, pictures, or guidebooks, and sentimental literature, which offers the vicarious experience of suffering.

The very possibility of consumption comes about through the rise of capitalism, which gives increased spending power to the middle class, while increasing poverty and hastening the social and economic displacement of the poor. The contradictions of capitalism are symbolically "resolved" via consumption of the picturesque experience, which allows a fantasy of empathy for the unfortunate without requiring any real social action, since the people and the villages of the picturesque are all kept at a distance; all is simply a "secret pleasure," as Goldsmith's visitor is quick to observe. The enjoyment of that pleasure is provided by the artist, whose voice confers the necessary aesthetic distance.

Between 1704, when Pope wrote his "Discourse on Pastoral Poetry," and 1770, when Goldsmith published *The Deserted Village*, a significant change took place in the nature of nostalgia. Whereas Pope acknowledges the use of "illusion" to make the shepherd's life appear "delightful," the consciousness of artifice is submerged in Goldsmith's nostalgic texts; whereas Pope foresees the restoration of "peace and plenty" to the land and looks forward to England's prosperity under the reign of Queen Anne, Goldsmith has seen the material consequences of the growth of trade and the adoption of commercial values on the smaller villages and laments the depopulation and destruction of those villages and the way of life they represent. Both Pope and Goldsmith create themselves as writers. Pope's nostalgia leads him to recreate classical themes and poetry, by which he can position himself as a public poet, despite his own real alienation from English society as a result of his religion, his physical deformity, and his lack of formal education; Goldsmith's nostalgia, on the other hand, drives him to assume the role of exile, writing poetry for a commercial society that cannot fully appreciate the artist. The luxury of nostalgia has a price, however: in the writings of both Pope and Goldsmith, the burden of nostalgia is borne by women, in whom are invested the values of tradition, stability, and continuity.

5

"In a world so changed": Feminine Nostalgia and Sarah Scott's *A Description of Millenium Hall and the Country Adjacent*

FICTIVE DOMAINS GREW OUT OF MY INITIAL CURIOSITY ABOUT SAMuel Richardson's representation of Clarissa Harlowe's prolonged illness and subsequent death. I began by wondering about the effects of cultural forces and social change on the body, and the ways in which those effects were perceived and represented in eighteenth-century literature; because the bodies of women are so often linked to bodies of land, as they are in *Clarissa*, *Sir Charles Grandison*, *Julie*, and "Windsor Forest," I wanted to examine the ways in which bodies and land might both be sites of cultural nostalgia. The trajectory of this project has led me from the body to the home and the garden, and finally to the landscape. In this final chapter, I will look at yet another text in which bodies and landscapes are constructed in response to eighteenth-century cultural nostalgia, Sarah's Scott's 1762 novel, *A Description of Millenium Hall, and the Country Adjacent*.

Both bodies and landscapes, as I have argued throughout this book, are likely locations for cultural nostalgia: that is, imaginary bodies and landscapes are constructed through nostalgia and invested with desire. The idea of nostalgia actually *began* in the body, as a physical "disease," a longing for home that we usually call homesickness; body, place, and nostalgia, therefore, have been intertwined from the very foundation of our modern concept of nostalgia.

Although nostalgia celebrates loss, it is not melancholia or mourning; nor is it grief. As a cultural practice, nostalgia is sentimental, paralyzing, conservative, resistant: it marks a certain reluctance to move forward, to change, or to break tradition. Nostalgia is a repetitive pleasure that is difficult to surrender. For those who are the object of a nostalgic fantasy that precludes agency—such as Deborah Primrose, locked into her own epitaph—nostalgia is a burden to be borne rather than a pleasure to be indulged.

The psychoanalytic roots of nostalgic desire for a return to a golden age may lie in the desire for reunion with the mother, from whom the child has been separated upon the entry into subjectivity. While nostalgia's resistance to change may make it seem to arrest the mourning process, nostalgia can be experienced *only* from a position of full subjectivity; nostalgia *depends* precisely upon the successful entry into subjectivity.

I claim that nostalgia can only exist once subjectivity is in place because if the split, or separation from the mother, and the entry into subjectivity have not taken place (as is the case in incomplete mourning), there would not be an object to mourn, nor would there be anything about which to feel nostalgic. Nostalgia only seems to defer mourning; actually, nostalgia is a way to play with loss. If loss is unacknowledged, then melancholia sets in, and symbolization is impossible.[1] Nostalgia, on the other hand, is a symbolic practice, a pleasurable "looking backward" at the past, without the danger of actually tipping back into the semiotic or preoedipal.[2] Because it requires that subjectivity rooted in sexual difference be secured firmly in place, nostalgia is a safe substitution for the pleasure of the preoedipal.

The Problem of Nostalgia: The Daughter's Case Is Different

Is there a feminine nostalgia, and, if so, what form would it take? Jessica Benjamin has argued that females enter into subjectivity in alternative ways.[3] The little girl need not experience the violent break with her mother because their gender is the same; separation is therefore less absolute, and her assumption of subjectivity through individuation runs a more ambivalent course. Jean Pfaelzer notes that "a girl's sense of herself is profoundly anchored in relationship, connection, and identification with her mother"; moreover, girls are encouraged to "tune in" to the feelings of others, so that empathy and connection are "self-enhancing," whereas, for boys, such dependency can be threatening and invasive.[4] Little boys, on the other hand, if they are to assume the gender identity of the father, must assume the father's subjectivity and agency, repressing all identification with the mother, who then becomes the object of desire. The little girl sees her mother as a subject, not a

mirror, while the relationship between the mother and the little boy requires that the mother reflect, not any subjectivity of her own, but the
desirability of the male subject. Women, associated with tradition and
the past, bear the burden of nostalgia; they are the objects of masculine
nostalgia and, as Deborah Primrose does, struggle to assert their
agency or subjectivity as the objects of masculine narratives or fantasies.

Because nostalgia symbolically reasserts the break from the mother,
it is especially self-enhancing, supporting a sense of the nostalgic's own
subjectivity. Women are often relegated to the spaces of nostalgia: a
quaint cottage, a deserted village, a picturesque landscape, or other
places associated with the past or tradition. Such circumscription effectively suppresses the material, maternal body; assignment to symbolic
spaces tends to deny subjectivity and agency.

Psychoanalytic theory alone, however, cannot adequately account for
the nostalgic cultural practices we see in the eighteenth century. The
nostalgia we see surfacing in eighteenth-century cultural practice derives from specific social and historical events: an increase in social mobility that eroded traditional class divisions, structures, and markers; an
acceleration in the enclosure of commons that had long provided a social and economic safety net for the landless laboring population; and
an inability to resolve—or ignore—the social and economic problems
resulting from the contradictions between a leftover feudal ideology of
social practice and new capitalistic economic systems. The new middle
classes also had an investment in "tradition." As Joseph Allen Boone
notes, "the insecurities bred of the bourgeoisie's sense of having just
arrived created their desire for a more civilized and refined existence;
companionate marriage became a fashionable vehicle by which a husband could advertise his successful achievement of a domestic kingdom
presided over by that most visible sign of status, a delicate, 'ladylike'
wife."[5]

Consistently, masculine nostalgia depends on a female object to bear
the burden of tradition, as it does with Deborah Primrose, Julie
d'Étange, Harriet Byron, and Clarissa Harlowe. Nostalgia serves as a
reinforcement for a male subjectivity, based on tradition and privilege,
facing social change that threatens its erosion, or for a new middle-class
male subjectivity attempting to assume a place for itself in society
through identification with tradition and privilege. Anxiety about class
or social change is transmuted into nostalgia for an undefined, but better, past.

With the social fabric beginning to unravel, domestic ideology assumed increasing importance: women were accorded a redemptive role in the family, and the household was called upon to maintain traditions that were disappearing from the wider social sphere. As Boone observes, the increasing idealization of women only served to reinforce the stereotype of the "delicate" woman that limited women's opportunities for work and independence.

But feminine nostalgia, based on a subjectivity formed through less violent individuation, may not necessarily attach itself to social factors in quite the same way. It may represent a less compromised desire for the mother that is not imbued with social anxiety: unlike the little boy, who seeks his father's agency or place in the social world, the little girl struggles to assume gradually a subjectivity that is individual and less defined by social forces outside the family, but more vulnerable to pressure from within the family. Her nostalgia may simply attach to motherhood itself, as a means by which she might attain the bliss of the mother-child dyad and at the same time assume the agency of the mother, who makes things happen for the child.

A history of feminine nostalgia requires consideration of the household's original function: that of a unit of production. With the move toward a capitalist economy, and subsequently to industrialization, which was already under way, women remained linked to the home; that link was vigorously reinforced by the development of a domestic ideology that is thoroughly rehearsed in the sentimental novels of the eighteenth century.

The question of women's work and the transition from a domestic to a capitalist economy has been examined extensively by many historians, including Alice Clark and Bridget Hill, who observe that a division of labor existed early on. As A. M. Hayford notes in "The Geography of Women: An Historical Introduction," the precapitalist household was a locus of economic, political, and social relationships effected through kinship networks. Attempting to account for the restriction of women to the private sphere, Hayford disputes the idea that motherhood "naturally" keeps women tied to the domestic sphere; rather, Hayford argues, the economic, political, and symbolic roles of motherhood align women with the domestic. Such roles require periodic reinforcement, especially at moments of social and economic change. As capitalism began to grow, the household was divested of its economic and political strength, which was then subsumed into the public sphere. Hayford suggests that men were able to assume control over the new, public area of production "because they traditionally had more external connections than did women, and thus moved logically into capitalist productive relations during the period when women remained at the eroding core of the household."[6]

The domestic sphere did not disappear. It survives, despite its loss of economic and political power, precisely because capitalism depends on the household to provide care and support for those who cannot work; to be a refuge that allows workers to recuperate their strength and morale sufficiently to be able to resume work again the following day; and, of course, to reproduce the labor force in the form of new human beings. In short, the domestic sphere absorbs the social and economic contradictions and inequities that are inherent in a capitalist economic system, while mothers produce the new workers that the capitalist system needs to operate. Public and private spheres are interdependent; one cannot exist without the other, and the functions of each permeate the other. While a capitalist economic system depends on the household's material support for its economic activity, the household itself is imbued with the values, frustrations, and pressures of the outside world.

If nostalgia is a combination of psychoanalytic and sociohistorical factors, then masculine nostalgia would be a reaction to an increasingly alienating world of work and uncertain social status that manifests itself in a longing for a more comforting and secure world, represented in contemporary life as the home; feminine nostalgia, on the other hand, might attempt to validate and empower the domestic sphere as a means of recuperating the real economic and political power once held by the household, and now lost. Without genuine political power, however, women were faced with few means by which to validate the power of the household—unless it was to be complicit with the domestic ideology currently in circulation. Such complicity, as we will see, surfaces in the conflicted ideology of Sarah Scott's *Millenium Hall*, in which Scott's view of a feminine utopia nevertheless privileges domesticity. As work was removed from the domestic unit of production, women of the emerging middle class were left without gainful employment; for a constellation of reasons, mothering became women's work.

Nostalgia, with its appeal to tradition and its evocation of a lost "golden age," was a polyvalent sentiment and was put to various uses by different writers. The nostalgia of the privileged male author of the eighteenth century, arising from rapid social change, was displaced onto representations of the body and the land and sought reinforcement through gender and domestic ideologies that restricted women to the spaces of the body and the home, while aligning men with the spaces of the mind and the public arena. The complicated use of nostalgia by a female writer of the period, such as Sarah Scott, is worthy of consideration for the light it sheds on the ways in which the public and private spheres, apparently so separate, actually interact.

MILLENIUM HALL AND FEMININE NOSTALGIA

Sarah Scott's *Millenium Hall* offers an alternative view of nostalgia. It is true that the novel describes what Mary Louise Pratt calls a "feminotopia," or place of "female autonomy, empowerment, and pleasure";[7] it also offers a model for widespread social action, something that a typically nostalgic text—because nostalgia resists change—does not. The model offered, however, is a nostalgic one reminiscent of those of Mary Astell or Sir Charles Grandison. The political ideology and literary form of Scott's novel are uneven, resulting, perhaps, from the need to present a radical vision of social change within the terms of the prevailing social discourse.[8] While Scott's community of women has a plan to improve their local community by providing for everyone according to his or her needs, the women do not attempt to take their plan outside the enclosure of their estate; the male narrator, revealed in a later novel to be Sir George Ellison, gives the estate its name, Millenium Hall, and tells the story of this community of women to the world outside the estate.

The central contradiction of Scott's novel emerges early, in the scene where Sir George and his traveling companion, Lamont, approach the hall. After praising the arcadian qualities of the estate, the narrator claims that he and his companion were "desirous to see still more of this earthly paradise" and "imagined" that "the Primum Mobile of all we had yet beheld" was residing in the "ancient structure."[9] Gary Kelly claims that Sir George is here suggesting that the women "are god-like directors and motivators of the world they have designed and set in motion. In other words, the female proprietors of Millenium Hall are agents in a powerfully original and originating way, by having returned to an 'original' and pre-lapsarian state of society."[10] Nostalgia doubles back on itself: Sir George's fantasy here is of the phallic mother, but of the phallic mother *contained* in every possible way—within a physical structure, within the past, and within his narrative. The similarities to Deborah Primrose, trapped within her own epitaph, are striking.

Jean Pfaelzer notes that a hallmark of some nineteenth-century female utopias appearing in works by Charlotte Perkins Gilman, Mary E. B. Lane, and other female writers are the subjectivity, agency, and initiative accorded to mothers.[11] But Scott's novel differs from a "feminotopia" in its prescription for broad social action; its end is not a utopian community of women, but a model for widespread social change. In *Millenium Hall*, despite the proliferation of maternal role models and relationships modeled on the mother-daughter dyad, no actual mothers are in residence. Women, in Scott's model community, achieve subjectivity by sacrificing actual motherhood and marriage and retiring from the public world. The idea of a retired community of unmarried women, informed by Mary Astell's *A Serious Proposal to the Ladies* of 1694–97, is nostalgic in itself; rather than attempting social change through intervention in domestic ideology—changing the role of the mother, for example—these women choose a backward gesture toward earlier models of female communities such as Astell's. The female community of Millenium Hall may represent a productive structure, but it lacks a reproductive structure.

The women of Millenium Hall, by rejecting marriage, attempt to deny the possibility of being sexual objects. But to refuse objectification is not sufficient; by physically isolating themselves within the seclusion of the estate, they are unable to negotiate what Jessica Benjamin calls "intersubjective space," where subject meets subject, and where the individual acts in a social context.[12] True intersubjectivity requires praxis, but as the women in Scott's novel immure themselves, their subjectivity is necessarily limited; despite its originality, their economic plan is not fully realized in a broad social space until Sir George implements a version of it on his own estate.

The model community of Millenium Hall embodies the contrast between nostalgia and utopianism. While nostalgia is linked to the home, it is also rooted in the past; a utopia, on the other hand, is an idealized place that includes a visionary plan for an ideal society. A utopia may call on aspects of the past as models of perfection, but it is essentially directed toward change, whereas nostalgia is often focused on maintaining the status quo and resisting change.

The Millenium Hall project is nostalgic in its attempt to reproduce social relations based on the mother-child relation among its members, and in its integrated domestic economy, in which all contribute according to their abilities and are cared for according to their needs. Its utopian vision calls on an older economic model in which the public and private spheres were not so widely separated. The nostalgia of *Millenium Hall* is a feminine nostalgia that seeks to recuperate power and agency for the home and for the women whose work is in the home. This utopia is not without a price, however; the women of Scott's model community sacrifice actual motherhood and sexuality in their quest for agency.

MILLENIUM HALL AND THE BODY

Bodies are foregrounded in *Millenium Hall* from the novel's inception. Sir George Ellison writes that "I was advised by an eminent physician to make a very extensive tour through the western part of this kingdom, in order, by frequent change of air, and continued exercise, to cure the ill effects of my long abode in the hot and unwholsome climate of Jamaica, where, while I increased my fortune, I gradually impaired my constitution" (54). Sir George is broken, in poor health, as a result of his quest for economic gain in the colonies. His "tour," during which he encounters the female arcadia that he calls Millenium Hall, is a quest for redemption, ostensibly of his health, but also of his spirit, for Sir George is a slave owner. As does Dr. Primrose or the narrator of "The Deserted Village," he invests a place with virtue. James Cruise notes the nostalgia of Sir George's immediate association of the estate with "the days of Theocritus" and observes that "the wholeness of body and soul that he seeks becomes a matter of personal fulfillment that he universalizes and superimposes upon Millenium Hall through his typologies. Thus, even when most apparently benevolent, Sir George's sympathy is streaked with paternalism."[13]

In a sense, Scott's novel is the articulation of Sir George's own nostalgic fantasy; bound by the terms of the prevailing social discourse, Scott unwittingly creates a utopia that is complicit in masculine nostalgia, where progress is associated with men (Sir George's venture in the colonies) and tradition is associated with women. Sir George needs this community of women to redeem his broken body and soul.

Brought into being through Sir George's precarious health[14] and attempt to cure his damaged constitution, the novel painstakingly details the plights of the bodies within the estate. The physical appearance of nearly all the women of the Millenium Hall community is irregular in some way. Early in his narrative, Sir George describes the "persons of the ladies": we learn that Mrs. Maynard has a "complexion agreeable, though brown"; Mrs. Selvyn has "features too irregular to be handsome"; Mrs. Mancel "excels in every beauty but the bloom"; Mrs. Trentham has a complexion "injured by the small pox"; Lady Mary Jones is "thin and pale" with "a countenance, which sickness has done its utmost to render languid"; and Mrs. Morgan is "plump" (59–60).

Injury or illness saves some of the women from marriage. Lady Mary, tempted to run off to Scotland with the trifling Mr. Lenman, escapes disgrace when her coach overturns the day before the planned departure. Louisa Mancel is saved from Mr. Hintman's lecherous designs when he drops dead "in a fit of apoplexy" (100), while her potential marriage to Sir Edward is prevented by his death in battle. Miss Melvyn, on the other hand, is forced into marriage with Mr. Morgan. In a passage reminiscent of Clarissa Harlowe's revulsion for Mr. Solmes, Miss Melvyn confesses that she dreads marriage to a man she does not love and asserts, "The grave . . . appears to me far more eligible than this marriage. . . . If he really loved me, he could not suffer me to be forced into a marriage which he well knows I detest" (128). Later, her friends will claim that "she suffered less uneasiness from his illhumour, brutal as it was, than from his nauseous fondness" (135).

Missing from Scott's utopia is the women's sexuality. Apart from Miss Melvyn's experience with Mr. Morgan's "nauseous fondness," most of the women seem to avoid sexual contact and feeling altogether. The story that most carefully explores sexual attraction, or the lack of it, is that of Harriot Trentham. Significantly, Harriot has not been acculturated into domesticity, since her mother died within a month of her birth; raised by her father, Harriot has "never been taught the little arts of behaviour, which mothers too commonly inculcate with so much care" (224). Friends with Mr. Alworth from childhood, Harriot finds that social pressures intrude on their friendship and push the young couple toward marriage. Despite their pleasure at being together, sexual attraction seems to have no place in their relationship; nevertheless, since "every one talked of their mutual passion . . . they began to fancy it was true, but were surprized to find that name should be given to an affection calm and rational as theirs, totally free from that turbulency and wildness, which had always appeared to them the true characteristics of love" (229). The relationship, of course, is doomed. Despite their engagement, "they saw no very good reason for their marrying; they enjoyed each others society already, and did not wish for any more intimate tie" (230). Mr. Alworth breaks off their engagement when he meets the vivacious Miss Melman, who attracts him despite her "light and unsteady mind" (231); the frosty Harriot gracefully lets him go.

Opposed to Miss Melman, "the incomparable Harriot" is a catalog of masculine virtues. Her wit, we are told, "was as sound as her judgment solid and sterling, free from affectation, and all little effeminate arts and airs. Reason governed her thoughts and actions, nor could the greatest flow of spirits make her for a moment forget propriety. . . . [S]he was always constant and uniform, and a stranger to caprice" (231). Her mind is completely rational, her body completely absent.

When Mr. Alworth later repents of his folly—sexual attraction is fleeting, apparently—he realizes that true love can be found in friendship, but it is too late to remedy his mistake. He continues to adore Harriot, while she keeps him at a distance. Stricken with smallpox, she is almost relieved, upon her recovery, to find that smallpox "had entirely destroyed her beauty." In fact, Harriot is "perfectly contented with the alteration this cruel distemper had made in her. Her love for reading returned, and she regained the quiet happiness of which flutter and dissipation had deprived her without substituting any thing so valuable in its place" (241). Typical of the women at the hall, Harriot achieves her limited subjectivity at the expense of her sexuality.

Marriage and sexual contact, indeed, are seen as a sort of sacrifice. Sir George questions the awarding of dowries to young women of the parish when the women of the Hall seem so clearly opposed to marriage for themselves, only to be told by Mrs. Melvyn that the women "consider matrimony as absolutely necessary to the good of society," even a "general duty"; nevertheless, she observes that the women, as do medieval knights called to service, reserve the right to send "deputies to supply their places," or, as Roman Catholics do, to pay others to pray for them (163). This view of marriage as social duty—in which one group of women essentially pays another group to marry—reveals the class differences at work in this utopia. The contradiction does not escape Sir George, who observes that should such a program become widespread, "it would confine matrimony to the lower rank of people" (163).

The relationships among the women are modeled on the mother-daughter relationship; that between Miss Mancel and Mrs. Morgan is the model for all others in the novel. Mrs. Morgan, who at fourteen lost her mother, is one of the few children in the novel to have had the nurturing love of a mother—Lady Melvyn's legacy is "the memory of mother-love" that allows Miss Melvyn to love unselfishly and unconditionally, providing "a model of good mothering" that influences the Millenium Hall project, as Linda Dunne observes.[15] Miss Melvyn then becomes a surrogate mother to the orphaned Louisa Mancel, and they eventually develop a romantic friendship.

Another set of close "friends," Harriot Selvyn and Lady Emilia Reynolds, are revealed to be daughter and mother when Lady Emilia confesses her secret on her deathbed. Harriot Selvyn rejects marriage because she is so happy living with her mother-friend. Significantly, when her mother is freed from the position of inculcator of patriarchy, she is also free to teach the daughter how to love and be a friend. It is the position of mother within a patriarchal society that is problematic. Linda Dunne notes that the traditional heroine of the marriage-plot novel survives an inhospitable world through "finding a suitable heterosexual marriage and a country estate," while the women in *Millenium Hall* "escape that world by finding each other and Millenium Hall" (64). [16]

The role of the mother is not a simple one, however. We may agree that mothers are the object of nostalgia, always lost and longed for, but we must recall that mothers are the agents, however unwitting, of patriarchy. Once within the system as wives, they assume the responsibility of initiating their children—especially their daughters—into the patriarchal system in order to keep that system intact. The mother's own desire is necessarily suppressed when she becomes the agent of patriarchy; if her own nostalgia has been invested in motherhood, whereby she can recuperate the union of the mother-child dyad, her subjectivity is least compromised in that union and, for the child, she is a powerful subject who makes things happen. Marriage compromises the mother's subjectivity; her role as socializing agent requires that she assume a false consciousness. Mothers within the patriarchal system have no choice but to inculcate their daughters into the system: witness the conflict of Mrs. Harlowe. To escape this system, they would have to opt out of marriage and motherhood within the patriarchal system, as do the women of Millenium Hall. Scott emphasizes this point: "The first thing a girl is taught is to hide her sentiments, to contradict the thoughts of her heart, and tell all the civil lies which custom has sanctified, *with as much affectation and conceit as her mother*, and when she has acquired all the folly and impertinence of a riper age, and apes the woman more ungracefully than a monkey does a fine gentleman, the parents congratulate themselves with the extremest complacency in the charming education they have given their daughter" (224, my emphasis).[17] The women of Millenium Hall are motherless, yet they mother each other. By choosing not to marry, they also remain childless. They are totally out of the economy that Clarissa Harlowe gives her life to escape.

George E. Haggerty claims that Scott is rewriting motherhood. The only "bad" mother is Lady Melvyn, who is actually a stepmother. Lady Melvyn, a consummate schemer, pretends to be distressed at discovering that Miss Melvyn is engaging in a romance with a farmer's son, when she is actually visiting her friend, Miss Mancel. Haggerty observes that Lady Melvyn's "violent (and feigned) hysteria at illicit sexuality, so clearly a function of patriarchal control, suggests more than the usual fear of female self-determination. Lady Melvyn insists on marriage as a way of separating the two women, whose own relation could be more threatening to patriarchal order (and her own hopes for a secure financial future) than even a liaison with a farmer would be."[18]

Lacking the genuine love of a mother, Lady Melvyn is free to exercise the most violent oppression of her stepdaughter in order to ensure all the imperatives of patriarchy. Scott, Haggerty observes, is distinguishing between a mutually supportive relationship based on goodwill that can only exist in isolation, exemplified in the relationship between Miss Mancel and Miss Melvyn, and the violence of motherhood entrapped within patriarchy.[19]

Isolated on the estate, however, the bodies of the women are desexualized; these bodies, lacking beauty, are an unmarked category in comparison with other bodies on the estate. All but two of the household staff are disabled: the housekeeper has a maimed hand, the cook walks with crutches, the kitchen maid has only one eye, and the dairy maid is deaf. Even the musicians' bodies are unhealthy, one suffering from asthma, another from kidney stones. Most curious of all, however, is the asylum for dwarfs and giants—or "monsters" as they are called—that the women have established on the estate. The monsters live enclosed inside a pale that has been painted green and lined with a hedge of thick evergreens that rises to seven or eight feet. Sir George and Lamont are curious about this enclosure, and wonder whether it is a zoo like the one in which Lord Lamore keeps a collection of exotic animals. The women at first refuse to explain, but Lamont breaks down their resistance. "[S]till I am puzzled," he tells Mrs. Mancel; "what we behold is certainly an inclosure, how can that be without a confinement to those that are within it?" (72). Mrs. Mancel explains that the enclosure contains "an asylum for those poor creatures who are rendered miserable from some natural deficiency or redundancy" (72). By keeping the "poor creatures" enclosed on the estate, Mrs. Mancel asserts that the women are protecting them from abuse by those who would exploit them for financial gain. The fence, she explains, is used to protect them from being seen, not to imprison them.

Linda Dunne notes that the presence of these disabled monsters is a measure of the degree of Christian charity practiced by the ladies. But Miss Mancel's reference to the story of Procrustes suggests that physical difference combined with a lack of money is the real problem. The monsters, Dunne asserts, are "a distorted mirror image of the ladies of Millenium Hall,"[20] who are also "different" in their rejection of marriage and sexuality.

Within this orderly society, sexuality and all strong emotion are repressed or at least hidden. Just as the monsters, so hard to look at, are enclosed, these unruly emotions are left unacknowledged. Dunne suggests that the monsters stand as metaphors for the sexuality of the ladies of the hall,[21] while George Haggerty considers the relationship between Miss Mancel and Mrs. Morgan in the tradition of "romantic friendships" and asserts that the maternal relations in the novel are actually highly eroticized, functioning as a model that presents new forms of female subjectivity and challenges patriarchal culture.[22] Felicity Nussbaum observes that close relationships between women in the novel are frequently represented in "maternal terms" despite "an undercurrent of homoerotic bonding [that] unsettles the narrative"; nevertheless, Nussbaum considers the women's refusal to marry nothing more than an "agreeable deformity," consistent with other examples of deformity or disability in the novel.[23]

While the workers on the estate are maimed, they are productive; because their disabilities are the result of accident or disease, these workers are already integrated into the system of work and continue to work in the sheltered environment of Millenium Hall. The dwarfs and giants, on the other hand, are nature's aberrations, unwitting spectacles to be gawked at. There is a continuum of disability on the estate, which allows the women the privilege of seeming entirely normal within this limited society; they will not be the ones gawked at as long as they remain inside their community.

The confinement of the "monsters," however, is a curious reflection of the position of women in society, whereby women have come to bear the burden of tradition and domesticity. Writing in another context, Judith Williamson has remarked that women, "the guardians of 'personal life,' become a dumping ground for all the values society wants off its back but must be perceived to cherish: a function rather like a zoo, or nature reserve, whereby a culture can proudly proclaim its inclusion of precisely what it has excluded."[24] Even within the pastoral utopia of Scott's Millenium Hall, the structures of patriarchal society are reproduced: the keeping of the "monsters" in their own preserve, like the maintenance of the poor women in cottages off the estate, or the housing of gentlewomen without means in separate quarters, geographically represents the exclusions and displacements of the society the women of the hall are trying to escape. The founders of the estate wish to establish a benevolent social model; nevertheless, this model is achieved by geographically isolating those who are different—in body, class, or means. The presence of these pockets of difference is then proclaimed as benevolence, and the society is represented as inclusionary, despite an internal structure that tells a very different story.

The geography of the estate reveals other displacements and exclusions. The land itself is pastoral and idyllic: there are open pastures teeming with sheep and cattle, woods filled with wildlife, streams stocked with fish, elaborate gardens, and lush hedges. The fertility of this community is all contained in the land; in this feminine Arcadia, the women's bodies are mapped as sexless. There is no sex in the house; all sexuality has been relegated to the land, which is productive in ways that the women's bodies are not.

The women of Millenium Hall have escaped the primary male-controlled economic system with an alternative economy based on communal and feminist principles, which "appropriates financial resources not to build or maintain private family fortunes but to nurture and protect the poor and unfortunate, the creatures of the natural world, and most importantly, other women."[25] The model community of Millenium Hall, removed from society, is relatively (if artificially) free of gender constraints but is not entirely without implications of class: it does, after all, take a certain amount of money to fund this community of women. The model, moreover, is that of a convent, or a feudal society in which the leaders of the community (that is, the ones with the money) assume management of the estate and care of the poor, aged, or disabled.

The nostalgia of Scott's novel is decidedly uneven. It articulates a feminine nostalgia in its construction of a unified community modeled on a mother-child relation and based on a domestic, self-sufficient economy in which the home is empowered, a place of productive work, a complement to worksites outside the home; nevertheless, a traditional, masculine nostalgia occasionally surfaces in the women's discourse, as we shall see in the speech of Harriot Trentham. Despite the radical vision of the Millenium Hall social project, the model retains a paternalistic, benevolent approach to social action.

Millenium Hall represents the unevenness of Scott's ideology. The apparently seamless community of the estate is achieved only at the price of exclusion and bracketing of difference, and retirement from society and the repression of sexuality; the entire novel is, as Vincent Carretta has observed, "a utopia of confines" due to the many "restrictions and boundaries" of "a benevolent hierarchy overseen by a loving patriarch that Scott sees as necessary to the happiness and order of human existence."[26] The estate itself is enclosed by the group of trees that are so evident in the book's often-reproduced frontispiece, which shows the narrator and his companion, Lamont, at the moment of their "discovery" peering through the enclosure of the trees at the hall.

THE GEOGRAPHY OF *MILLENIUM HALL*

Millenium Hall, ultimately, is nothing more than Julie's Elysee garden, a small island of freedom that is encapsulated. It is an illusory, harmonious space that does not engage its surrounding world, whatever implications it may have for an idealized world, or future utopia. This space requires protection and careful cultivation, just as the asylum for the dwarfs and giants does.

The women, significantly, do not all live at the hall. Those women who do not marry and have no resources, the poor unmarried gentlewomen, will be sent to live in the ruined mansion that is being restored, thereby segregating them from the ladies of modest fortune living in the main house. Women cannot live without money; the women of resources who operate Millenium Hall are restoring this ruined mansion to house women who cannot "earn" a living through an economic system based on marriage.

Ironically, the women come into possession of the mansion because the previous owner was a wealthy miser: having refused to spend money to keep up the house, he dies sprawled out on a chest of gold, his estate in decay all around him. An impoverished and libertine nephew inherits the gold, but because he squanders it through decadent living, he must sell the mansion to satisfy his gambling debts. The patriarchal system, which prevents a free flow of resources by placing those resources instead into the hands of socially irresponsible individual men,

Frontispiece from Sarah Robinson Scott's *A Description of Millenium Hall, and the Country Adjacent* (London: Printed for J. Newbery, 1764). With permission from the University of Chicago Library, Special Collections Research Center.

results in ruin; a communal approach to economy, on the other hand, in which all share resources according to their need and give according to their ability, results in adequate housing for all.

In addition to the communal house of the six main characters and the restored mansion for the poor gentlewomen, there are the single-person cottages for the old peasant women, each of whom contributes whatever services she can. There are also cottage schools for the children of the poor villagers, in which girls receive education limited only by interest and ability. Another group of girls are taught service skills and are given dowries. The ladies also purchase and manage a carpet factory that serves as a sheltered workshop for the villagers. In this benevolent workplace, children and old people who cannot work as quickly as younger people are paid at a higher rate so that their income will not be unequal to that of the faster workers. It remains, however, a system of wages and piecework; there is no true domestic economy or cottage industry in the novel. Class distinctions clearly obtain in the community: the girls who live in the hall study art and music, while the children of the poor are prepared to go into service and are trained to be content with their lot in life. There is little, if any, social mobility.

Like the social structure of the community, the geography and landscape of *Millenium Hall* are contained and orderly: pastures, gardens, and vegetable beds are all neatly tended. Such tidiness reflects the clearly defined segments of the Millenium Hall community. Despite the women's desire to do good works, it is not an accident that the monsters, those with essential differences, are enclosed in a "natural" asylum behind a nearly invisible pale, partly obscured by tall hedges—a "natural" enclosure for "natural" deformities. The concealing and confinement of difference within the estate are an exercise of power, an attempt to render the space of Millenium Hall neutral or transparent by erasing bodies that are inscribed with physical difference. The visual is central to claims to know, and by enclosing the monsters and impeding the gaze, the women of Millenium Hall simultaneously resist the claim to know of the (male) observer and exercise their own imperative and authority.[27]

The unevenness of Scott's model community is evident in the nostalgia articulated by Harriot Trentham. "The poor man," observes Harriot, "sighs after the days when his father married; then cleanliness was a woman's chief personal ornament, half the quantity of silk sufficed for her cloaths, variety of trumpery ornaments were not thought of, her husband's business employed her attention, and her children were the objects of her care. When he came home, wearied with the employment of the day, he found her ready to receive him. . . . But in a world so changed, a man dare not venture on marriage which promises him no comfort, and may occasion his ruin, nor wishes for children, whose mother's neglect may expose them to destruction" (164–65). Curiously, Harriot Trentham expresses the nostalgia of the "poor man"—she articulates his desires, which are entirely consistent with contemporary domestic ideology. She does not articulate any specifically feminine nostalgia, although she laments a breakdown of maternal care and attention to children. This "world so changed" suffers from the loss of the traditional household, for which, in Mrs. Trentham's formulation, women are blamed: their frivolity and love of luxury, according to her, have contributed to the erosion of the family. This nostalgia is quaint, almost picturesque, and one that must be borne by both women and the poor. Maintaining tradition and the status quo always has a price, one that is usually paid by oppressed or marginalized groups, so that privileged groups can enjoy a "tradition" that benefits them alone.

The Author and the Textual Landscape

Gillian Rose notes that when historically specific bodies are repressed in the service of geography, imaginary bodies are constructed in their place. Rose observes that "fundamental to its construction and possession of other imaginary bodies is the masculinist denial of the male body; others are trapped in their brute materiality by the rational minds of white men. This erasure of his own specificity allows the master subject to assume that he can see everything."[28]

In the traditional geographical work that Rose discusses here, the middle-class male body becomes invisible, an unmarked category. Geographers become "invisible observers of social life . . . making sense of it all, its reproductions, resistance and contradiction."[29] This invisible position is that of Richardson, Rousseau, Pope, and Goldsmith, who were both empowered and threatened by their authorial privilege, a privilege they were able to take for granted but that nevertheless left them keenly aware of the sterility and loss associated with that disembodied authorial privilege. By aligning the body with the feminine, these male authors attempted to rise above their own "brute materiality," yet recuperate the passion associated with the body.

In order to assume some sort of visibility, these authors must reconstruct themselves within the texts; their position is so tenuous, so invisible, that they must assume a presence in the text by walking onto the stage of their text or by inserting themselves into it. In Richardson's case, he makes himself visible as the editor of the huge textual body of *Clarissa*, the one who can keep the narrative under control. As the creator of Sir Charles Grandison, the "good" man, Richardson is that invisible point, that empty geographer's space from which he can gaze at every surrounding place or person. In the case of Sir Charles, the peculiar emptiness of his character, which so many critics have noticed, is perhaps due to his own position as master subject who defines and prescribes the behavior of everyone around him.

In "Eloisa to Abelard," Pope also struggles with invisibility; he adopts Eloisa's voice to connect with her passion. The castrated Abelard—truly an empty space—is able to assume the position of the one who knows, ruled as he is by pure rationality. The price of his mastery, however, is high. Rousseau, as does Richardson, asserts a presence in *Julie* as the editor, controlling access to the letters of Julie and Saint-Preux, holding back some and editing others. His creation of Saint-Preux as the sentimental man, one who can live in the body, nevertheless acknowledges the failure of this "new" man to assert any type of authority: Saint-Preux does not have the power of Julie's father or husband; nor does he have property, wealth, or social position. While Julie is able to redeem herself and those around her by yielding up her body as sacrifice, Saint-Preux merely disappears from the text; his life in the body has no symbolic importance.

Oliver Goldsmith uses a series of narrators or personas to negotiate his own presence in his texts, rather than inserting himself directly into it as Richardson, Rousseau, and Pope do. The narrators of "The Revolution in Low Life" and "The Deserted Village" assume personas that are consistently nostalgic, just as Dr. Primrose is nostalgic; they concur in longing for an imaginary golden age, locating this earthly paradise in a village, or, in the Vicar's case, in the home and family, and in placing the burden of nostalgia on the bodies of women.

Sarah Scott's *Millenium Hall* exhibits a different relation to the fictive domains of body and landscape. The women of the hall are aware that the invisibility of the masculine subject is not available to them in society at large: by enclosing the monsters within the asylum, and by enclosing themselves within the estate, the women of Millenium Hall are able to assume the invisibility of the unmarked category. Scott chose a different sort of authorial presence for herself: rather than insert herself into the text as editor, or through the co-opting of a female voice, she wove her own story into the text and gave each of the characters an autonomous voice. While all the stories are contained within Sir George Ellison's frame, each story is nevertheless an individual vignette recounted in a distinct voice; Sir George may provide the frame narrative and take these stories out to the world, but the women's voices, their individual points of view and their occasional inconsistencies, resist any overarching, seamless narrative.

Scott allows the women in her novel their own voices. She is, of course, present in the novel as a character: that of Mrs. Morgan, who suffers through an unhappy marriage before retiring to a community of women.[30] This story is Scott's own thinly disguised autobiography; she is present in her novel as a character, ostensibly minimizing her role as observer—unlike Richardson, Rousseau, or Pope, who assert their presence boldly as the "editors" of their texts, remaining external to the texts themselves. Mrs. Morgan's character provides the money and energy to found the community, but despite the agency assigned to Mrs. Morgan, Scott relegates the narrative frame to a fictional male narrator. By integrating her own narrative into the novel, by fictionalizing her identity, by surrendering the narrative thread to the voices of the characters, and by allowing a male character to provide the frame of the novel, Scott shares narrative control of her text. She conceals, rather than proclaims, her presence in the novel; while Richardson, Rousseau, Pope, and Goldsmith consciously position themselves outside their texts—making *objects* of their texts—Scott breaks down the distance between herself and her text. She embeds herself and her story within *Millenium Hall*, thereby renegotiating her own relationship to the space, or body, of her book.

The retirement celebrated by Pope in "Windsor Forest" and Goldsmith's narrators in "The Revolution in Low Life" and *The Deserted Village* is enjoyed by the women of the Millenium Hall community. Sir George Ellison, weary of a world that has broken his body and health, nevertheless resists the idea of retirement; ironically, he "discovers" Millenium Hall on a tour taken just prior to a planned rest at his country estate. As in the case of geographers, Sir George's ostensible "self-erasure" through the gesture of allowing the women to tell their own stories is "contradicted by the narcissistic assertion of self through what is seen"[31] and the use made of that claim to knowledge.

In contrast, Rousseau's Julie, in her garden, assumes a different position from which to view the land. She continually insists on this position in her confrontation with Saint-Preux, who chooses to see it much in the same way Sir George Ellison sees Millenium Hall—from the position of the white male colonist. Nevertheless, her garden is walled and her consciousness, like that of Harriot Trentham, is false.

How would a true feminine reworking of space, and nostalgia, look? Writing about the mother and child paintings of Mary Cassatt and Berthe Morisot, Griselda Pollock has observed that a feminine rearticulation of space would have that space resist functioning as the object of the mastering gaze and become instead the "locus of relationships,"[32] a concept that describes the attempts of Sarah Scott to re-negotiate space in Millenium Hall.

What Scott and the women of Millenium Hall achieve is precisely this transference of the point of vision: enclosed within their own space, perspective changes. But in order to stop functioning as a space subject to masculine gaze, they must immure themselves. The presence of Sir George as narrator reveals the impossibility, for Scott, fully to cease being the object of the gaze. No matter how tightly the community functions, it is always subject to "discovery" by a colonizing explorer. The story of the discovery must be taken into the world by that male explorer, while the women of Millenium Hall can only realize happiness and fulfillment through retirement from the world. In a novel that is all too ready to abandon the past and look forward to the future, there is no need for these women to bear the burden of nostalgia or to be locked into an imagined past that seems to be a golden age.

In Conclusion: Body, Landscape, and Nostalgia

The cultural nostalgia of the eighteenth century developed out of the rapid social and economic change of that century. The sense of loss, the longing for a golden age, contributed to the textual production of the period; often, as we have seen, that longing—the "desire to desire"—was invested in the fictive domains of body and landscape. The female body, especially, became an object of fascination, invested with nostalgia for some imaginary coherence and assigned the burden of tradition and redemption.

The land—so frequently linked to the female body in material ways, as we see in the cases of Clarissa Harlowe, Clementina della Porretta, and Julie d'Étange—also bears the burden of tradition. The fascination for the picturesque, evident at least as early as Pope's "Eloisa," gains ground in the second half of the eighteenth century. Social anxiety about changes in land ownership and a related increase in social mobility are reflected in the attempt to preserve, in nostalgic fantasy, an image of an older countryside that is "natural" and unmarked by rapid enclosure. These picturesque landscapes, as portrayed in both literature and art, are invested with social values that reflect an imaginary golden age of uncomplicated social relations. The burden of nostalgia, however, is consistently placed onto the bodies of women and the poor.

Because the growth of domestic ideology and the erosion of women's work in the eighteenth century increasingly confined women to the home, it is not a coincidence that the texts I have chosen as the focus for this book return again and again to questions of the family and home. The psychoanalytic basis for nostalgia is likely found within the family itself: in the formation of male subjectivity, the denial of dependency leads to domination and power imbalance. Jessica Benjamin observes that "since the child continues to need the mother, since man continues to need woman, the absolute assertion of independence requires possessing and controlling the needed object. The intention is not to do without her but to make sure that her alien otherness is either assimilated or controlled, that her own subjectivity nowhere asserts itself in a way that could make his dependency upon her a conscious insult to his sense of freedom."[33]

The implications of these observations for the textual strategies of the authors I have examined seem obvious: Richardson creates and controls the body of Clarissa Harlowe, constructing his own text in the process; Pope likewise co-opts the passion of Eloisa and Lodona; Rousseau assigns Julie the burden of redemption, and although he allows her a garden, it is, as Scott's Millennium Hall is, a limited utopia; Goldsmith places the burden of tradition onto women and the poor. By assigning the burden of nostalgia and the past to the bodies of women, or to bodies of land, some eighteenth-century authors negotiated their own social and authorial anxiety; their works, in turn, reflect a larger sentiment within society in general, one that increasingly restricted women to that most segregated of spaces, the home, where nostalgia is so often located.

The longing for a golden age is a sentiment that has appeared in literature since long before Johannes Hofer coined the term in 1688. That homesickness would be medicalized is an interesting mark of the times; that Hofer's new term would be readily adopted and the "disease" quickly absorbed into the cultural and social milieu is hardly surprising. It was a development, in some ways, long overdue. The seventeenth and

eighteenth centuries were centuries of rapid change: new ways of looking at the world were reflected in new models of the human body and
new relationships to the landscape. Political change, imperial expansion, and the development of consumerism helped create new kinds of
social and economic relations, resulting in increased social anxiety that
sought consolation through the displacement of anxiety onto gender relations and the household. As social relations became increasingly unstable, a new ideology of gender and domesticity would provide the
structural stability missing in the world at large.

The nostalgia of the eighteenth-century texts I have examined is a
conservative reaction to change that is also a pleasurable indulgence,
offering a fantasy of plenitude and wholeness in stark contrast to everyday realities. The psychoanalytic root of nostalgia may be a longing for
uninterrupted union with the mother that exists prior to the child's
entry into subjectivity, but as such, nostalgia represents a longing for a
sense of wholeness that is more theoretical than actually remembered.
In social terms, nostalgia is also a longing for an imaginary golden age,
for "the way things used to be," a time never experienced, yet perceived
as simpler and better. The objects of nostalgic desire are imagined referents that require constant reinforcement through the contemporary performance of our nostalgia; such performance, in turn, convinces us that
our nostalgia is real.

We have much to learn from studying the development of nostalgia
as a cultural category as it emerged in the eighteenth century. Cultural
nostalgia is not an uncomplicated celebration of the past. By oversimpli-
fying and reducing the past to its pleasing elements, nostalgia can be
dangerously reductive, a false consciousness. By refusing to acknowledge the social contradictions of the past and escaping those of the present through immersion in "memories" of a glorified past, nostalgia as a
social and cultural posture can thwart the possibility of constructive social change. The pleasures of nostalgia are tempting, and its potential
for generating creative work is rich; such pleasures and possibilities,
however, should not blind us to nostalgia's pitfalls. By studying the
emergence of nostalgia as a cultural phenomenon in the eighteenth century, we can place contemporary nostalgia in its historical context. Like
eighteenth-century nostalgia, the nostalgia of the twenty-first century is
a response to rapid social change; by recognizing the history of our nostalgia, we can learn to use nostalgia for creative social, political, and
artistic ends. As a society, we have a responsibility to acknowledge all
of our past, and to look critically at our own nostalgia.

Notes

NOTES TO CHAPTER 1

1. Sigmund Freud, "On Transience," *The Standard Edition of the Complete Psychological Works*, ed. James Strachey (London: Hogarth, 1974; repr., 1986), 14:305. All subsequent citations are to this edition. Freud wrote "On Transience" in 1915, several months after he wrote his "Thoughts for the Times on War and Death" and "Mourning and Melancholia" (which would be published two years later, in 1917). The young poet and the silent friend were identified by Herbert Lehmann in 1966 as Rainer Maria Rilke and Lou Andreas-Salomé. See John Paul Russo's discussion of Freud's "On Transience" in "Logos and Transience in Franco Rella," *Differentia* 1 (1986): 187–223. It can hardly be a coincidence that Freud's essays on loss were written in direct response to a real historical situation: the shock and destruction of World War I. Freud's reaction to the shattering of the world as he had known it was to produce some of the richest and most significant writing of his career: in addition to his essays on loss, he wrote "On Narcissism" (1914), "The Unconscious" (1915), "Instincts and Their Vicissitudes" (1915), and "Repression" (1915) during this period.

2. See Harvey Kaplan, "The Psychopathology of Nostalgia," *Psychoanalytic Review* 74 (1987): 465–86.

3. Joseph Banks, *The Endeavour Journal of Joseph Banks*, August 25, 1768–July 12, 1771, 2 vols, page 319. *The Papers of Sir Joseph Banks*. arranged by B. P. Sandford, 1998, Mitchell Library of New South Wales, http://www.sl.nsw.gov.au/banks/series_03/03_741.cfm. February 16, 2006.

4. Jonathan Lamb, *Preserving the Self in the South Seas, 1680–1840* (Chicago: University of Chicago Press, 2001), 120–21. In chapter 4, "Scurvy," Lamb examines the links among the intense cravings, mood swings, and acute sensory perceptions experienced by those suffering from scurvy, reporting an unusual cure: "burying the sick up to the neck in soil," literally satisfying the longing for land (123).

5. Robert Markley, "Sentimentality as Performance: Shaftesbury, Sterne, and the Theatrics of Virtue," in *The New Eighteenth Century: Theory, Politics, English Literature*, ed. Felicity Nussbaum and Laura Brown (New York: Methuen, 1987), 212.

6. The best-known study of the companionate marriage is Lawrence Stone, *The Family, Sex and Marriage in England 1500–1800* (New York: HarperCollins, 1977). Stone's study, despite its considerable influence, has been widely criticized for its male perspective and its failure to consider the lives of women outside marriage and the family; his use of primary sources has also been criticized as inadequate. See, for example, Lois G. Schwoerer, "Seventeenth-Century English Women Engraved in Stone?" *Albion* 16 (1984): 389–403; David Cressy, "Foucault, Stone, Shakespeare and Social History," *ELH* 21,2 (Spring 1991): 121–33.

7. Lefebvre, *The Production of Space*, trans. Donald Nicholson-Smith (Oxford and

159

Cambridge, Mass.: Blackwell, 1994), 28–30. Lefebvre calls on the body to help explain social space, observing that

> the relationship to space of a "subject" who is a member of a group or society implies his relationship to his own body and vice versa. Considered overall, social practice presupposes the use of the body. . . . As for *representations of the body*, they derive from accumulated scientific knowledge, disseminated with an admixture of ideology: from the body's relations with nature and with its surroundings or "milieu." Bodily *lived* experience, for its part, may be both highly complex and quite peculiar, because "culture" intervenes here, with its illusory immediacy. . . . (40, italics in original)

8. Lefebvre, *Production of Space*, 30.

9. Jordanova, *Sexual Visions: Images of Gender in Science and Medicine Between the Eighteenth and Twentieth Centuries* (Madison: University of Wisconsin Press, 1989), 156.

10. John Urry observes that once history has been cleaned up and commodified, "it is made safe, sterile and shorn of its capacity to generate risk and danger, subversion and seduction." See *Consuming Places* (London: Routledge, 1995), 219. The "danger" that lurks in social space, for both Urry and Lefebvre, must be continually negotiated.

11. Butler, *Bodies That Matter: On the Discursive Limits of "Sex"* (New York and London: Routledge, 1993), 108–9. Writing of castration anxiety, Butler describes the anxiety not as one of loss, but as *"the spectre of the recognition that* [the phallus] *was always already lost, the vanquishing of the fantasy that it might ever have been possessed—the loss of nostalgia's referent"* (101, italics in original).

12. On loss, melancholia, and creativity see Julia Kristeva, *Desire in Language: A Semiotic Approach to Literature and Art* : *Revolution and Poetic Language*, trans. Leon S. Roudiez (New York: Columbia University Press, 1980); Kristeva, *Black Sun: Depression and Melancholia*, trans. Leon S. Roudiez (New York: Columbia University Press, 1989); Melanie Klein, "Infantile Anxiety-Situations Reflected in a Work of Art and in the Creative Impulse" and "The Importance of Symbol Formation in the Development of the Ego" *Contributions to Psycho-Analysis 1921–1945* (London: Hogarth Press, 1948), 227–50; and Hanna Segal, "Notes on Symbol Formation," *International Journal of Psychoanalysis* 38 (1957): 391–405.

13. Stewart, *On Longing: Narratives of the Miniature, the Gigantic, the Souvenir, the Collection* (Baltimore, MD: Johns Hopkins University Press, 1983), 133.

14. Williams, *The Country and the City* (New York: Oxford University Press, 1975), 35.

15. See, for example, Johanna Spyri's *Heidi*, in which Heidi's sleepwalking is cured by a return to her mountain village.

16. Williams, *Country and the City*, 43.

17. Jameson, "Beyond the Cave: Demystifying the Ideology of Modernism," in *Contemporary Marxist Literary Criticism*, ed. Francis Mulhern (London: Longman, 1972), 172.

18. Stewart, *On Longing*, 23.

19. Jameson, *The Political Unconscious: Narrative as a Socially Symbolic Act* (Ithaca, NY: Cornell University Press, 1981), 82, italics in original.

20. Brooks, *Body Work: Objects of Desire in Modern Narrative* (Cambridge, MA and London: Harvard University Press, 1993), xiii.

21. Ibid., xii–xiii.

22. Ibid., 5.

23. Burton, *The Anatomy of Melancholy* (1621; repr., New York: Dutton, 1932), 355.

Much of the thought on nervous diseases in the eighteenth century was influenced by Burton. Among the diseases suffered by young unmarried women was "greensickness," defined by Samuel Johnson in his *Dictionary* as "The disease of maids, so called from the paleness which it produces." Greensickness would be more thoroughly explored in the nineteenth century as a form of anemia that gives a greenish pallor to the skin; "chlorosis," as it was called, was also linked to pica and other eating disorders.

24. Turner, *The Body in Society: New Explorations in Social Theory* (Oxford: Basil Blackwell, 1984), 112–13.

25. Ibid., 41.

26. Mackenzie, *The Man of Feeling*, ed. Kenneth C. Slagle (New York: Norton, 1958), 66. Hereafter parenthetically cited in text.

27. Mullan, *Sentiment and Sociability: The Language of Feeling in the Eighteenth Century* (Oxford: Clarendon, 1988), 213. Mullan's examination of the connections among the sentimental novel, sociability, and medical writing in the eighteenth century has been an important source in my thinking about nostalgia, and its influence will be apparent throughout this study.

28. On the topic of "new" diseases, Turner notes that "disease" is as much a cultural category as "health" or "illness," as all these categories depend on a judgment that evolves from a theoretically "ideal state." Disease, therefore, is "not a fact, but a relationship [that] is the product of classificatory processes," and "new" diseases represent "a shift in explanatory frameworks or the identification of a new niche" within a categorical frame (*Body in Society*, 208).

29. George Rosen, "Nostalgia: A 'Forgotten' Psychological Disorder," *Clio Medica* 10 (1975): 30.

30. Stanley Jackson, *Melancholia and Depression: From Hippocratic Times to Modern Times* (New Haven, CT: Yale University Press, 1986), 373.

31. Rosen, "Nostalgia," 32.

32. Ibid., 30–33.

33. Qtd. in ibid., 34.

34. Willis McCann, "Nostalgia: A Review of the Literature," *Psychological Bulletin* 38 (1941): 180; Rosen, "Nostalgia," 35.

35. Samuel Richardson, *Clarissa, or the History of a Young Lady*, ed. Angus Ross (Harmondsworth, UK: Penguin, 1985), letter 338, p. 1075. Hereafter cited in text by letter and page number.

36. Qtd. in Rosen, "Nostalgia," 36.

37. Jackson, *Melancholia and Depression*, 376.

38. Rosen, "Nostalgia," 42.

39. Kaplan, "The Psychopathology of Nostalgia," 467–69. Kaplan suggests that this nostalgic compromise is often a solution to the disillusionment of adolescence, leading to the glamorizing of a particular object or situation and overvaluing a certain object by minimizing or denying other characteristics of that object; moreover, issues of "valor, courage, virtue, and morality"—issues that predominate in *Clarissa*—are overcathected ("Psychopathology," 471–73).

40. Kaplan, "Psychopathology," 470, 482.

41. The quintessential example of such textual pleasure is, of course, Proust—an example that Kaplan does not fail to acknowledge. See "Psychopathology," esp. pp. 467–68.

42. Jameson, "Nostalgia for the Present," *South Atlantic Quarterly* 88 (1989): 523.

43. Cheyne himself was on this diet, as was Richardson. After arriving in London

from Aberdeen, Cheyne enjoyed an active social life centered around coffeehouses and other places of diversion. To his dismay, his weight ballooned to over four hundred pounds; hence, the development of the low diet.

44. Jocelyn Harris notes that this letter is radically different from the rest of the work, and she quotes the *Gentlemen's Magazine* as observing that this section is distinguished by "curious particulars in geography, which the reader would not expect" (November 1753, xxxiii, qtd. in Harris, introduction to *The History of Sir Charles Grandison* by Samuel Richardson [Oxford: Oxford University Press, 1986], 498n445). Harris also notes the unusual language of the fifth paragraph, in which the vehicle for travel through the mountains is described as being "a kind of horse, as it is called with you, with two poles"; the phrase "as it is called with you," Harris observes, seems to indicate that this section was likely written by someone from outside England (*Grandison*, 499n446).

45. Pope, "Eloisa to Abelard" in *The Poems of Alexander Pope*, ed. John Butt. Reduced version of the Twickenham text. (New Haven, CT: Yale University Press, 1963), line 106. Hereafter cited in text by line number.

46. Bermingham, *Landscape and Ideology: The English Rustic Tradition, 1740–1860* (Berkeley: University of California Press, 1986), 67.

Notes to Chapter 2

1. Doody, *A Natural Passion: A Study of the Novels of Samuel Richardson* (Oxford: Clarendon, 1974), 171; Eagleton, *The Rape of Clarissa: Writing, Sexuality and Class Struggle in Samuel Richardson* (Minneapolis: University of Minnesota Press, 1982), 90; Barker-Benfield, *The Culture of Sensibility: Sex and Society in Eighteenth-Century Britain* (Chicago: University of Chicago Press, 1992), 35; Frega, "Speaking in Hunger: Conditional Consumption as Discourse in Clarissa," *Studies in the Literary Imagination* 28, no. 1 (1995), 87.

2. Samuel Richardson, *Clarissa, or the History of a Young Lady*, ed. Angus Ross (Harmondsworth, UK: Penguin, 1985), letter 338, p.1075. Hereafter cited in text by letter and page number.

3. Barker-Benfield, *Culture of Sensibility*, xxvi–xxvii.

4. Pope, "Epistle II. To a Lady" in *The Poems of Alexander Pope*, ed. John Butt. Reduced version of the Twickenham text (New Haven, CT: Yale University Press, 1963), line 216. Hereafter cited in text by line number.

5. Laqueur, *Making Sex: Body and Gender from the Greeks to Freud* (Cambridge, MA: Harvard University Press, 1990), 3.

6. Williams, *The Country and the City* (New York: Oxford University Press, 1975), 43.

7. Butler, *Bodies That Matter: On the Discursive Limits of "Sex"* (New York: Routledge, 1993), 108–9.

8. See Robert Markley's discussion of the way Shaftesbury's writings were nevertheless co-opted by "writers less interested in defending upper-class privilege than in pressing their own claims to the social status of gentlemen" in "Sentimentality as Performance: Shaftesbury, Sterne, and the Theatrics of Virtue" in *The New Eighteenth Century: Theory, Politics, English Literature*, ed. Felicity Nussbaum and Laura Brown (New York: Methuen, 1987), 212.

9. Barker-Benfield, *Culture of Sensibility*, 112–14.

10. Brooks, *Body Work: Objects of Desire in Modern Narrative* (Cambridge, MA: Harvard University Press, 1993), 15.

11. In *Literary Fat Ladies: Rhetoric, Gender, Property,* Patricia Parker writes of dilated female bodies that defer closure of the text; significantly, though, that deferral is (necessarily) always temporary because texts must come to an end eventually. Seldom does the female body, dilated or otherwise, maintain any real control over the text; a more usual model is one in which closure is deferred after "a topsy-turvy middle space of female rebellion," finally ending in "the proper marital hierarchy" (London: Methuen, 1987), 19. The alternative to marriage for female characters is, of course, death. In the case of Clarissa, the meaning of her body is overwhelmingly dilated, even while her physical body shrinks and dissolves.

12. Turner, *The Body and Society: New Explorations in Social Theory* (Oxford: Basil Blackwell, 1984), 41.

13. Chronic disease, however, does not require the sick role; for example, a diabetic who actively manages his or her diabetes, despite being under the supervision of a medical professional, can reject the "sick role" and consider himself or herself a healthy person who is able to participate in an unrestricted variety of social activities.

14. Barker-Benfield, *Culture of Sensibility,* 26.

15. Of course, men were also advised to take the waters at spa towns, and Richardson himself visited Tunbridge Wells.

16. The relationship between women and food is explored in the studies of Joan Jacobs Brumberg, *Fasting Girls: The History of Anorexia Nervosa* (Cambridge, MA: Harvard University Press, 1988), and Caroline Walker Bynum, *Holy Feast and Holy Fast: The Religious Significance of Food to Medieval Women* (Berkeley: University of California Press, 1987). See also Donnalee Frega, "Speaking in Hunger: Conditional Consumption as Discourse in *Clarissa.*" *Studies in the Literary Imagination,* 28, no. 1 (1995): 87–103.

17. Turner cites anorexia as an example of a doomed attempt to "master" the body: although the anorexic tries to control the body through exercise and restriction of food intake, the body always has the last word, by shutting down functions, such as menstruation, or even by ceasing to live.

18. *Clarissa* was indeed a body for Richardson: in a letter to Aaron Hill on October 29, 1746, Richardson remarks that some friends have suggested a manner of shortening *Clarissa,* but Richardson objects, "I must not part with a Limb, nor yet with any of the Sentiments; but do as the *above-weight* Jockeys at Newmarket, whatever I take away, sweat it out of the Whole." *Selected Letters,* ed. John Carroll (Oxford: Clarendon Press, 1964), 70.

19. The excess of letters describing Clarissa's slow death hints at textual "repetition," in which the trauma that leads to her death is not remembered or narrated, but is compulsively "repeated" in the continual act of writing. The analysand, Freud reminds us in "Remembering, Repeating, and Working Through," always acts instead of remembering, in *The Standard Edition of the Complete Psychological Works,* vol. 12, ed. James Strachey (London: Hogarth, 1974).

20. Eagleton, *Rape of Clarissa,* 61.

21. Price, *The Anthology and the Rise of the Novel: From Richardson to George Eliot* (Cambridge: Cambridge University Press, 2000), 28. Also see Terry Castle, *Clarissa's Ciphers: Meaning and Disruption in Richardson's "Clarissa"* (Ithaca, NY: Cornell University Press, 1982).

22. At this moment in the text, Lovelace seems particularly like Clarissa, or even Richardson himself: a collector and editor of letters.

23. Ferguson, "Rape and the Rise of the Novel," *Representations* 20 (1987): 106.

24. Gwilliam, *Samuel Richardson's Fictions of Gender* (Stanford, CA: Stanford University Press, 1993), 107.

25. Eagleton, *Rape of Clarissa*, 62–63.

26. William Warner seems to read Richardson's writing project into that of Clarissa herself. Warner suggests that Clarissa's death is "the crucial initial act" in the writing of her book, enabling her to "tie the ends of life into a neat circle, something complete and secure." Indeed, Warner asserts, Clarissa writes her book as a linguistic substitute for herself, a means by which she can fix a meaning to her own life; moreover, Clarissa is convinced her death will give her book credibility (*Reading Clarissa: The Struggles of Interpretation* [New Haven, CT: Yale University Press, 1979], 76). I am convinced, on the other hand, that her death gives credibility to Richardson's book, and meaning to his project. The story of Clarissa's "long illness" would be much less compelling.

27. Phillippe Ariès observes that human "insignificance" is a Pascalian idea and quotes from Jacques-Bénigne Bossuet's *Meditation sur la brièveté de la vie* (1648): "I am nothing. . . . I am a nonentity; the world had no need of me" (*The Hour of Our Death*, trans. Helen Weaver [New York: Knopf, 1981], 343).

28. Everett Zimmerman observes that the letters gathered by Clarissa help her create a "monument" of herself; the letters may be fragmentary, but their collection and arrangement form a "history" (*The Boundaries of Fiction: History and the Eighteenth-Century Novel* [Ithaca, NY: Cornell University Press, 1996], 117).

29. The erotic aspects of death had been well incorporated into literature and art by the eighteenth century. Sculptures of swooning and suffering holy women, such as Bernini's *Ecstasy of St. Teresa* (1645–52) or *The Ecstasy of the Blessed Ludovica Albertoni* (1671–74), testify to the intricate relation between death and desire. Notes Phillippe Ariès, the "mystical ecstasies" of these holy women are "ecstasies of love and death. . . . The confusion between death and pleasure is so total that the first does not stop the second, but on the contrary, heightens it. The dead body becomes in its turn an object of desire" (*The Hour of Our Death*, 373). Death, with its prolonged suffering, becomes a pleasurable ideal for Clarissa, and serves, to borrow Freud's phrase, as a "substitute for the lost narcissism of childhood in which [the child] was [her] own ideal." Moreover, notes Freud, the formation of such an ideal is connected to sublimation, or the redirection of libido "towards an aim other than, and remote from, that of sexual satisfaction" ("On Narcissism: An Introduction," *The Standard Edition of the Complete Psychological Works*, trans. and ed. James Strachey (London: Hogarth, 1974), vol. 14, 94.

30. Harvey Kaplan, "The Psychopathology of Nostalgia," *Psychoanalytic Review* 74, no. 4 (1987): 471.

31. Doody, *Natural Passion*, 172–73.

32. Ibid., 174–75. The dramatic impact of Clarissa's coffin is so great that an illustration of *Clarissa's House* appears as the frontispiece to vol. 7, in *Clarissa*, 7th ed. See Doody, *Natural Passion*, plate 2.

33. Visual imagery is a part of Richardson's writing style as well. See Doody, *Natural Passion*, esp. chap. 9, and Janet E. Aikens, "Richardson's 'Speaking Pictures'" in *Samuel Richardson: Tercentenary Essays*, ed. Margaret Anne Doody and Peter Sabor (Cambridge: Cambridge University Press, 1989).

34. See Elizabeth Kowaleski-Wallace's discussion of Mrs. Sinclair's death scene in *Consuming Subjects: Women, Shopping, and Business in the Eighteenth Century* (New York: Columbia University Press, 1997), esp. the chapter on "Businesswomen."

35. Kristeva, *The Power of Horror: An Essay on Abjection*, trans. Leon S. Roudiez (New York: Columbia University Press, 1982), 3–4, italics in original.

36. Ibid., 4.

37. It is worth noting that childbirth would have been associated with a high risk of bodily infection in the eighteenth century; despite the early work of physicians such as Charles White and Alexander Gordon, death of puerperal fever was disturbingly frequent prior to the work of Ignaz Semmelweis in the midnineteenth century. More curious still, for my analysis, is the peculiar conjunction of life and death found in Semmelweis's work: the source of infection in one of the Vienna Hospital's maternity wards was traced to the failure of medical students to wash their hands between sessions in the dissecting room and sessions in the maternity ward. The spread of infection worked both ways, of course; Semmelweis began his study of puerperal sepsis after his mentor died of the disease as a result of pricking his finger while dissecting a cadaver and subsequently performing a vaginal examination (Richard A. Leonardo, *History of Surgery* [New York: Froben Press, 1943], 332–33; Owen H. Wangensteen and Sarah D. Wangensteen, *The Rise of Surgery: From Empiric Craft to Scientific Discipline* [Minneapolis: University of Minnesota Press, 1978], 410–17).

38. Cheyne, *The English Malady: or a Treatise of Nervous Diseases of all kinds, as Spleen, Vapours, Lowness of Spirits, Hypochondriaca, and Hysterical Distempers, etc.* (1733; repr., Delmar, NY: Scholars' Facsimiles & Reprints, 1976), 38.

39. Cheyne, *English Malady,* 38–39.

40. Kristeva, *Power of Horror,* 155.

41. Gwilliam, *Fictions of Gender,* 58.

42. Richardson's hypochondria is legendary. See *Selected Letters of Samuel Richardson,* ed. John Carroll (Oxford: Clarendon Press, 1964 and *The Letters of Doctor George Cheyne to Samuel Richardson (1733–1743),* ed. Charles F. Mullett, University of Missouri Studies 28.1 (Columbia: University of Missouri, 1943). Also see Richardson's "Preface" to *Sir Charles Grandison.*

43. Samuel Richardson, *The History of Sir Charles Grandison,* ed. Jocelyn Harris (Oxford: Oxford University Press, 1986), vol. 6, p. 68. Hereafter cited in text by volume and page number. All italics appear in the original text, unless otherwise indicated.

44. Sir Charles is a baronet, a rank created by James I so that it could be sold in order to raise cash; approximately £100,000 was generated by the sale of these titles (Bridget Hill, *Women, Work and Sexual Politics in Eighteenth-Century England* [London: U[niversity] C[ollege] L[ondon] Press, 1994], 45).

45. Tassie Gwilliam notes Sir Charles's "glacial presence" and observes that many readers have found the novel "lacking at the core" (*Fictions of Gender,* 111); Gerard A. Barker claims that Richardson "willingly sacrificed probability for the sake of idealizing his hero" (*Grandison's Heirs: The Paragon's Progress in the Late Eighteenth-Century English Novel* [Newark: University of Delaware Press, 1985], 24); Margaret Doody writes that Richardson's creation of Sir Charles is an "abstraction" (*Natural Passion,* 248). For an example of Sir Charles's contradictory nature, see Mary V. Yates, "The Christian Rake in *Sir Charles Grandison,*" *SEL: Studies in English Literature, 1500–1900* 24 (1984).

46. Gwilliam, *Fictions of Gender,* 112.

47. Ibid., 113.

48. The idea of castration in *Sir Charles Grandison* has been explored by more than a few critics. Jocelyn Harris specifically contrasts and compares Sir Charles to Abelard, observing that "Sir Charles is not, like Abelard, thwarted in his potency, but a certain cold rectitude in his dealings with Clementina, together with his known chastity and irresistibility to women, make them not dissimilar. . . . Sir Charles' lack of sexual feeling could well have resulted from Richardson's commitment, imaginatively, to Abelard and

Eloisa's tale (*Samuel Richardson* [Cambridge: Cambridge University Press, 1987], 159–60). David Robinson explores the friendship of Sir Charles and Jeronymo, which seems to tip over into homosexual attraction as a result of Jeronymo's feminization and submission to Sir Charles's control after his wounding; see "Unravelling the 'Cord Which Ties Good Men to Good Men': Male Friendship in Richardson's Novels" in Margaret Anne Doody and Peter Sabor, *Samuel Richardson: Tercentenary Essays* (Cambridge: Cambridge University Press, 1989) 167–87. The most thorough discussion of castration in the novel is that of Tassie Gwilliam, who notes that Sir Charles's rescues of Sir Hargrave, Mr. Merceda, and Jeronymo implicate him in their woundings by placing him at the "scenes-of-the-crime." Gwilliam observes that although "the burden of castrating others never settles on Sir Charles . . . like the Freudian/Lacanian father, he presides over the threat of its performance" (*Fictions of Gender*, 124–25).

49. In "*Sir Charles Grandison*: Richardson on Body and Character," Juliet McMaster notes the "felt presence of the body" in this novel (*Eighteenth Century Fiction* 1 [1989]: 85); while I agree that the body is very much present in the text, I argue that it is the deviant body—ill or maimed—that is brought to the reader's consciousness. Sir Charles's health is always viewed in relation to these other bodies.

50. Wiltshire, *Jane Austen and the Body: The "Picture of Health"* (Cambridge: Cambridge University Press, 1992), 8. See also Drew Leder, *The Absent Body* (Chicago: University of Chicago Press, 1990).

51. Although Jocelyn Harris has characterized Clementina as a "reductionist version" of Clarissa (*Samuel Richardson*, 135), I believe that Clementina needs to be read in her own right, and not necessarily through the filtering lens of Clarissa. As Margaret Doody points out, Clarissa's madness is only temporary, while Clementina's illness defines her and "makes her at last an individual," able finally to differentiate herself from her family, whose seamless love is suffocating (*Natural Passion*, 330, 325). The Harlowe family conflict is always articulated; the conflict in the della Porretta family, on the other hand, is always suppressed. As Doody remarks, "the controlled serenity" of the della Porrettas has "encas[ed] Clementina in a love as smooth as marble" (*Natural Passion*, 320), as smooth as marble and every bit as monolithic and unyielding.

52. Sir Charles, in fact, blames Clementina's illness on her religion: "For my own part," he tells Father Marescotti and Clementina's brother, the bishop of Nocera, "I have been recollecting the behaviour of your admirable sister throughout every stage of her delirium, respecting myself: And I have not been able to call to mind one instance in it of an attachment *merely* personal. I need not tell you, Father, nor you, my Lord, what a zealous Catholic she is. . . . Her unhappy illness was owing to her zeal for religion, and to her concealing her struggles on that account. She never hinted at marriage in her resveries. She was still solicitous for the SOUL of the man she wished to proselyte" (5:585–86).

53. Gwilliam, *Fictions of Gender*, 155, 154.

54. Brooks, *Body Work*, 5.

55. See Gillian Rose, *Feminism and Geography: The Limits of Geographical Knowledge*, for her discussion of the middle-class male body as an unmarked category, and of traditional geographical practice, in which male geographers become "invisible observers of social life . . . making sense of it all" (Minneapolis: University of Minnesota Press, 1993), 39.

Notes to Chapter 3

1. A French translation, by Jean de Meun, of Abelard's *Historia calamitatum* had existed since the late thirteenth century; a version of the lovers' story, by Jacques Al-

luis, was published in 1675. In 1687, Roger de Rabutim, Comte de Bussy, paraphrased two letters by Héloïse and a reply by Abelard, and sent them to his cousin, Mme. de Sévigné. He would publish this paraphrase in 1697, but not before the letters had been plagiarized and rewritten, and then published, along with Alluis's history, by F. N. Du Bois in 1695. The translated paraphrase of the letters into English by John Hughes, variously dated 1713 or 1714, is actually a translation of Du Bois's 1695 text. Richard Rawlinson's Latin version of the letters was published in 1718, but Hughes's translation was widely read, surpassed only by that of the Reverend Joseph Berington, published in 1787. See the discussion of the history of the letters in Linda S. Kauffman's *Discourses of Desire: Gender, Genre, and Epistolary Fictions* (Ithaca, NY: Cornell University Press, 1986), 84–89, and in Peggy Kamuf's *Fictions of Feminine Desire: Disclosures of Héloïse* (Lincoln: University of Nebraska, 1982), introduction.

2. Pope's epistle, which appeared a year prior to Rawlinson's Latin version, is based on Hughes' translation. Although Hughes had read the letters in the 1616 Latin text, he reportedly used a "much more romantic" French translation published in 1693 as the basis for his 1713 translation (Nicolson and Rousseau 152 and 152n37); Linda Kauffman ascribes his source to Du Bois's text of 1695 (85).

3. The Paraclete was abandoned and neglected until 1129, when Abelard learned that Héloïse, prioress at Argenteuil, was evicted from the wealthy Argenteuil monastery along with all her sisters. Abelard reopened the Paraclete monastery and installed Héloïse as abbess; legally, they were still husband and wife.

4. Pope, "Eloisa to Abelard" in *The Poems of Alexander Pope*, ed. John Butt, reduced version of the Twickenham text (New Haven, CT: Yale University Press, 1963), lines 17, 19. Hereafter cited in text by line number.

5. See Elizabeth Grosz's discussion of the body image in *Volatile Bodies: Toward a Corporeal Feminism* (Bloomington and Indianapolis: Indiana University Press, 1994). For Grosz, the body image mediates between the lived body and culture; the body image, or schema, consists of libidinal investments in various body parts, the relation of the body to its surrounding space, and the relation of the body to other objects and other bodies (chap. 3, 67–68, 79–85).

6. In Kleinian aesthetic theory, the creation of a work of art or body of text can represent the reparation of the mother's body, destroyed in fantasy by the infant's aggressive urges and later mourned as lost.

7. Seidler, "Reason, Desire, and Male Sexuality," in *The Cultural Construction of Sexuality*, ed. Pat Caplan (London: Tavistock, 1987), 96–99.

8. Pope's other heroic epistle, also written in the voice of a woman, is "Sapho to Phaon," written circa 1707 and published in Pope's translation of *Ovid's Epistles* (1712).

9. Pollak, "Pope and Sexual Difference: Woman as Part and Counterpart in the 'Epistle to a Lady,'" *SEL: Studies in English Literature, 1500–1900* 24 (1984): 474, 479–81.

10. Peter Abelard and Héloïse, *The Letters of Abelard and Héloïse*, trans. Betty Radice (Harmondsworth, England: Penguin, 1974), 75–76. Hereafter cited in text by page number. Radice drew on several sources in the preparation of her translation: Victor Cousin, *Petri Abaelardi opera*, 2 vols. (Paris: 1849); *Historia calamitatum* and Letters 1–7, ed. J. T. Muckle and T. P McLaughlin, *Mediaeval Studies*, vols. 12, 15, 17, 18 (Toronto: Pontifical Institute of Mediaeval Studies, 1950, 1953, 1955, 1956); and *Patrologia Latina*, vol. 178 (Paris: J. P. Migne, 1855).

11. Radice notes that Abelard's *Historia* was most likely written for public circulation, despite its ostensible creation as a letter to a friend (introduction, 25).

12. In Héloïse's first letter to Abelard she writes that she was eager to read his "letter of consolation" to a friend when she saw it had been written by Abelard: "I hoped for

renewal of strength, at least from the writer's words which would picture for me the reality I have lost" (109). The very materiality of his letters, the fact that the letters were once in his actual possession and that his own handwriting is inscribed on the sheets, seems to thrill Héloïse. She cites a passage from Seneca that celebrates writing as "the one way in which you can make your presence felt": "If pictures of absent friends give us pleasure . . . how much more welcome is a letter which comes to us in the very handwriting of an absent friend" (*Epistulae ad Lucilium*, 40.I, qtd. in letter 1, p. 110). Moreover, Héloïse explicitly connects desire to writing, reminding Abelard, "When in the past you sought me out for sinful pleasures your letters came to me thick and fast" (117).

13. In her reading of the *Letters*, Peggy Kamuf convincingly demonstrates the various ways in which Abelard attempts to maintain rhetorical mastery over Héloïse and the unruly passion that breaks through her writing. See *Fictions*, 26–43.

14. Pope's chronic illness, Pott's disease or tuberculosis of the spine, had begun when he was only twelve years old, resulting in extremely stunted growth and a grotesque double curvature of the spine known as kyphoscoliosis.

15. Pope's sexual life has been a frequent topic of speculation. Marjorie Hope Nicolson and G. S. Rousseau cite medical opinion that a urethral stricture suffered by Pope in 1740 was "probably the result of gonorrhea, contracted in youth" (*"This Long Disease, My Life": Alexander Pope and the Sciences* [Princeton, NJ: Princeton University Press, 1968], 66); Maynard Mack suggests that Pope's medical condition would have prohibited sexual activity (*Alexander Pope: A Life* [New York: Norton, 1985], 293); James Winn acknowledges that the evidence is not conclusive but believes that Pope's poor health made sexual activity unlikely ("Pope Plays the Rake: His Letters to the Ladies and the Making of the Eloisa" in *The Art of Alexander Pope*, ed. Howard Erskine-Hill and Anne Smith [New York: Harper & Rowe 1979], 93).

16. Cf. Héloïse's letter to Abelard: "Everything here is your own creation. This was a wilderness open to wild beasts and brigands, a place which had known no home nor habitation of men. In the very lairs of wild beasts and lurking-places of robbers, where the name of God was never heard, you built a sanctuary to God and dedicated a shrine in the name of the Holy Spirit" (111).

17. Paulson, *Breaking and Re-Making: Aesthetic Practice in England, 1700–1820* (New Brunswick, NJ: Rutgers University Press, 1989), 71.

18. Rousseau, *Julie, ou la nouvelle Héloïse*, ed. Michel Launay (Paris: Garnier-Flammarion, 1967). Hereafter cited in text by page number. All translations are my own, unless otherwise indicated.

19. O'Dea, "The Dialogics of Desire in *La nouvelle Héloïse*," *Eighteenth-Century Fiction* 7, no. 1 (1994): 40. O'Dea notes that Saint-Preux, on the other hand, claims Julie as his "natural" wife and attempts to integrate the sexuality that Julie's forgetfulness denies.

20. Rousseau, *Julie*, 18.

21. Miller, *The Heroine's Text: Readings in the French and English Novel 1722–1782* (New York: Columbia University Press, 1980), 99.

22. Thompson, *The Making of the English Working Class* (New York: Vintage, 1966), 11.

23. Tanner, "Julie and 'La Maison Paternelle': Another Look at Rousseau's *La nouvelle Héloïse*," *Daedalus* 105, no. 1 (Winter 1976): 28.

24. It should be noted that in the "Preface," Rousseau casts doubt on the authenticity of the collection of letters, noting that "having been several times in the region of the two lovers, I have never heard talk of the Baron d'Étange, nor of his daughter,

nor of M. d'Orbe, nor of Lord Edward Bomston, nor of M. de Wolmar" (3). Bernard Duyfhuizen observes that Rousseau's declaration "suggests an inherent indeterminateness between fiction and reality" and finds such a statement unusual in the eighteenth century, when "editors" such as Richardson or Defoe prefaced their novels with assurances that the narratives are true, assurances they knew their readers would disbelieve ("Epistolary Narratives of Transmission and Transgression," *Comparative Literature* 37, no.1 [1985]: 12). Ultimately, Rousseau the editor leaves the origin of this collection of letters a mystery.

25. Ohayon, "Rousseau's Julie: Or the Maternal Odyssey," *College Language Association Journal* 30, no. 1 (1986): 69.

26. Ibid., 73. For a discussion of Julie's relationship with her father, see Tony Tanner, "Julie," 28–35.

27. O'Dea, "Dialogics of Desire," 40.

28. Another tradition—the dressing room poem—is a subtext here. See, for example, Swift, "The Lady's Dressing Room."

29. In Jean Starobinski's classic study of Rousseau's work, *Le Transparence et l'obstacle* (1971; translated as *Transparency and Obstruction* by Arthur Goldhammer [Chicago: University of Chicago Press, 1988]), he suggests that the veil, which assumes a central role in *Julie,* is an obstacle that stands between Rousseau and "limpid space," or "a transparent self look[ing] out upon transparent surroundings," which he calls "the sum of Rousseau's desires." Starobinski recognizes these desires as Rousseau's "nostalgia for . . . moments of transparent perfection," moments of pleasure that he compares to Saint-Preux's description of pleasure in his letter extolling the beauty of Le Valais (83).

30. It might be argued that whether Julie is actually pregnant is irrelevant; what matters is the possibility of pregnancy. The question of pregnancy would have been undecidable in any case; until fairly recently, the only medical "proof" of pregnancy was considered to be the birth of a baby.

31. Lechte, "Woman and the Veil—or Rousseau's Fictive Body," *French Studies: A Quarterly Review* 39, no. 4 (1985): 429–31.

32. Danielle Montet-Clavié explores Rousseau's attitude toward women and sexual difference in the *Confessions, Julie,* and *L'Émile,* as revealed through Thérèse, Julie, and the role of the tutor ("La femme comme nature morte dans l'oeuvre de J.-J. Rousseau" in *La femme et la mort,* ed. Groupe de Récherches Interdisiplinaire d'Étude des Femmes [Toulouse: Université de Toulouse-Le Mirail, 1984], 59–76). Thérèse, she finds, is silent and absent, despite the fact that she is Rousseau's constant companion; Julie dies; and the tutor, finally, is able to step in and assume a paternal role without any female intervention. Woman is eventually totally effaced, and the tutor takes on a superhuman, even divine role, as creator of both Sophie and Émile. Montet-Clavié argues that, in this way, Rousseau is able to establish an origin that denies sexual difference.

33. It is worth noting that the names of both the Elysée and the Paraclete are linked to other literary and historical names: the Elysée suggests the Greek Elysium, a paradise, or abode of virtuous people after death, located at the edge of the world; the Paraclete evokes the Holy Spirit, the intercessor, advocate, or comforter, as part of redemption necessitated by the corruption or fall of the world. I am grateful to Patrick A. McCarthy for this insight.

34. See discussions of this scene in Jonathan Lamb, *Preserving the Self in the South Seas, 1680–1840* (Chicago: University of Chicago Press, 2001), chap. 7, and in Christopher Thacker, "'O Tinian! O Juan Fernandez!': Rousseau's 'Elysee' and Anson's Desert Islands," *Garden History* 5, no. 9 (1977), 41–47.

35. Rousseau, *The First and Second Discourses Together with the Replies to Critics and the Essay on the Origin of Languages* [1750–55], ed. and trans. Victor Gourevitch (New York: Harper Torchbooks, 1990), 170, italics in original.

36. Rousseau, "Second Discourse," 198–99.

37. Kamuf, *Fictions*, 117.

38. In *L'Émile*, Rousseau distinguishes between the social order and the natural order: "In the social order where all positions are determined, each man ought to be raised for his. If an individual formed for his position leaves it, he is no longer fit for anything. Education is useful only insofar as fortune is in agreement with the parents' vocation. In any other case it is harmful to the student, if only by virtue of the prejudices it gives him. . . . But among us where only the ranks remain and the men who compose them change constantly, no one knows whether in raising his son for his rank he is not working against him. In the natural order, since men are all equal, their common calling is man's estate and whoever is well raised for that calling cannot fail to fulfill those callings related to it. . . . Prior to the calling of his parents is nature's call to human life (Rousseau, *L'Émile ou de l'éducation* [1762], trans. Allan Bloom as *Emile, or on Education* [New York: Basic, 1979], 41. Hereafter cited in text by page number). Cf. Sir Charles Grandison's speech on the social order.

39. Starobinski, *Transparency*, 98, italics in original.

40. Ibid., 99.

41. Donald, "The Natural Man and the Virtuous Woman: Reproducing Citizens," in *Cultural Reproductions*, ed. Chris Jenks (London: Routledge, 1993), 40.

42. Ibid., 40–41.

43. Brooks, *Body Work*, 5.

44. Francesco Petrarca, *Rime sparse* 338, 12–13. Translated by Robert Durling as *Petrarch's Lyric Poems: The* Rime sparse *and Other Lyrics* (Cambridge, MA: Harvard University Press, 1976). Rousseau's title page includes a translation into French as well: "Le monde la posséde sans la connaîte, / Et moi, je l'ai connue, je reste ici-bas à la pleurer."

Notes to Chapter 4

Pope, "A Discourse on Pastoral Poetry" (1704), in *The Poems of Alexander Pope*, ed. John Butt, reduced version of the Twickenham text (New Haven, Conn.: Yale University Press, 1963), 120. Hereafter cited in text by page number. Oliver Goldsmith, "The Revolution in Low Life. To the Editor of *Lloyd's Evening Post* (June 14–16, 1762)," in *British Literature 1640–1789: An Anthology*, ed. Robert DeMaria (Oxford and Cambridge, Mass.: Blackwell, 1996), 1052–54. Hereafter cited in text by page number.

1. Pope, "Discourse," 119.

2. Ibid., 120, my emphasis.

3. Malcolm Andrews, *The Search for the Picturesque: Landscape Aesthetics and Tourism in Britain, 1760–1800* (Stanford, CA: Stanford University Press, 1989), 5.

4. Stewart, *On Longing: Narratives of the Miniature, the Gigantic, the Souvenir, the Collection* (Baltimore, MD: Johns Hopkins University Press, 1984), xii.

5. John Rennie Short, *Imagined Country: Society, Culture, and Environment* (New York: Routledge, 1991), 28–30.

6. Ibid., 31–32.

7. Williams, *The Country and the City* (New York: Oxford University Press, 1975), 43.

8. See John Barrell, *The Dark Side of the Landscape: The Rural Poor in English Painting 1730–1840* (Cambridge, MA: Harvard University Press 1980): "As the rustic figures become less and less the shepherds of French or Italian Pastoral, they become more and more ragged, but remain inexplicably cheerful. The effort is always to claim that the rural poor are as contented, the rural society as harmonious, . . . as it must have been in Arcadia. The jolly imagery of Merry England, which replaced the frankly artificial imagery of classical Pastoral, was in turn replaced when it had to be by the image of a cheerful, sober, domestic peasantry, more industrious than before; this gave way in turn to a picturesque image of the poor, whereby their raggedness became of aesthetic interest, and they became the objects of our pity." Eventually, Barrell goes on to say, the picturesque (with its characteristic affection for "raggedness") will disappear into a romantic fantasy of harmony in nature, and the actual workers will merge with their surroundings, "too far away from us for the questions about how contented or how ragged they were to arise" (16).

9. The picturesque movement has been the subject of much critical interest in the twentieth and twenty-first centuries. Some of the early work on the picturesque, notably Christopher Hussey's 1925 study, *The Picturesque: Studies in a Point of View* (Hamden, CT: Archon Books, 1967), has been ambivalent toward the topic, asserting its importance through critical attention, but nevertheless struggling to find a suitable niche for the picturesque, vis-à-vis the sublime and beautiful. Hussey finds his way out of this dilemma by describing the picturesque as a liminal stage, a "phase" through which various arts, including painting, architecture, poetry, gardening, and even the "art of travel," must pass as a "prelude to Romanticism" (4). Despite a book that, it may be argued, marks the beginning of contemporary interest in the picturesque, Hussey turns out to be an apologist for the movement, reading it through the later lenses of romanticism and impressionism. Hussey's own nostalgia as a possible source of his project on the picturesque shows through when he notes, in 1925, that "there is no denying that the gradual disappearance of [the landowning] class is resulting in the blighting of the countryside" (129).

In *Italian Landscape in Eighteenth Century England: A Study Chiefly of the Influence of Claude Lorrain and Salvator Rosa on English Taste 1700–1800* (New York: Oxford University Press, c. 1925), Elizabeth Manwaring dates the appearance of the picturesque from the late 1730s, noting, however, that the fashion for collecting pictures was already well established. The "sentiment" for the picturesque, observes Manwaring, "rises into frequency by 1760, is general after 1780, and ridiculously hackneyed after 1800" (167). Early "pioneers" of the picturesque include Dr. Thomas Herring, bishop of Bangor, who wrote his impressions of a trip through Wales in 1738; Horace Walpole, whose letters to Thomas West and others describe the mountains, forests, rocks, cliffs, waterfalls, cottages, and hermitages he observed on the Grand Tour; and Thomas Gray, who accompanied Walpole on his travels and was equally transported by the natural beauty of the French and Italian landscapes (170–71). Manwaring notes that women were "among the first to perceive the picturesque," citing the travel descriptions of Lady Hertford in 1740, as well as those of Elizabeth Montagu, Elizabeth Carter, Hestor Chapone, and Mary Delany later in the century. Manwaring's intriguing observation stops with her suggestion that the attraction of the picturesque for these women derived from their love of sketching and drawing (171–75). Manwaring's book, if deficient in analysis, is an excellent catalogue of picturesque references in the poetry and novels of the eighteenth century.

More recently, critical work on landscape, tourism, and aesthetics in the eighteenth century has taken a fresh look at the picturesque. In *The Genius of the Place: The English Landscape Garden, 1620–1820,* John Dixon Hunt and Peter Willis collect a wide variety of seminal writings on the picturesque. John Dixon Hunt's *The Figure in the Landscape: Poetry, Painting, and Gardening During the Eighteenth Century* (Baltimore, MD: Johns Hopkins University Press, 1976) and Malcolm Andrews's *The Search for the Picturesque: Landscape Aesthetics and Tourism in Britain, 1760–1800* (Stanford, CA: Stanford University Press, 1989) examine the interrelationships of landscape gardening, poetry, and the visual arts in the context of picturesque theory. Barrell's *The Dark Side of the Landscape* (1980) and Ann Bermingham's *Landscape and Ideology: The English Rustic Tradition, 1740–1860* (Berkeley: University of California Press, 1986) delineate some of the political implications of the picturesque. The conference "Romanticism and the Picturesque," held in July 1991 at the University of Wales, resulted in a collection of essays edited by Stephen Copley and Peter Garside entitled *The Politics of the Picturesque: Literature, Landscape and Aesthetics Since 1770* (Cambridge: Cambridge University Press, 1994), which greatly extends and enriches the critical conception of the picturesque as a political and ideological construct. Also see *The Picturesque in Late Georgian England: Papers Given at the Georgian Group Symposium, 22nd October, 1994* (London: The Georgian Group, 1994), and John Dixon Hunt, *The Picturesque Garden in Europe* (London: Thames and Hudson, 2002).

10. Qtd. in Morris R. Brownell, *Alexander Pope and the Arts of Georgian England* (Oxford: Clarendon Press, 1978), 122.

11. See Smith's *Uneven Development: Nature, Capital and the Production of Space* (Oxford: Basil Blackwell, 1984), 32. While Smith is primarily considering our concepts of space and geography in the twentieth century, I find his model useful for illuminating the ways in which the rapid social and economic changes of the eighteenth century surface in the aesthetic representation (and production) of landscape during that period.

12. Freud observes that, upon recognizing castration anxiety, the therapist believes that he or she has "penetrated all the psychological strata and reached 'bedrock,'" for "in the psychical field the biological factor is really the rock-bottom" ("Analysis Terminable and Interminable" in *Therapy and Technique,* ed. Philip Rieff [New York: Collier/Macmillan, 1963], 271).

13. As we see in Richardson's *Clarissa,* however, the natural body cannot be separated from the social body: when Clarissa Harlowe attempts to remove her social body from a patriarchal economy that would make that body an object of exchange, her natural body does not survive.

14. Smith, *Uneven Development,* 13–14.

15. Ibid., 32.

16. And, perhaps, with Pope's own personal nostalgia. Pope's family had moved to Windsor Forest in 1700, when Pope was about twelve years old. He spent the following years in the relative solitude of that home, reading and writing; Windsor Forest embodies, for Pope, very fond memories. Because of his family's Roman Catholicism, they would eventually be forced to move from Windsor Forest in 1716, an occasion that grieved Pope. In a letter to his friend John Caryll he notes, "I write this from Windsor Forest, which I am come to take my last look and leave of. We here bid our papist-neighbours adieu, much as those who go to be hanged do their fellow-prisoners" (March 20, 1716, qtd. in John Paul Russo, *Alexander Pope: Tradition and Identity* [Cambridge, Mass.: Harvard University Press], 76). Howard Erskine-Hill notes that the legislation requiring Catholics to register their estates for punitive taxation was the cause

of the Popes' sale of their land and home in Binfield ("Alexander Pope: The Political Poet in His Time," *Eighteenth Century Studies* 15.2 (1981–82): 132. Pope, then, was dispossessed of his land, much as the farmers of Virgil's *Eclogues*.

17. "Windsor Forest" in *Poems*, line 7. Hereafter cited in text by line number.

18. See Laura Brown's discussion of the Peace of Utrecht in *Alexander Pope* (Oxford: Basil Blackwell, 1985), 40.

19. The formal terms of the *asiento*, however, were widely ignored. England was officially allowed to import 4500 adult slaves per year into Latin America, and one "free ship" was entitled to trade directly with the empire. Because 4500 slaves could not possibly satisfy the need for labor in the Spanish American colonies, this limit was frequently circumvented, and slave ships were often loaded with contraband goods. The single free ship was often reloaded with goods from other ships, a tactic that was difficult to control (Isser Woloch, *Eighteenth-Century Europe: Tradition and Progress, 1715–1789* [New York: Norton, 1982], 127).

20. See Carole Fabricant's "Binding and Dressing Nature's Loose Tresses: The Ideology of Augustan Landscape Design" in *Studies in Eighteenth-Century Culture*, vol. 8, ed. Roseann Runte, (Madison: University of Wisconsin Press, 1979), for her analysis of the feminization and containment of landscape as expressed in Pope's garden at Twickenham (110).

21. The similarity to Clarissa Harlowe, whose retreat from sexuality also causes her body to disappear, is striking here: as Pan pursues the "fainting, sinking, pale" Lodona, "her Flight increas'd his Fire" so that "his shorter Breath with sultry Air / Pants on her Neck, and fans her parting Hair" (191, 184, 194–95). Valerie Rumbold observes another similarity to Richardson and to gothic novelists in Pope's "fascination with female helplessness," noting that Pan's pursuit of Lodona "anticipates the ambiguous excitement" of *Clarissa* and some gothic novels, in which the reader and author (and perhaps the victim, if we take the rake's word for it) share (*Women's Place in Pope's World*, Cambridge Studies in Eighteenth-Century Literature and Thought 2 [Cambridge: Cambridge University Press, 1989], 92).

22. Brown, *Alexander Pope*, 30.

23. Ibid., 40.

24. Brown, *Ends of Empire: Women and Ideology in Early Eighteenth-Century English Literature* (Ithaca, NY: Cornell University Press, 1993), 118.

25. When Goldsmith's father decided to pay a four-hundred-pound dowry for Goldsmith's sister's marriage to prevent the impression that she was marrying for money, the capital that was to have funded Goldsmith's university education was gone, necessitating that he attend university as a sizar.

26. Goldsmith's politics in this regard have been discussed by various critics. Richard C. Taylor, in "The Politics of Goldsmith's Journalism," traces Goldsmith's ambivalent and seemingly contradictory political positions in his writings in various periodicals. Taylor also notes Goldsmith's remarkable silence on Irish issues such as the inclusion of the Irish in the Militia Bill (*Philological Quarterly* 69, no. 1 [1990]: 71–89). James P. Carson traces the nostalgia of Goldsmith's politics as they are represented in *The Vicar of Wakefield*, observing that the novel provides "a resolution on a fantasy level for the problems inherent in an advanced commercial state" ("'The Little Republic' of the Family: Goldsmith's Politics of Nostalgia," *Eighteenth-Century Fiction* 16, no. 2 [2004]: 178).

27. The improbable and contrived plot of *The Vicar of Wakefield* has contributed to its uncertain status as a major eighteenth-century novel; in fact, it is not even mentioned

in the 1996 *Cambridge Companion to the Eighteenth-Century Novel,* ed. John Richetti (Cambridge: Cambridge University Press, 1996). Patricia Meyer Spacks attempts a fresh reading of plots as revelatory of desire and notes that toward the end of the 1760s "new ideological possibilities emerge, as plot structure also weakens" (*Desire and Truth: Functions of Plot in Eighteenth-Century Novels* [Chicago: University of Chicago Press, 1990], 6); nevertheless, Spacks chooses not to analyze the desire, nostalgia, that props up the weak plot structure in Goldsmith's *Vicar.*

28. Goldsmith, *The Vicar of Wakefield* (Harmondsworth, UK: Penguin, 1982), 39. Hereafter cited in text by page number.

29. The similarities between Goldsmith's Vicar and Pope's country parson are hard to ignore. While Deborah is known for her pickling, preserving, and gooseberry wine, Pope's parson has a wife who "makes conserves," and the ragged horse that eventually carries the Primrose women to church is an echo of the parson's "*Steed* / That carries double when there's need" ("The Happy Life of a Country Parson," in *Poems,* 20.3–4). Hereafter cited in text by line number.

30. Laslett, *The World We Have Lost: England before the Industrial Age,* 3rd ed. (New York: Scribner's, 1984), 18.

31. This structure is also at work in Sarah Scott's 1762 novel *Milennium Hall,* the subject of the next chapter.

32. Laslett, *The World We Have Lost,* 20.

33. Dr. Primrose's epitaph of Deborah—displayed in full view—is an attempt at a panoptical device, designed to ensure Deborah's own self-monitoring; see Foucault's description of Jeremy Bentham's design for the modern prison, which was designed to create "a state of conscious and permanent visibility that assures the automatic functioning of power. So to arrange things that the surveillance is permanent in its effects, even if it is discontinuous in its action; that the perfection of power should tend to render its actual exercise unnecessary; . . . in short, that the inmates should be caught up in a power situation of which they are themselves the bearers" (*Discipline and Punish: The Birth of the Prison,* trans. Alan Sheridan [New York: Random/Vintage, 1995], 201). As we shall see, Dr. Primrose's epitaph fails to make Deborah fully self-policing.

34. Stewart, *On Longing,* 145, emphasis in original.

35. Ibid., 150.

36. There is, perhaps, an ironic reference to the graveyard school of poets in Dr. Primrose's writing of an epitaph; significantly, however, while a typical "graveyard" poem, such as Gray's "Elegy Written in a Country Church-Yard," laments death and lost opportunity, the epitaph pointing to the poet's own mortality, Dr. Primrose declines to ponder his own death and seeks fame instead through the dead body of his wife. Dr. Primrose, by being in love with the dead and missing Deborah (instead of the living, uncontrollable Deborah), is following a well-established poetic tradition here: cf. Petrarch's *Rime sparse,* written about the distant, silent—and finally dead—Laura.

37. The strict timetable is another (doomed) attempt by Dr. Primrose at disciplining his wife and daughters. See Foucault on timetables and "docile bodies" in *Discipline and Punish,* 149–52.

38. Durant, "*The Vicar of Wakefield* and the Sentimental Novel," *Studies in English Literature* 17 (1977): 477.

39. In fact, Dr. Primrose has never been especially well paid as a clergyman. See Jeffrey G. Williamson's "The Structure of Pay in Britain, 1710–1922," in which he sets the nominal annual earnings for clergymen as £99.66 in 1710, £96.84 in 1737, and £91.90 in 1755 (*Research in Economic History* 7 [1982]: 1–54).

40. Dykstal, "The Story of O: Politics and Pleasure in *The Vicar of Wakefield*," *ELH* 62, no. 2 (1995): 333.

41. Ibid., 334.

42. Ibid., 340.

43. While Timothy Dykstal claims that Olivia's song "remains the single most memorable feature of her presence in the novel" (339), I would point out that the song is not truly hers: she has not composed it, but merely sings, at her mother's behest, "'that little melancholy air your pappa was so fond of'" (148). While Dykstal claims that by singing this lyric Olivia "declare[s] a willingness to regulate herself" ("Story of O," 340), the song Olivia sings is really the Vicar's song—a song she has apparently sung before and now takes up again in order to please him. As is Charlotte Harlowe, Deborah Primrose is complicit in the patriarchal project of the family.

44. Lonsdale, "'A Garden and a Grave': The Poetry of Oliver Goldsmith," in *Oliver Goldsmith*, Modern Critical Views, ed. Harold Bloom (New York: Chelsea House, 1987), 52.

45. Bermingham, *Landscape and Ideology*, 9.

46. See Christopher Tilley, *A Phenomenology of Landscape: Places, Paths, and Monuments* (Oxford and Providence, R.I.: Berg, 1994), chap. 1, for a full discussion of how space becomes place.

47. Barrell and Guest, "On the Use of Contradiction in the Eighteenth-Century Long Poem," in *The New Eighteenth Century: Theory, Politics, English Literature*, ed. Felicity Nussbaum and Laura Brown (New York: Methuen, 1987), 143.

48. Ibid., 141.

49. Ibid.

50. Ibid.

51. Goldsmith, *The Deserted Village* in *Eighteenth-Century Poetry: An Annotated Anthology*, 2nd edition, ed. David Fairer and Christine Gerrard (Oxford: Blackwell, 2004), 459–69, l. 29. Hereafter cited in text by line number.

52. Mulvey, "Visual Pleasure and Narrative Cinema." *Screen* 16, no. 3 (1975): 7.

53. The allusion to Olivia Primrose and Mr. Thornhill in *The Vicar of Wakefield* is obvious here.

54. Williams, *Country and the City*, 78–79.

NOTES TO CHAPTER 5

1. In her 1957 essay "Notes on Symbol Formation," Hanna Segal proposes that symbolization results from the infant's need to recuperate and restore its absent mother. She emphasizes, however, that "the symbol proper" is not merely an equation, or "symbol-substitute," which the infant feels "to *be* the original object"; rather, the symbol "is felt to *represent* the object." Segal's distinction is crucial: she recognizes that true symbolization "is used not to deny but to overcome loss"; that is, symbolization can only take place when separation and loss can be "experienced and tolerated." The denial—rather than the acceptance—of loss would result in an inability to symbolize (*International Journal of Psychoanalysis* 38 [1957]: 395, italics in original).

2. Julia Kristeva contends that the semiotic continually surfaces in creative work, because the thetic is permeable, and subjectivity is continually renegotiated in the practice of creative work such as writing or painting. I agree with her thesis. Nostalgia as cultural practice, on the other hand, does not tap into the semiotic or preoedipal; rather,

it depends on distance and on maintenance of a gendered subjectivity firmly in place. See *Revolution in Poetic Language*, trans. Margaret Waller (New York: Columbia University Press, 1984), esp. chap. 9, "The Unstable Symbolic."

3. Benjamin claims that subjectivity does not proceed in a straightforward course from oneness to separateness; rather, the self evolves gradually through simultaneous differentiation and recognition of the other, by alternating between "being with" and "being distinct." See *The Bonds of Love: Psychoanalysis, Feminism, and the Problem of Domination* (New York: Pantheon, 1988), esp. chap 1, "The First Bond."

4. Pfaelzer, "Subjectivity as Feminist Utopia," in *Utopian and Science Fiction by Women: Worlds of Difference*, ed. Jane L. Donawerth and Carol A. Kolmerten (Syracuse, NY: Syracuse University Press, 1994), 99–100.

5. Boone, *Tradition Counter Tradition: Love and the Form of Fiction* (Chicago: University of Chicago Press, 1987), 60.

6. Hayford, "The Geography of Women: An Historical Introduction," *Antipode* 6 (1974): 14. Also see Clark, *The Working Life of Women in the Seventeenth Century* 3rd. ed. (1919; repr., New York: Routledge, 1992), and Hill, *Women, Work and Sexual Politics in Eighteenth-Century England* (London: U[niversity] C[ollege] L[ondon] Press, 1994).

7. Pratt, *Imperial Eyes: Travel Writing and Transculturation* (New York: Routledge, 1992), 155–71.

8. I use the term *uneven* in the sense that Mary Poovey uses it: to denote the sense in which Scott's novel may appear (as a novel) "coherent and complete," while it is nevertheless "fissured by competing emphases and interests." See Poovey's *Uneven Developments: The Ideological Work of Gender in Mid-Victorian England* (Chicago: University of Chicago Press, 1988), esp. chap. 1, "The Ideological Work of Gender."

9. Sarah Robinson Scott, *A Description of Millenium Hall*, ed. Gary Kelly (Peterborough, Ont.: Broadview Press, 1995), 58. Hereafter cited in text by page number.

10. Kelly, introduction to *A Description of Millenium Hall*, 36.

11. Pfaelzer also notes that traditional narratives that describe the development of subjectivity fail to account for female development. In these narratives, moreover, the self exists in isolation, outside society, while intimacy, bonding, and empathy are relegated to the preoedipal. Feminist psychoanalysis, however, resists any definition of intimacy as "regressive," hence, Benjamin's notion of simultaneous differentiation and union. The self must be separate as well as part of a social entity. Empathy is not merger; rather it requires an articulated and differentiated image of the other. "Feminist utopians," observes Pfaelzer about nineteenth- and twentieth-century writers, "invoke a particularized image of the other as the basis for intimacy, and intimacy is essential to their vision of an egalitarian society. In other words, feminist utopians have a common view of radical subjectivity that derives, in part, from mother-daughter relations" ("Subjectivity," 99). This alternate view of the psychic development of subjectivity would seem to preclude feminine nostalgia; if nostalgia is a longing for the mother, or for preoedipal symbiosis, then the fragility of male subjectivity would derive from its construction on the already-fragile basis of gender. Male subjectivity is dependent on gender differentiation, while female subjectivity is more flexible and durable, and hence, not prone to nostalgia.

12. Benjamin, "A Desire of One's Own: Psychoanalytic Feminism and Intersubjective Space" in *Feminist Studies/Critical Studies*, ed. Teresa de Lauretis (Bloomington: Indiana University Press, 1986), 78–101.

13. Cruise, "A House Divided: Sarah Scott's *Millenium Hall*," *SEL: Studies in English Literature, 1500–1900* 35 (1995): 558.

14. As we saw in chapter 2, the writing of *Sir Charles Grandison* is likewise related to Richardson's own fragile health.

15. Dunne, "Mothers and Monsters in Sarah Robinson Scott's *Millenium Hall*," in *Utopian and Science Fiction by Women: Worlds of Difference*, ed. Jane L. Donawerth and Carol A. Kolmerten (Syracuse, NY: Syracuse University Press, 1994), 61.

16. Ibid., 64.

17. Such an "education" is one that Mary Wollstonecraft would later argue against as one that "would render women an object of desire for a *short* time." See her *Vindication of the Rights of Women*, 2nd ed., ed. Carol Poston (New York: Norton, 1988), 90, italics in original.

18. Haggerty, "'Romantic Friendship' and Patriarchal Narrative in Sarah Scott's *Millenium Hall*," *Genders* 13 (1992): 115–16.

19. Ibid., 116.

20. Dunne, "Mothers and Monsters," 67.

21. Ibid., 71.

22. Haggerty, "'Romantic Friendships,'" 112–13.

23. Nussbaum, "Feminotopias: The Pleasures of 'Deformity' in Mid-Eighteenth-Century England," in *The Body and Physical Difference: Discourses of Disability*, ed. David T. Mitchell and Sharon L. Snyder (Ann Arbor: University of Michigan Press, 1997), 164, 170.

24. Williamson, "Woman Is an Island," in *Studies in Entertainment: Critical Approaches to Mass Culture*, ed. Tania Modleski (Bloomington: Indiana University Press, 1986),106.

25. Dunne, "Mothers and Monsters," 58.

26. Carretta, "Utopia Limited: Sarah Scott's *Millenium Hall* and *The History of Sir George Ellison*," *The Age of Johnson* 5 (1992): 323.

27. On the role of the male observer, see Gillian Rose, *Feminism and Geography: The Limits of Geographical Knowledge* (Minneapolis: University of Minnesota Press, 1993), esp. p. 38.

28. Ibid., 39.

29. Ibid.

30. Scott's own experience of marriage was short and was disastrous by all accounts. Subsequent to her removal from her husband's home by her father and brothers, she went to live with Lady Barbara Montagu at Bath, where she enjoyed, on a much smaller scale, of course, a life of charity and domesticity similar to that enjoyed by the ladies of Millenium Hall.

31. Rose, *Feminism and Geography*, 107.

32. Pollack, *Vision and Difference: Femininity, Feminism and Histories of Art* (London: Routledge, 1988), 87.

33. Benjamin, "A Desire of One's Own," 80.

Bibliography

Abelard, Peter, and Héloïse. *The Letters of Abelard and Héloïse*. Translated by Betty Radice. Harmondsworth, England: Penguin, 1974.

Addison, Joseph. "Pleasures of the Imagination." *Spectator* 417 (June 28, 1712).

———. *Remarks on Several Parts of Italy*. 1705.

Aikens, Janet. "Richardson's 'Speaking Pictures.'" In Doody and Sabor, 146–66.

Andrews, Malcolm. *The Search for the Picturesque: Landscape Aesthetics and Tourism in Britain, 1760–1800*. Stanford, Calif.: Stanford University Press, 1989.

Ariès, Phillippe. *The Hour of Our Death*. Translated by Helen Weaver. New York: Knopf, 1981.

Astell, Mary. *A Serious Proposal to the Ladies*. 1694–97.

Auenbrugger, Leopold. *Inventum novum*. 1761.

Banks, Joseph. *The Endeavour Journal of Joseph Banks*, August 25, 1768–July 12, 1771, 2 vols. *The Papers of Sir Joseph Banks*. Arranged by B. P. Sandford. 1998. Mitchell Library of New South Wales. http://www.sl.nsw.gov.au/banks/series_03/03_741.cfm. February 16, 2006.

Barker, Gerard A. *Grandison's Heirs: The Paragon's Progress in the Late Eighteenth-Century English Novel*. Newark, DE: University of Delaware Press, 1985.

Barker-Benfield, G. J. *The Culture of Sensibility: Sex and Society in Eighteenth-Century Britain*. Chicago: University of Chicago Press, 1992.

Barrell, John. *The Dark Side of the Landscape*. Cambridge, MA: Harvard University Press, 1980.

———. *The Idea of Landscape and the Sense of Place, 1730–1840*. Cambridge, MA: Harvard University Press, 1972.

Barrell, John, and Harriet Guest. "On the Use of Contradiction in the Eighteenth-Century Long Poem." In Nussbaum and Brown, 121–43.

Benjamin, Jessica. *The Bonds of Love: Psychoanalysis, Feminism, and the Problem of Domination*. New York: Pantheon, 1988.

———. "A Desire of One's Own: Psychoanalytic Feminism and Intersubjective Space." In *Feminist Studies/Critical Studies*, edited by Teresa de Lauretis, 78–101. Bloomington: Indiana University Press, 1986.

Bermingham, Ann. *Landscape and Ideology: The English Rustic Tradition, 1740–1860*. Berkeley: University of California Press, 1986.

Bondi, Liz. "Progress in Geography and Gender: Feminism and Difference." *Progress in Human Geography* 14 (1990): 438–45.

Bondi, Liz, and Mona Domosh. "Other Figures in Other Landscapes: On Feminism,

Postmodernism and Geography." *Environment and Planning D: Society and Space* 10 (1992): 199–213.

Boone, Joseph Allen. *Tradition Counter Tradition: Love and the Form of Fiction*. Chicago: University of Chicago Press, 1987.

Bowlby, S., et al. "The Geography of Gender." In *New Models in Geography. Volume 2: The Political Economy Perspective*, edited by R. Peet and N. Thrift, 157–75. London: Unwin Hyman, 1989.

Boym, Svetlana. *The Future of Nostalgia*. New York: Basic Books, 2001.

Bright, Timothy. 1586. *A Treatise of Melancholie*. Reprint, New York: DaCapo Press, 1969.

Brissenden, R. F. *Virtue in Distress: Studies in the Novel of Sentiment from Richardson to Sade*. New York: Barnes & Noble, 1974.

Brooks, Peter. *Body Work: Objects of Desire in Modern Narrative*. Cambridge, MA: Harvard University Press, 1993.

Brown, Laura. *Alexander Pope*. Oxford: Basil Blackwell, 1985.

———. *Ends of Empire: Women and Ideology in Early Eighteenth-Century English Literature*. Ithaca, NY: Cornell University Press, 1993.

Brownell, Morris R. *Alexander Pope and the Arts of Georgian England*. Oxford: Clarendon Press, 1978.

Brumberg, Joan Jacobs. *Fasting Girls: The History of Anorexia Nervosa*. Cambridge, MA: Harvard University Press, 1988.

Burton, Robert. 1621. *The Anatomy of Melancholy*. Reprint, New York: Dutton, 1932.

Butler, Judith. *Bodies That Matter: On the Discursive Limits of "Sex."* New York: Routledge, 1993.

Bynum, Caroline Walker. *Holy Feast and Holy Fast: The Religious Significance of Food to Medieval Women*. Berkeley: University of California Press, 1987.

Carretta, Vincent. "Utopia Limited: Sarah Scott's *Millenium Hall* and *The History of Sir George Ellison*." *The Age of Johnson* 5 (1992): 303–25.

Carson, James P. "'The Little Republic' of the Family: Goldsmith's Politics of Nostalgia." *Eighteenth-Century Fiction* 16, no. 2 (2004): 173–96.

Castle, Terry. *Clarissa's Ciphers: Meaning and Disruption in Richardson's Clarissa*. Ithaca, NY: Cornell University Press, 1982.

Cheyne, George. 1733. A facsimile of the first edition of *The English Malady: or a Treatise of Nervous Diseases of all kinds, as Spleen, Vapours, Lowness of Spirits, Hypochondriaca, and Hysterical Distempers, etc.* with an introduction by Eric T. Carlson. Delmar, NY: Scholars' Facsimiles & Reprints, 1976.

———. *The Letters of Doctor George Cheyne to Samuel Richardson (1733–1743)*. Edited by Charles F. Mullett. University of Missouri Studies, vol. 28, no. 1. Columbia: University of Missouri Press, 1943.

Clark, Alice. *The Working Life of Women in the Seventeenth Century*. 3rd ed. New York: Routledge, 1992.

Copley, Stephen, and Peter Garside. *The Politics of the Picturesque: Literature, Landscape and Aesthetics Since 1770*. Cambridge: Cambridge University Press, 1994.

Cosgrove, Dennis. *Social Formation and Symbolic Landscape.* London: Croom Helm, 1984.

Cruise, James. "A House Divided: Sarah Scott's *Millenium Hall.*" *SEL: Studies in English Literature, 1500–1900* 35 (1995): 555–73.

Donald, James. "The Natural Man and the Virtuous Woman: Reproducing Citizens." in *Cultural Reproductions,* edited by Chris Jenks, 36–54. London: Routledge, 1993.

Donawerth, Jane L., and Carol A. Kolmerten, eds. *Utopian and Science Fiction by Women: Worlds of Difference.* Syracuse, NY: Syracuse University Press, 1994.

Doody, Margaret Anne. *A Natural Passion: A Study of the Novels of Samuel Richardson.* Oxford: Clarendon Press, 1974.

Doody, Margaret Anne, and Peter Sabor. *Samuel Richardson: Tercentenary Essays.* Cambridge: Cambridge University Press, 1989.

Duifhuyzen, Bernard. "Epistolary Narratives of Transmission and Transgression." *Comparative Literature* 37, no. 1 (1985): 1–26.

Dunne, Linda. "Mothers and Monsters in Sarah Robinson Scott's *Millenium Hall.*" In Donawerth and Kolmerten 54–72.

Durant, David. "*The Vicar of Wakefield* and the Sentimental Novel." *SEL: Studies in English Literature* 17 (1977): 477–91.

Dykstal, Timothy. "The Story of O: Politics and Pleasure in *The Vicar of Wakefield.*" *ELH* 62, no. 2 (1995): 329–46.

Eagleton, Terry. *The Rape of Clarissa: Writing, Sexuality and Class Struggle in Samuel Richardson.* Minneapolis: University of Minnesota Press, 1982.

Erskine-Hill, Howard. "Alexander Pope: The Political Poet in His Time." *Eighteenth Century Studies* 15, no. 2 (1981–82): 123–48.

Fabricant, Carole. "Binding and Dressing Nature's Loose Tresses: The Ideology of Augustan Landscape Design." *Studies in Eighteenth-Century Culture.* Vol. 8, edited by Roseann Runte, 109–35. Madison: University of Wisconsin Press, 1979.

Ferguson, Frances. "Rape and the Rise of the Novel." *Representations* 20 (1987): 88–112.

Foucault, Michel. *Discipline and Punish: The Birth of the Prison.* Translated by Alan Sheridan. New York: Vintage/Random, 1995.

Frega, Donnalee. "Speaking in Hunger: Conditional Consumption as Discourse in *Clarissa.*" *Studies in the Literary Imagination* 28, no. 1 (1995): 87–103.

Freud, Sigmund. "Analysis Terminable and Interminable." 1937. In *Therapy and Technique,* edited by Philip Rieff, 233–72. New York: Collier/Macmillan, 1963.

———. *The Standard Edition of the Complete Psychological Works.* 24 vols. Translated and edited by James Strachey. London: Hogarth, 1974.

———. "Instincts and Their Vicissitudes." 1915. *SE* 14: 111–40.

———. "Mourning and Melancholia." 1917. *SE* 14: 239–58.

———. "On Narcissism: An Introduction." 1914. *SE* 14: 67–102.

———. "Remembering, Repeating, and Working Through." 1914. *SE* 12: 145–56.

———. "Repression." 1915. *SE* 14: 143–58.

———. "On Transience." 1915. *SE* 14: 304–7.

———. "Thoughts for the Times on War and Death." 1915. *SE* 14: 274–303.

———. "The Unconscious." 1915. *SE* 14: 161–215.

Gilpin, William. *Three Essays: On Picturesque Beauty; On Picturesque Travel; and On Sketching Landscape*. 1792.

Goldsmith, Oliver. *The Deserted Village*, in *Eighteenth-Century Poetry: An Annotated Anthology*, 2nd ed., edited by David Fairer and Christine Gerrard, 459–69. Malden, MA, and Oxford: Blackwell, 2004.

———. "The Revolution in Low Life. To the Editor of *Lloyd's Evening Post* (14–16 June 1762)." In *British Literature 1640–1789: An Anthology*, 2nd ed. edited by Robert DeMaria, 814–15. Oxford and Cambridge, MA: Blackwell, 2001.

———. *The Vicar of Wakefield*. Harmondsworth: Penguin, 1982.

Gray, Thomas. "Elegy Written in a County Churchyard." 1751. In *Gray and Collins: Poetical Works*, edited by Roger Lonsdale, 33–39. Oxford: Oxford University Press, 1977.

Grosz, Elizabeth. *Volatile Bodies: Toward a Corporeal Feminism*. Bloomington: Indiana University Press, 1994.

Gwilliam, Tassie. *Samuel Richardson's Fictions of Gender*. Stanford, CA: Stanford University Press, 1993.

Haggerty, George E. "'Romantic Friendship' and Patriarchal Narrative in Sarah Scott's *Millenium Hall*." *Genders* 13 (1992): 108–22.

Harris, Jocelyn. Introduction to *The History of Sir Charles Grandison*, by Samuel Richardson. Oxford: Oxford University Press, 1986.

———. *Samuel Richardson*. Cambridge: Cambridge University Press, 1987.

Hayford, A. M. "The Geography of Women: An Historical Introduction." *Antipode* 6 (1974): 1–19.

Hill, Bridget. *Women, Work and Sexual Politics in Eighteenth-Century England*. London: U[niversity] C[ollege] L[ondon] Press, 1994.

Hill, Christopher. *The Century of Revolution, 1603–1714*. New York: Norton, 1980.

Hofer, Johannes. "De nostalgia oder Heimwehe." Diss. Basel, 1678. Translated by Carolyn Kiser Anspach as "Medical Dissertation on Nostalgia." *Bulletin of the History of Medicine* 2 (1934): 376–91.

Hunt, John Dixon. *The Figure in the Landscape: Poetry, Painting, and Gardening during the Eighteenth Century*. Baltimore, MD: Johns Hopkins University Press, 1976.

Hussey, Christopher. *The Picturesque: Studies in a Point of View*. Hamden, CT: Archon Books, 1967.

Jackson, Stanley. *Melancholia and Depression: From Hippocratic Times to Modern Times*. New Haven, CT.: Yale University Press, 1986.

Jameson, Fredric. *The Political Unconscious: Narrative as a Socially Symbolic Act*. Ithaca, NY: Cornell University Press, 1981.

———. "Nostalgia for the Present." *South Atlantic Quarterly* 88, no. 2 (1989): 517–37.

———. "Beyond the Cave: Demystifying the Ideology of Modernism." In *Contemporary Marxist Literary Criticism*, edited by Francis Mulhern, 168–87. London: Longman, 1972.

Jordanova, Ludmilla. *Sexual Visions: Images of Gender in Science and Medicine between the Eighteenth and Twentieth Centuries*. Madison: University of Wisconsin Press, 1989.

Kamuf, Peggy. *Fictions of Feminine Desire: Disclosures of Héloïse.* Lincoln: University of Nebraska Press, 1982.

Kaplan, Harvey. "The Psychopathology of Nostalgia." *Psychoanalytic Review* 74, no. 4 (1987): 465–86.

Kauffman, Linda. *Discourses of Desire: Gender, Genre and Epistolary Fictions.* Ithaca, NY: Cornell University Press, 1986.

Kelly, Gary. Introduction to *A Description of Millenium Hall,* by Sarah Robinson Scott. Edited by Gary Kelly. Peterborough, Ont.: Broadview Press, 1995.

Klein, Melanie. *Contributions to Psycho-Analysis 1921–1945.* London: Hogarth, 1948.

———. "The Importance of Symbol-Formation in the Development of the Ego." In Klein, *Contributions,* 236–50.

———. "Infantile Anxiety-Situations Reflected in a Work of Art and in the Creative Impulse." In Klein, *Contributions,* 227–35.

Knight, William Payne. *The Landscape.* 1794.

Kowaleski-Wallace, Elizabeth. *Consuming Subjects: Women, Shopping, and Business in the Eighteenth Century.* New York: Columbia University Press, 1997.

Kristeva, Julia. *Black Sun: Depression and Melancholia.* Translated by Leon S. Roudiez. New York: Columbia University Press, 1989.

———. *Revolution in Poetic Language.* Translated by Margaret Waller. New York: Columbia University Press, 1984.

———. *The Power of Horror: An Essay on Abjection.* Translated by Leon S. Roudiez. New York: Columbia University Press, 1982.

Lamb, Jonathan. *Preserving the Self in the South Seas, 1680–1840.* Chicago: University of Chicago Press, 2001.

Laslett, Peter. *The World We Have Lost: England before the Industrial Age.* 3rd ed. New York: Scribner's, 1984.

Laqueur, Thomas. *Making Sex: Body and Gender from the Greeks to Freud.* Cambridge, MA: Harvard University Press, 1990.

Lechte, John. "Woman and the Veil—Or Rousseau's Fictive Body." *French Studies: A Quarterly Review* 39, no. 4 (1985): 423–41.

Leder, Drew. *The Absent Body.* Chicago: University of Chicago Press, 1990.

Lefebvre, Henri. *The Production of Space.* Translated by Donald Nicholson-Smith. Oxford: Blackwell, 1994.

Leonardo, Richard A. *History of Surgery.* New York: Froben Press, 1943.

Lonsdale, Roger. "'A Garden and a Grave': The Poetry of Oliver Goldsmith." In *Oliver Goldsmith,* edited by Harold Bloom, 49–72. New York: Chelsea House, 1987.

Mack, Maynard. *Alexander Pope: A Life.* New York: Norton, 1985.

Mackenzie, Henry. *The Man of Feeling.* Edited by Kenneth C. Slagle. New York: Norton, 1958.

Manwaring, Elizabeth. *Italian Landscape in Eighteenth Century England: A Study Chiefly of the Influence of Claude Lorrain and Salvator Rosa on English Taste 1700–1800.* New York: Oxford University Press, [ca. 1925].

Markley, Robert. "Sentimentality as Performance: Shartesbury, Sterne, and the Theatrics of Virtue." In Nussbaum and Brown, 210–30.

Mason, William. *The English Garden*. 1771–81.

McCann, Willis. "Nostalgia: A Review of the Literature." *Psychological Bulletin* 38 (1941): 165–82.

McMaster, Juliet. "*Sir Charles Grandison*: Richardson on Body and Character." *Eighteenth Century Fiction* 1 (1989): 83–102.

Miller, Nancy K. *The Heroine's Text: Readings in the French and English Novel 1722–1782*. New York: Columbia University Press, 1980.

Montet-Clavie, Danielle. "La femme comme nature morte dans l'oeuvre de J.-J. Rousseau." *La femme et la morte,* edited by Groupe de Récherches Interdisciplinaire d'Étude des Femmes, 59–76. Toulouse: Université de Toulouse-Le Mirail, 1984.

Mullan, John. *Sentiment and Sociability: The Language of Feeling in the Eighteenth Century.* Oxford: Clarendon Press, 1988.

Mulvey, Laura. "Visual Pleasure and Narrative Cinema." *Screen* 16, no. 3 (1975): 6–18.

Nicolson, Marjorie Hope, and G. S. Rousseau. *"This Long Disease, My Life": Alexander Pope and the Sciences.* Princeton, NJ: Princeton University Press, 1968.

Nussbaum, Felicity. "Feminotopias: The Pleasures of 'Deformity' in Mid-Eighteenth-Century England." In *The Body and Physical Difference: Discourses of Disability,* edited by David T. Mitchell and Sharon L. Snyder, 161–73. Ann Arbor: University of Michigan Press, 1997.

Nussbaum, Felicity, and Laura Brown, eds. *The New Eighteenth Century: Theory, Politics, English Literature.* New York: Methuen, 1987.

O'Dea, Michael. "The Dialogics of Desire in *La Nouvelle Héloïse*." *Eighteenth Century Fiction* 7, no. 1 (1994): 37–50.

Ohayon, Ruth. "Rousseau's Julie: Or the Maternal Odyssey." *College Language Association Journal* 30, no. 1 (1986): 69–82.

Parker, Patricia. *Literary Fat Ladies: Rhetoric, Gender, Property.* London: Methuen, 1987.

Parsons, Talcott. "The Sick Role and the Role of the Physician Reconsidered." *Milbank Memorial Fund Quarterly / Health and Society* (Summer 1975): 257–77.

Paulson, Ronald. *Breaking and Re-making: Aesthetic Practice in England, 1700–1820.* New Brunswick, NJ: Rutgers University Press, 1989.

Petrarca, Francesco. *Petrarch's Lyric Poems: The* Rime sparse *and Other Lyrics*. Translated and edited by Robert Durling. Cambridge, MA: Harvard University Press, 1976.

Pfaelzer, Jean. "Subjectivity as Feminist Utopia." In Donawerth and Kolmerten, 93–106.

Pollak, Ellen. "Pope and Sexual Difference: Woman as Part and Counterpart in the 'Epistle to a Lady.'" *SEL: Studies in English Literature, 1500–1900* 24 (1984): 461–81.

Pollock, Griselda. *Vision and Difference: Femininity, Feminism and Histories of Art.* London: Routledge, 1988.

Poovey, Mary. *Uneven Developments: The Ideological Work of Gender in Mid-Victorian England.* Chicago: University of Chicago Press, 1988.

Pope, Alexander. *The Poems of Alexander Pope.* 1 vol. Edited by John Butt. A reduced version of the Twickenham text. New Haven, CT: Yale University Press, 1963.

————. "A Discourse on Pastoral Poetry." 1704. In *Poems*, 119–23.

————. "Eloisa to Abelard." 1717. In *Poems*, 252–61.

————. "Epistle II. To a Lady. Of the Characters of Women." 1735. In *Poems*, 559–69.

————. "Epistle III. To Bathurst." 1733. In *Poems*, 570–86.

————. "Epistle IV. To Burlington." 1731. In *Poems*, 586–95.

————. "The Happy Life of a Country Parson." 1727. In *Poems*, 20.

————. "Ode on Solitude." c. 1700. In *Poems*, 265.

————. "Sapho to Phaon." 1712. In *Poems*, 29.

————. "Windsor Forest." 1713. In *Poems*, 195–210.

Pratt, Mary Louise. *Imperial Eyes: Travel Writing and Transculturation*. New York: Routledge, 1992.

Price, Leah. *The Anthology and the Rise of the Novel: From Richardson to George Eliot*. Cambridge: Cambridge University Press, 2000.

Price, Uvedale. *An Essay on the Picturesque*. 1794.

Richardson, Samuel. *Clarissa, or the History of a Young Lady*. Edited with an introduction by Angus Ross. Harmondsworth, UK: Penguin, 1985.

————. *The Correspondence of Samuel Richardson*. 6 vols. Edited by Anna Laetitia Barbauld. London, 1804.

————. *The History of Sir Charles Grandison*. Edited with an introduction by Jocelyn Harris. Oxford: Oxford University Press, 1986.

————. *Pamela, or Virtue Rewarded*. Edited by T. C. Duncan Eaves and Ben D. Kimpel. Boston: Houghton Mifflin, 1972.

————. *Selected Letters of Samuel Richardson*. Edited by John Carroll. Oxford: Clarendon Press, 1964.

Richetti, John, ed. *The Cambridge Companion to the Eighteenth Century Novel*. Cambridge: Cambridge University Press, 1996.

Robinson, David. "Unraveling the 'Cord Which Ties Good Men to Good Men': Male Friendship in Richardson's Novels." In Doody and Sabor, 167–87.

Robinson, Sidney K. *Inquiry into the Picturesque*. Chicago: University of Chicago Press, 1991.

Rose, Gillian. *Feminism and Geography: The Limits of Geographical Knowledge*. Minneapolis: University of Minnesota Press, 1993.

Rosen, George. "Nostalgia: A 'Forgotten' Psychological Disorder." *Clio Medica* 10 (1975): 29–51.

Rousseau, Jean-Jacques. *The Confessions*. Translated by J. M. Cohen. Harmondsworth, UK: Penguin, 1982.

————. *Emile, or on Education*. Translated by Allan Bloom. New York: Basic, 1979.

————. *The First and Second Discourses Together with the Replies to Critics and the Essay on the Origin of Languages*. Edited and translated by Victor Gourevitch. New York: Harper Torchbooks, 1990.

————. *Julie, ou la nouvelle Héloïse*. Paris: Garnier-Flammarion, 1967.

Rumbold, Valerie. *Women's Place in Pope's World*. Cambridge Studies in Eighteenth-

Century Literature and Thought. Vol. 2. Cambridge: Cambridge University Press, 1989.

Russo, John Paul. *Alexander Pope: Tradition and Identity*. Cambridge, MA: Harvard University Press, 1972.

————. "Logos and Transience in Franco Rella." *Differentia: A Review of Italian Thought* 1 (Autumn 1986): 187–223.

Schama, Simon. *Landscape and Memory*. New York: Vintage/Random House, 1995.

Schwoerer, Lois G. "Seventeenth-Century English Women Engraved in Stone?" *Albion* 16 (1984): 389–403.

Scott, Sarah Robinson. *A Description of Millenium Hall*. Edited by Gary Kelly. Peterborough, Canada: Broadview Press, 1995.

————. *The History of Sir George Ellison*. Edited by Betty Rizzo. Lexington: University Press of Kentucky, 1996.

Seidler, Victor J. "Reason, Desire, and Male Sexuality." In *The Cultural Construction of Sexuality*, edited by Pat Caplan, 82–112. London: Tavistock, 1987.

Segal, Hanna. "Notes on Symbol Formation." *International Journal of Psychoanalysis* 38 (1957): 391–405.

Shaftesbury, Anthony Ashley Cooper, 3rd earl of. *Characteristics of Men, Manner, Opinions, and Times*. 3 vols. Edited by Douglas den Uyl. Indianapolis: Liberty Fund, 2001.

Short, John Rennie. *Imagined Country: Society, Culture, and Environment*. New York: Routledge, 1991.

Smith, Neil. *Uneven Development: Nature, Capital and the Production of Space*. Oxford: Basil Blackwell, 1984.

Spacks, Patricia Myers. *Desire and Truth: Functions of Plot in Eighteenth-Century Novels*. Chicago: University of Chicago Press, 1990.

Starobinski, Jean. *Transparency and Obstruction*. Translated by Arthur Goldhammer. Chicago: University of Chicago Press, 1988.

Stewart, Susan. *On Longing: Narratives of the Miniature, the Gigantic, the Souvenir, the Collection*. Baltimore, MD: Johns Hopkins University Press, 1984.

Stone, Lawrence. *The Family, Sex and Marriage in England 1500–1800*. Abridged ed. Harmondsworth, UK: Penguin, 1990.

Swift, Jonathan. "The Lady's Dressing Room." 1732. In *British Literature 1640–1789: An Anthology*, 2nd ed., edited by Robert De Maria, 430–33. Oxford and Cambridge, MA: Blackwell, 2001.

Tanner, Tony. "Julie and 'La Maison Paternelle': Another Look at Rousseau's *La Nouvelle Héloïse*." *Daedalus* 105, no. 1 (Winter 1976): 23–45.

Taylor, Richard C. "The Politics of Goldsmith's Journalism." *Philological Quarterly* 69, no. 1 (1990): 71–89.

Thompson, E. P. *The Making of the English Working Class*. New York: Vintage, 1966.

Tilley, Christopher. *A Phenomenology of Landscape: Places, Paths and Monuments*. Oxford: Berg, 1994.

Turner, Bryan S. *The Body and Society: New Explorations in Social Theory*. Oxford: Basil Blackwell, 1984.

Urry, John. *Consuming Places*. London: Routledge, 1995.

Wangensteen, Owen H., and Sarah D. Wangensteen. *The Rise of Surgery: From Empiric Craft to Scientific Discipline*. Minneapolis: University of Minnesota Press, 1978.

Warner, William. *Reading Clarissa: The Struggles of Interpretation*. New Haven, CT: Yale University Press, 1979.

Wesley, John. *Primitive Physick: Or, An Easy and Natural Method of Curing Most Diseases*. London: J. Palmar, 1751.

Williams, Raymond. *The Country and the City*. 1973. New York: Oxford University Press, 1975.

Williamson, Jeffrey G. "The Structure of Pay in Britain, 1710–1911." *Research in Economic History* 7 (1982): 1–54.

Williamson, Judith. "Woman Is an Island." *Studies in Entertainment: Critical Approaches to Mass Culture*, edited by Tania Modleski, 99–118. Bloomington: Indiana University Press, 1986.

Wiltshire, John. *Jane Austen and the Body: The "Picture of Health."* Cambridge: Cambridge University Press, 1992.

Winn, James. "Pope Plays the Rake: His Letters to the Ladies and the Making of the Eloisa." In *The Art of Alexander Pope,* edited by Howard Erskine-Hill and Anne Smith, 89–118. New York: Harper & Row, 1979.

Wollstonecraft, Mary. *A Vindication of the Rights of Woman*. 2nd ed. Edited by Carol Poston. Norton Critical Edition. New York: Norton, 1988.

Woloch, Isser. *Eighteenth-Century Europe: Tradition and Progress, 1715–1789*. New York: Norton, 1982.

The Women and Geography Study Group. *Geography and Gender: An Introduction to Feminist Geography.* London: Hutchinson, 1984.

Wotton, Henry. *Elements of Architecture*. 1624.

Yates, Mary V. "The Christian Rake in *Sir Charles Grandison*." *SEL: Studies in English Literature, 1500–1900* 24 (1984): 545–61.

Zelinsky, W. "The Strange Case of the Missing Female Geographer." *Professional Geographer* 25 (1973): 101–5.

Zimmerman, Everett. *The Boundaries of Fiction: History and the Eighteenth-Century British Novel*. Ithaca, NY: Cornell University Press, 1996.

Index